MANAGEMENT RESEARCH

MANAGEMENT RESEARCH

Edited by
G.S. BATRA

ANMOL PUBLICATIONS PVT. LTD.
NEW DELHI - 110 002 (INDIA)

ANMOL PUBLICATIONS PVT. LTD.
4374/4B, Ansari Road, Daryaganj
New Delhi - 110 002
Ph.: 3261597, 3278000
Visit us: www.anmolbooks.com

Management Research

ISBN 81-261-1288-3

PRINTED IN INDIA

Published by J.L. Kumar for Anmol Publications Pvt. Ltd., New Delhi - 110 002 and Printed at Mehra Offset Press, Delhi.

Preface

India has taken the decision to globalise its economy. The deregulation and the liberalisation initiatives have been undertaken with a view to increase production, improve quality and market the products and services abroad in competition with other multinationals. The concept of globalisation is based on the market size hypothesis. When it expands the size of the market, it yields to the economy of large scale production. Besides this, it ensures utmost utilization of resources for which we have been making endeavours so far.

There is growing realisation of the part of the Government that instead of doing some business, it should concentrate on creating an environment in which business prospers and entrepreneurial instincts are aroused so that the investors may get maximum output and reward from the efforts. Radical liberalisation has been ushered to make the Indian economy progressively market oriented and integrate it with the emerging global economic structure in a more meaningful way.

In this direction management is concerned with acquiring maximum prosperity with a minimum effort. Management is essential wherever group efforts are required to be directed towards achievement of common goals. It is now widely recognised that management is an important factor of growth of any country.

Management concentrates on achieving the objectives of the enterprise. The available resources of production are put to use in such a way that all sort of wastages and inefficiencies are reduced to a minimum. Workers are motivated to put in their best performance by the inspiring leadership. Managers create and maintain an environment conductive to highest efficiency and performance.

Researches conducted in their area indicate that through the optimum use of available resources, management accelerates the process of economic growth.

This volume deals with the analytical issues aimed at exhaustive treatment of almost all the leading aspects of the business management practices and policies. This book put together valuable papers contributed by the eminent scholars from different universities and institutions. I am grateful to all the contributors for their cooperation in this academic venture. I am also thankful to Sh. J.L. Kumar, of M/s Anmol Publications Pvt. Ltd., New Delhi for timely publication of this volume.

G.S. Batra

Contents

Preface v

1. Value Added Exports: A Case of Agro-Processing 1
   V.M. Rao

2. Management of Conflict between Tourism Industry and Environment in India 13
   Dev Malya Dutta

3. Strategic Management of International Business: Recent Trends 23
   Narinder Kaur and K.C. Singhal

4. Performance Evaluation of State Financial Corporations (A Case Study) 55
   B.S. Bhatia, K.C. Singhal and Pervinder Kaur

5. Emerging Dimensions in Services Management (A Case of India's Financial Services) 73
   G.S. Batra

6. Strategic Management of Indian Financial Markets: Taking Shape for Turbulent Times 93
   A.S. Chawla and G.S. Batra

7. Managing Privatisation: Global Developments and Strategic Issues 113
   G.S. Batra and Narinder Kaur

8. Industrial Relations in Indian Corporate Sector: Challenges Ahead 127
   B.S. Bhatia and G.S. Batra

9. Human Resource Valuation in India:
A Managerial View Point 141
G.S. Batra and B.S. Bhatia

10. Development Banking in Transition in India
(A Case Study) 151
B.S. Bhatia, G.S. Batra and Pervinder Kaur

11. Strategic Renaissance of Stock Markets:
An Appraisal for Recent Stock Market Reforms 173
G.S. Batra

12. Managing Transition in Indian Economy: An
Evaluation of Recent Public Sector Reforms 183
G.S. Batra and B.S. Bhatia

13. Management of Tourism in India (A Case Study) 197
G.S. Batra

14. Accountability of State Enterprises: Recent Trends 209
G.S. Batra, B.S. Bhatia and Harvinder Singh

15. Strategic Management of Industrial Sickness
in India —Challenges for 90's 219
B.S. Bhatia and G.S. Batra

16. Role of Public Sector in Industrialisation (A Case
Study of Garhwal Mandal Vikas Nigam) 227
R.C. Dangwal

17. Management Control Over Public Enterprises:
Emerging Dimensions 241
G.S. Batra

1

Value Added Exports : A Case of Agro-Processing

V.M. Rao*

Introduction

Agro-processing includes processing of agricultural raw materials, both ground and tree crops, as well as livestock and fisheries. According to Agricultural Credit Review Committee, those industries which use not less than 50% of the raw materials from agriculture and where the value added as a result of the processing is not more than 50% of the final value of output are considered as agro-processing industries.[1] It provides a crucial link between agriculture and industry. In the context of rural development, agro-based industries assumes a strategic place as they not only add value to primary products/commodities but also generate more employment in rural areas. An analysis of the Indian rural scene with reference to cooperative sugar, oilseeds, milk, fruits and vegetables, and other agro-based industries reveals four important things : (a) these industries add value to primary produce and its associated by-products thereby contribute to high economic development; (b) generate employment for rural people in the rural areas but away from farm sector; (c) provide employment to educated unemployed and unskilled labour in the rural areas thereby reducing pressure on urban areas of rural migrants; and (d) encourage leadership and cooperative entrepreneurship.

* Visiting Fellow, International Co-operative College, Leicestershire, U.K., Reader (Applied Economics), Vaikunth Mehta National Institute of Co-operative Management, University Road, Pune 411 007. The author is grateful to Shri K.C. Srivastava, IAS, Director of the Institute for Guidance during preparation of this paper.

Status of Food Processing Industries

India is blessed with a wide range of climatic and soil conditions across its land. It is, therefore, no wonder that India produces a large volume and a variety of crops. Potential for development of agro-industries is very large as it covers the entire canvas of agriculture. It covers the entire biomass. It consists of domesticated plants (food crops, commercial crops, horticulture, plantation crops, medicinal plants, floriculture, mushrooms, etc.), wild plants (sericulture, grasses, roots, tubers, etc.), domesticated animals (cattle, buffaloes, sheep, goat, pig, horses, camel, elephant, poultry, dog, fish etc.), insect kingdom (silk worms, bees, etc.), and micro organisms (algae, etc.). With the help of this biomass, organic matter can be converted into a variety of consumer and industrial products. However, we need a technology to convert this biomass into commercial and industrial products and there lies the need for agro-processing. So far, we have in the country achieved fairly good results in relevance to only a few crops such as sugarcane, milk, and oilseeds, and very little in other crops. Due to non-availability of necessary technology, post harvest losses of cereals and legumes are currently placed around 15-20%, and those of fruits and vegetables at 20-30% (NABARD, 1993).

Food processing industry in India is comprised of three groups: (a) primary food processing, (b) unorganised and cottage industries, and (c) processed food industries. The first group is made up of about 79000 rice hullers, 2.66 lakh chakkis, 10000 dhal mills, and 2.2 lakh oil mills. Unorganised sector is dominated by 54000 bakeries, 5000 paste food units, 15000 traditional food units, 2000 poha making units, 5000 fruits, vegetables, and spices processing units. There are about 18000 manufacturing units in the organised factory sector producing a variety of food products valued over Rs. 8 billion. As is evident from the above, a large part of food processing industries are in small scale and household sectors. For this purpose, a small scale sector shall mean an undertaking in which the investment in fixed assets in plant and machinery, whether held on ownership terms or by lease or by hire purchase, does not exceed Rs. 60 lakhs.

India produces Rs. 738 billion worth of agro-food materials which are converted into processed products. However, value additions by secondary and tertiary processing amounts to only 19% as against 64% in industrialised countries. Investment in this industry is only 5.2% of the total investment in the country, and employing about 17% of the total labour force (Potty, 1993). This industry contributes 19% of the total number of manufacturing units, 13% of output, and 6.4% of value added.

Trade in Agro-products

World trade in agricultural materials and foodstuffs has grown substantially over the last 20 years, from $65.4 billion in 1972 to $323.9 billion in 1990 (Anonymous, 1994). As of India, of the total exports of Rs. 325 billion in 1990-91, the share of agri-exports was Rs. 63.2 billion accounting 19.4% of total exports (Table I). They include tea, coffee, rice, cashew, oilmeals, marine products, raw cotton, spices, sugar and molasses, tobacco, fruits and vegetables, etc.

Government Support

Realising the importance of this prime sector, Government of India has created Ministry of Food Processing Industries with a view to create increased job opportunities in rural areas, enabling farmers to reap benefit from modern technology, create surplus for exports, and stimulating demand for processed foods. In the new economic policy, initiated in the year 1992, it was considered as a major sunrise sector; a variety of concessions were provided which was followed by a strong policy support for agro-industries. The recent draft Agricultural Policy Resolution prepared by the Government of India aims, inter alia, to give a thrust in increasing processing, marketing and storage facilities for value addition in agriculture (Sangita, 1993).

This sector was identified as a thrust area under the Eighth five year plan in the context of enhancing agricultural production and foreign exchange earnings. Government of India has targeted a level of Rs. 6000 crores by 1996-97 from exports of food processing sector. The plan provided for an outlay of Rs. 839.50 crores for agro-processing. Keeping in view the potential of this sector, the National Bank for Agriculture and Rural Development has been providing refinance support to integrated projects covering production and processing activities. A variety of other facilities are also provided by the National Cooperative Development Corporation. Agricultural and Processed Food Products Export Development Authority (APEDA) is another institution created by Government of India to promote agricultural and processed foods export. Further, recently constituted 'agri-business consortium' would also go a long way in promoting production, processing, and exports of agricultural products. As a result, food processing industry is in for a quantum leap with Rs. 4800 crores worth of investment coming in of which proposals to the tune of Rs. 3000 crores have already been cleared by Government of India.

In a recent workshop on 'Strategy for accelerating agro-processing industries : A development approach' held at the Vaikunth Mehta National Institute of Cooperative Management (VMNICM), Pune. Sh. S.L. Kapoor, Secretary, Ministry of Food Processing Industries, Government of India informed that 'granting priorities in allocation of land, quick power connection on priority basis, giving quick clearances, helping in arranging for water supply and granting priorities in financing by state financial corporations and lending agencies would go a long way in strength food processing sector. As the cost of processed food is slightly high, Government of India has reduced and/or even eliminated excise duties on a large segments of food products.'

It is to be mentioned here that of all agro-processing industries, grains processing, oilseeds processing, sugarcane processing, and milk processing account for over 71% of output and capital employed in all food processing industries in organised sector. Their share in value added is close to 60%. Similarly, their share in working capital and employment is over 65% (Desai and Namboodiri, 1993). The following is a description of various agro-processing sectors.

Grain Processing

Besides producing 50 million tonnes of pulses and coarse grains, India is the second largest producer of rice and the fourth largest producer of wheat in the world. Primary processors are estimated to account for 88% of production in this sector. Secondary and tertiary producers process the milled grain and its by-products. Total installed capacity of rice milling is around 285 million tonnes. In addition, there are 2000 units engaged in the manufacture of aval (poha) and puffed rice products. Further, there about 7000 cooperative food grain processing plants in the country. In 1991-92, 7.6 lakh tonnes of rice was exported. As of wheat, it is milled in 583 roller flour mills and 3 lakh flour atta chakkis. There are 75000 bakery units and 5000 units engaged in vermicelli and other extruded food products.

Milk Processing

India is having about 50% of world buffaloes, and 20% of cattle. It is the second largest milk producing country in the world by producing about 58 million tonnes in 1993. About 30% of this production is converted into products, mainly ghee and the rest, into butter, cheese, infant milk food, powdered milk, and malted milk food. There are 87 milk processing units in public, coopcrative, and private sectors. Co-operative dairy processing sector is comprised of 168 dairy plants which are integrated with chilling centres and cattle feed mixing plants.

The production of milk powder and infant milk food is estimated to be 1.65 lakh tonnes in 1992. Similarly, the production of malted milk food including malted food, cheese, and condensed milk is estimated to be 41300 tonnes, 2900 tonnes, and 8400 tonnes respectively. However, there are restrictions on the export of certain dairy products. Export of milk, baby milk, and sterilized milk is permitted only against a licence. Export of butter, powder, and ghee are permitted through agencies designated by the government. In 1990-91, 1125 tonnes of malted milk food, and 161 tonnes of ghee was exported.

Fruits and Vegetables Processing

India grows a variety of temperate to tropical fruits and vegetables. It is producing about 95 millions tonnes of fruits, vegetables, and tubers and about 25-30% of the production is being lost due to inadequate storage facilities and other infrastructure. Thus, about one per cent of this production is only processed. There are about 3700 units of varying capacities in this sector of which 90% are in small scale accounting for about 70% of the total production. Total installed capacity of fruits and vegetables processing industries is estimated to be 0.96 million tonnes in 1991 (Eipeson, 1993). The prominent processed items are fruit pulps and juices (27%), ready to serve beverages (13%), pickles (12%), squashes, tomato products, and canned vegetables (12%), jams and jellies (10%), synthetic syrups (8%), and others (18%). Of late, frozen pulps and vegetables, freeze dried fruits and vegetables, fruit concentrates and aromas, packaged vegetable currys, canned mushroom products, tomato paste, potato chips and oleoresin are added to the list. In 1991-92, value of export of fresh fruits and vegetables was about Rs. 3170 million and that of processed fruits and vegetables was Rs. 1200 million.

The fruits and vegetables processing cooperatives in India have emerged as farmer oriented enterprises. At present, there are 32 such cooperatives in operation that process mango, tomato, pineapple, orange, apple, and cherries. It is estimated that the annual production of processing cooperatives amount to about Rs. 30 million.

Sugar Processing

There are 400 sugar mills (120 in private sector and 280 in cooperative sector) producing 9.5 million tonnes annually. Thus, cooperative sugar mills occupy a dominant position in the Indian sugar industry contributing about 60% of national sugar production.[2] These sugar mills are owned and managed by 2.2 million members who are sugarcane growers and have invested Rs. 1927 million in the form of share capital in these mills.

Oilseeds Processing

These are nine oilseeds grown in India : groundnut, rapeseed/mustard, soybean, sunflower, sesamum, safflower, niger, linseed, and castor. With about 20 million ha. under cultivation, India produces about 19 million tonnes of oilseeds annually. Rice bran and cotton seed are among the non-conventional oilseeds. Further, 67% of coconut production is used for purposes other than extraction of oil, and over 50% of total output is used for industrial purposes (Asian Productivity Oraganisation, 1991). Oilseeds processing industry is highly fragmented and comprised of small capacity units and very big integrated plants with wide spectrum of technologies. In this sector, there are 2.5 lakh primitive bullock driven oil extraction units (ghanis/kohlus), 50,000 oil mill expellers, and 500 solvent extraction units (Adsule, 1993). India is one of the major exporters of castor oil and the value of foreign exchange earnings are about 0.7% of total Indian exports (Tewari and Rao, 1991). Further, India also exports large quantity of oilmeals to Europe.[3] There are 8 Oilseeds Growers' Cooperative Federations, and 135 mills in the cooperative sector manufacturing edible oil and processing by products (Rao, 1993[c]). The value of products generated in this sector is estimated at Rs. 3067 million (1992). Products like peanut candy, sesamum candy, etc. based on oilseeds are getting popular in India.

Fish Processing

India has a vast coast line of about 75000 km. Marine and inland water resources have been mostly tapped by local fishermen to meet domestic demand. Indian fish production is estimated to be 4 million tonnes (1991-92) and the export value of sea foods was around Rs. 1424 million in the same year. There are 150 units engaged in deep sea fishing in the country. Frozen shrimps account for 45% in terms of quantity and 73% in terms of value of the country's total sea food export and the major markets are Japan, United States of America, Italy, Spain, The Netherlands, France, and others.

The Marine Products Export Development Authority (MPEDA) came into existence in 1972 for the development of marine products industry and allied matters. MPEDA has contributed in improving the infrastructure facilities for post harvest operations like landing, berthing, pre-processing and processing facilities, upgradation of technology, modernisation of seafood industry, etc. Government of India has identified fishery development as a high priority area and $1180 million is the export target for the year 1996-97 (MPEDA, 1993).

Fisheries cooperatives are promoted as an integral part of government to exploit the potential of the industry, and to provide fishermen with gainful employment. These cooperatives market fresh, processed, and fish products to the tune of Rs. 450 million annually.

Meat and Poultry Processing

Traditionally, meat and poultry producting industry in India is largely in the unorganized sector. Of late, processed products based on meat and poultry have become common mainly meant for export and consumption in hotels and restaurants. The current production of meat and poultry products is estimated to be 2.2 million tonnes (1992). There are 150 meat processing units, 150 pork processing units, and 3 poultry processing units.

Spices Processing

India is known for the production spices like pepper, cardamom, ginger, chillies, turmeric, clove, nutmeg, cinnamon, cassia, celery, fennel, fenugreek coriander, cumin, and saffron. Drying, cleaning, grinding, and packaging of these spices are important operations in the small scale sector. There are about 2000 spices processing units in the country. Pepper worth of Rs. 110 crores was exported from India in 1990-91 (George and Charles, 1993).

Beer and Alcoholic Beverages

Liquor made in India is generally categorized as beer, country liquor and Indian made foreign liquor. There are 32 breweries, and 212 distilleries in the country. In 1990-1991, alcoholic beverages worth Rs. 69 million were exported.

A very useful information on various other export oriented food processing projects in India were provided in Gupta and Sinha (1993). Thus, there is a vast scope for producing value added agro-processing commodities to meet both domestic and international markets.

Problems of Agro-processing Industries

The problems of agro-processing industries were neatly expounded in Mahajan (1993), which included multiple taxation, development of new crop varieties, lack of processing technology, lack of storage and distribution mechanisms, lack of quality raw material, and the market itself. Packaging is another important factor which makes the processed foods costlier. Packaging industry is highly decentralized and there are about 13000 packaging units in the country (Ministry of Food Processing Industries, 1993). Large corporations like Tetrapak, India Foils, Cosmo Films, Garware Polyester and Plastics, Mazda Packaging, Bajaj Plastics, Pearl Polymers, Kesoram Industries, Metal Box. Asian Cans and Closures, and Poysha Industries are functioning in the field. In the recent years, many of these problems faced by the industry were attended to, licensing system was liberalised and a lot of concessions were provided to set up units in this sector.

Role of Cooperatives in Food Processing

Cooperative movement in India has been assigned a key role in the agricultural and rural development strategy of the country. In this, processing of agricultural commodities has been given a high degree of importance as it provides a wide base for rural industrialization and creates opportunities for building up new industrial and leadership based on agriculture in rural areas. Organisations like National Cooperative Development Corporation,[4] National Agricultural Cooperative Marketing Federation of India Limited, Tribal Cooperative Marketing Federation of India Limited, State Cooperative Agricultural and Rural Development Banks, State Cooperative Banks, etc. are helping for the development of the agro-processing industries in rural India. Sectoral progress of cooperatives was already provided in this paper. In a recent workshop held at the VMNICM, Pune, Sh M P Pinto, Secretary, Department of Agriculture Marketing, Government of Maharashtra stressed the problems of raising funds for cooperatives and suggested that 'scarce NCDC funds should not be used to fund term loan requirement and that can be met from institutional banking sector. If financial institutions can be asked to fund loan portion of such projects, NCDC funds can be reserved for equity assistance'.

The said workshop thoroughly discussed two important issues related to cooperatives: (a) appropriate organisational/federal structure, supply of raw materials to plant by members, and problems of seasonal raw material and resultant under utilization, and supply of production enhancement inputs to members; and (b) policy issues related to technology upgradation, marketing and role of export promotion agencies, incidence of taxes, and liberalisation and its impact. The workshop came out with concrete recommendations to solve the above problems.[5]

Need for an Agri-business Bureau[6]

If one look at the profile of each sector, one feels that there is vast potential, but so far we have not been able to reap benefits fully from them. Among others, following are three reasons: (a) information about this potential is not readily available to entrepreneurs, (b) information regarding the availability of the technology in the country and/or from abroad is not available to them,[7] and (c) sometimes suitable technology for converting a particular biomass into specific product is not readily available and needs to be developed. Thus, it is absolutely imperative today that cooperative entrepreneurs be guided properly with respect to: (a) potential of producing high quality agricultural produce, (b) vast potential for developing agro-processing industry in the country, (c) availability of technology and its suitability for a given agricultural raw material, (d) availability of plants and machineries in the country or from abroad, and (e) internal and external markets.

The proposed bureau would act as a link between industry and research institutes by bringing problems (such as suitable technology, plant and machinery design for production, transport, packaging, storage, etc.) by the entrepreneurs to a research institute or a group of institutes for appropriate modifications. The bureau would also undertake research studies/consultancies its own behalf and on the behalf of clientele to find out the problems and prospects of such sub-sector.

An added advantage of the above efforts will be that material generated from research studies/consultancies, etc. will be available as case material for teaching/training programmes. As an extension effort the bureau may also start publishing a journal on agri-business[8] for the benefit of the entrepreneurial community. Once sufficient case material on different agri-commodities is available, the bureau could think of conducting workshops/training programmes for managers of various cadres working in agri-business sectors. Infact, the idea of training managers of agri-business sectors can be persuaded as a major activity in course of time. Thus, in all the bureau aims to plug infrastructure bottleneck of information required by every entrepreneur.

GATT and Indian Agricultural Exports

GATT proposals promotes Indian agricultural exports to large extent. It stipulates that the aggregate measure of support in the form of product specific and general agricultural subsidies, each should not be more than 10% value of agricultural produce raised. At present, the level of agricultural subsidies in India is much below 10% whereas in developed countries these subsidies range between 20-40%. Thus, when these proposals are implemented, developed countries need to cut their agricultural subsidies which would make their agricultural produces costlier in the international market (Selvam, 1994), and Indian products would be cheaper. India should make use of the changing world economic scenario into her advantage.

Table I
Trends in Indian Exports

Year	*Total Exports (rupees in billions)*	*Agricultural exports*	
		Amount	*% to total Exports*
1990-91	325.5	63.2	19.4
1991-92	440.4	82.3	18.7
1992-93	533.5	89.8	16.8
1993-94*	660.0	120.0	18.2

* Estimated.

REFERENCES

1. Through out the text words 'food processing' and 'agro-processing' are used synonymously.
2. For an excellent review on Indian cooperative sugar industry, see Rao, 1993.[a]
3. For more details on exports of oilmeals, see Rao, 1993.[b]
4. For more details on NCDC finance to agro-processing industries, see Mathur, 1993.

5. Those who are interested in detailed recommendations may get in touch with the author.
6. Based on a proposal prepared by the author and submitted to NABARD for finance under Cooperative Development Fund during 1994.
7. This happens even when institutions such as Central Food Technological Research Institute, Indian Institute of Technology, Indian Institute of Packaging, National-Dairy Research Institute, Indian Horticultural Research Institute; Vasantdada Sugar Institute, and other commodity boards (horticultural crops, coffee, tea, leather, etc.) develop necessary technology for food processing.
8. It includes all those business and management activities performed by firms that provide inputs to farm sector, produce farm products, and/or process, transport, finance, handle, or market farm products (Downey and Erickson, 1987). Thus, agro-processing is an important sub-system of agri-business system.

BIBLIOGRAPHY

1. Adsule, P.G. (1993), **Status of Small Scale Food Industries in India,** (mimeo), Office of the Development Commissioner (SSI), Government of India, New Delhi.
2. Anonymous (1994), Trade takes off, but who for?, **International Agricultural Development,** 14 (1) : 11-13.
3. Asian Productivity Organisation (1991), **Food processing industry in Asia and Pacific,** APO, Tokyo.
4. Desai, B M, and N V Namboodiri (1993), Development of food processing industries, **Economic and Political Weekly,** March 28, pp. A37-A42.
5. Downey, W.D., and SP Erickson (1987), **Agribusiness Management,** McGraw-Hill Book Company, New York, p. 6.
6. Eipeson, W.E. (1993), **Fruit and Vegetable Processing in Rural Areas,** Paper presented at the seminar on 'Financing food/agro-processing activities by ARDBs' at Kochi during April 15.17.
7. George C.K., and CK Charles (1993), **Techno-economic Aspects of Processing Spices : Scope, Potential, Infrastructure Support Available,** (mimeo), Spices Board, Ministry of Commerce, Government of India, Kochi.
8. Gupta R.K., and R.K. Sinha (1993), **Exported Oriented Food Processing Projects,** (mimeo), SBP Consultant and Engineers Private Limited, New Delhi.
9. Mahajan, V.B. (1993), **Marketing of Food Products,** (mimeo), National

Agricultural Cooperative Marketing Federation Limited, New Delhi.

10. Mathur, B.C. (1993), **NCDC's Role and Experience in Financeing Agro-Processing Industries,** (mimeo), NCDC, New Delhi.

11. MPEDA (1993), **Role of MPEDA in Promoting Fish Processing,** Paper presented at the seminar on 'Financing food/agro-processing activities by ARDBs' at Kochi during April 15-17.

12. Ministry of Food Processing Industries (1993), **Opportunities for Food Processing Industries in India,** (mimeo), Government of India, New Delhi.

13. NABARD (1993), **NABARD's Refinance Support for Agro-processing Sector : Policy, Procedure, and Programme,** Paper presented at the seminar on 'Financing food/agro-processing activities by ARDBs', at Kochi during April 15-17.

14. Potty, V.H. (1993), **Food Processing Industry in India : An Overview,** (mimeo), Central Food Technological Research Institute, Mysore.

15. Rao, V.M. (1993[a]), **Cooperative Sugar Industry in India : A Time Series Analysis,** (mimeo), VMNICM, Pune.

16. Rao, V.M. (1993[b]) Indian oilmeals/cakes scenario : 1961-90, **Agricultural Situation in India,** 46 (12) : 912-916.

17. Rao, V.M. (1993[c]), **Management Development Programme for the Excutives of Oilseeds Cooperatives,** (mimeo), VMNICM, Pune.

18. Sangita, G. (1993), **The Role of Cooperatives in Agro-processing,** (mimeo), Department of Agriculture and Cooperation, Ministry of Agriculture, Government of India, New Delhi.

19. Selvam, M. (1994), Scope to boost farm exports, **Financial Express,** January 21.

20. Tewari, D.D. and V.M. Rao (1991), **Castor Economy : A Profile and Analysis of Indian and International Market,** Oxford and IBH, New Delhi.

2

Management of Conflict between Tourism Industry and Environment in India

Dev Malya Dutta*

Introduction

Today tourism is perhaps the biggest global business activity after oil. World spending on tourism exceeds $ 2 trillion and world tourist arrivals are in excess of 360 million (Hussain, 1989). In India, too, tourism has emerged as one of the valuable foreign exchange earning industry. The country is expected to earn Rs. 3500 crores from this trade by 92-93; d and Rs. 10,000 crores by the end of century. The employment generation potential of this industry can not be overlooked. 5.3 million people are involved directly and another 13.8 million people are indirectly related to the tourism and travel industry in this country. The growth of super and infrastructure, nourishment of culture, national and international integration, and an all round development — all flow from the tourism and travel industry.

India is a fascinating country for tourists, with a variegated wealth of its rich cultural heritage, religious centres, natural spots, adventure sports, captivating fairs and festivals. India has everything for every tourist. The tourist promotional agencies in this country are exploiting these sources to earn the proverbial foreign exchange earnings from the trade. However, this mad rush for foreign exchange earning is

* Lecturer in Marketing, Faculty of Management, L.N. Mishra Institute of Economic Development and Social Change, Patna.

causing irreparable damages to the nations fragile environment, specially in the Himalayan regions and beach resorts.

Surprisingly the environmentalists in India while discussing the causes of environmental problems in the country, always give stress on the growing human and animal populations, indifference of the industrial sectors on matter of environmental safety, the low level of environmental literacy etc. But they often forget to identify tourism, specially the sight-seeing, pilgrimage and adventure tourism, as one of the major reasons for environmental pollution in the country. In the present paper an effort has been made to identify the types of environmental pollution caused by the tourism trade in the Himalayan regions and beach resorts and possible remedial strategies to reduce the risk of pollution in these tourist spots.

Tourism : Environment-Inerrelationship

Environment is one the major elements, which forms the foundation of the tourism industry of a nation. Both, the natural environment in the form of land, water, plants and animals, and the man made environment constitute the attraction, which tourists look for in a destination. Thus, in the absence of an attractive environment, tourism industry of a country can not succeed.

As the environment is an integral component of tourism industry, it is expected that tourism developers of a country should take special care to ensure that the environment is properly cared for and preserved. But, such an ideal situation is very rare; since the impact of tourism and tourists on both the man-made and natural environment is far from beneficial and often the impact proves to be quite harmful. This situation is further strengthened by the discovery of the following two types of tourism related impact on the environment :

1. Harmonious coexistence between tourism and the environment, and
2. Conflicting relationship between tourism and the environment (Davidson, 1990).

When there is a harmony between tourism and the environment the latter benefits from the former or vice versa. One of the major tourism related benefits which a country can gain from the trade is the conservation of its natural and man-made environment. The palace hotels are a source of great fascination for tourists and provide revenue for those who own them (Misra, 1989). Similarly, the natural environment too, has benefited from tourism in a number of ways; Establishment of wildlife parks and sanctuaries have led to the conservation of wildlife and rare plants and flowers. In India 'Project Tiger' has contributed considerably in the protection of rare species of the Indian tigers. Not only does tourism provide a reason for the conservation of the natural and man-made environment, it can also provide the money which pays for the conservation. Income generated from tourism can be reused to preserve the environment of a country. Tourism also gives a fillip to the local handicrafts industry as the local crafts make the most popular souvenirs. Such examples demonstrate how tourism can benefit the environment by saving what otherwise would have been lost completely with the passage of time.

On the other hand tourism is said to be in a conflict with environment when a large number of visitors arriving at destinations lead to over-crowding of the place. Over-crowding further leads to untreated sewage, supply of polluted water and causes damage to the surroundings. Vegetation of a place suffers from constrant trampling and crushing by feet. Car wheels can lead to erosion and to the disappearance of fragile species. Fumes emiting from the exhaust pipes of the automobiles also cause wanton destruction to the fragile environment of the place. An important example of wanton destruction of environment by tourism can be found in the beach resort of Digha in West Bengal where deforestation and overcrowding has made the Bay of Bengal to eat a large portion of landmass and no wonder it is now threatening the small beach town. Further over-crowding of beach during the winter months and fumes of the trawlers are causing immense danger to rare marine life in that beach resort.

Types of Tourism Environment Conflict in India

The role of the Himalayas, environmentally and economically, in providing water resources, vegetation and special climatic conditions, is unique. The rivers rising from this range are major source of India's prosperity. Not only this, stretching 2,700 kms in an unbroken range from Ladakh in the north to Sikkim in the east, the Himalayas have treasure troves of flora and fauna systems. Also, being the highest mountains in the world, they can provide an array of rugged adventure sports that a tourist needs in this region. But, in the last 50 years, the forests of the Himalayas have been cut heavily. Now, the result is that most hills, mountains and valleys are barren. Its effect is being felt in the form of floods, soil erosion, landslides, drying up of water sources and severe droughts. A recent addition to this wanton destruction of the Himalayas rich flora and fauna, is the tourism induced pollution in region. Similar is the case with Indian beach resorts.

In fact, the various types of negative or underirable environmental impacts which have generated by tourism in India are those described below:

Population Hazard

During the peak tourist seasons the concentration of high volumes of tourism lead to congestion in the tourist places. Sudden increase in the number of population creates shortage of water, fuel transport, even food articles in the area. This leads to increase in the problems of the local populace, and finally to popular resentment against tourists.

Creation of Concrete Jungles

Growing number of tourists visiting a particular spot create a demand for accommodation. As a result of this, unintegrated tourists resorts are being rapidly construced with little consideration for regional planning. In order to construct low cost houses, box like, high-rise type pigeon holes with no architectural or aesthetic merits, are developed at tourist sites. These concrete structures lead to soil erosion and excavated debris pushes up the level of the streams and rivers.

Visual-Pollution

Poorly designed hotels and other tourist facility buildings, inadequate or inappropriate landscaping create visual pollution in the area. For example makeshift wooden structures mushroom all along the Manalsu bank, in Sial and Aleo Villages of Manali, creating a visual pollution (Singh, 1989).

Improper Waste Disposal

Littering of debris on the landscape or on the trekking trails generates both litter and environmental health problems. Not only this, plastic cans and bags carried by the trekkers and mountaineers once thrown into the rivers, create severe blocking of the stream. It also leads to the flooding of downstream areas.

Water Pollution

In the absence of proper sewage disposal system for a hotel, resort or other tourist facilities, there occurs the pollution of ground water from the Sewage. Further if a sewage outfall has been constructed into a nearby river and there is no water treatment plant, the polluted water of the river is bound to cause diseases like cholera, jaundice etc. Such type of diseases are common among the tourists and local people of Mussorie, Darjeeling, Nainital during the peak summer seasons. While describing about the sewage system of Manali the most horrifying fact is the absence of a central sewage system for 170 registered hotels and guest houses (Bhasin, 1992).

Air Pollution

The improperly maintained exhaust system of vehicles, campfire by the trekkers and mountaineers, use of firewoods for picnics increase the danger of forest fires as well as air pollution. This can lead to the destruction of vast range of forest and wildlife. These steps put a question mark to tourism industry claim as clean industry 'in the Himalayan region. The story is in no way different at beach resorts.'

Noise Pollution

Noise generated by a concentration of tourists or tourist vehicles or helipads for tourist helicopters can result, into ear damage and psychological stress to both the tourists and locals. Even the screeching sounds of tourist vehicles inside a wildlife park can create behavioural changes and fear among the wild animals. Recently in the Jim Corbett National Park a little girl was pulled out of her grand-father's arm in a bus by a ferocious horde of tigers (Sudhir, 1992). This is a clear case of the sound of the vehicles causing mental trauma to the wild animals. Further, the plying of vehicles inside the wildlife parks scares off the animals and birds. Photographing the wild animals and birds at close range can lead to great disruption in their lives. Their feeding and breeding patterns are interrupted. Different species are also prevented from laying their eggs in their usual places as a result of influx of visitors.

Ecological Damages

Several types of ecological problems result from uncontrolled and unplanned tourism developments in the tourist regions. Felling of trees to make way for tourist facilities, ski slopes and ski lifts cause suffering to forests. Further, construction of hill roads also causes irreparable losses to ecological surroundings of the area. It is estimated that the cumulative effect of building just one kilometer of road length can dislodge upto 12,000 cubic meters of debris, with neighbouring Nepal's contribution 6,000 million tons of silt annually find their way to the

Bay of Bengal (Bhasin, 1992). The construction of mountain roads causes extensive damages to the trees and top soil along the track. It also effects the hills natural angle of repose so badly that repeated landslides in Darjeeling, Sikkim, Shillong regions of the Himalayas have become a regular feature.

The excavated soil debris alongwith wilted trees down the hill slopes push up the level of the stream and rivers causing siltation and floods in the Gangetic plains. The overcrowding of the areas on the way to the valley of flowers and Hemkund from Govind ghat, Kedarnath from Gaikund and Yamunotri has caused destruction to conifer trees and pollution of the sites. The search for herbal flowers of rare varieties has led to their wanton destruction in the region of valley of flowers and Alkananda Valley. One of the species of rare Brahmakund flowers is disappearing because of the visitors to these areas, (Bagri, 1990).

The oars of the boats of the river rafting tourists in the streams of the Alakananda can cause extensive damages to the rare aquatic species. River rafting can also cause the loose pebbles in the waters to go down stream thereby choking the flow of water and causing floods. The department of tourism's under weightage to adventure tourism has led Shri Ashish Kothari of the Indian Institute of Public Administration to exclaim, "our greed for foreign exchange is making us overlook the influx of tourists that means havoc for our environment. In less than 30 years we won't have anything left except may be dollars to lure the foreign tourist with'' (Kothari, 1992).

Social Pollution

An extensive study of tourist literature indicates that tourism is closely related to increase in the sale of sex, crime of various kinds and organised gambling. There is the example of neighbouring Shri Lanka where AIDS has spread along the tourist trails into the interior (Bhatia, 1992). Moreover, the presence of a large number of prostitutes from the hill regions in the red light areas of Indian metropolis testifies to the fact that the poor innocent hill girls become easy prey to the dubious visitors to their areas and leave their homes for the promised land from where there is no return.

Remedial Strategies for Reducing Conflict Between Tourism and Environment

Since long the tourism planners, environmentalists, government officials and people at large have ignored the negative impact of tourism on the environment. This is more true in case of tourist sites and types of tourism practised in the Himalayan region and at beach resorts. Now a time has come when ignorance is no longer a bliss. A fresh look at the burning point of conflict between tourism and the environment has to be taken into consideration at the earliest. Strategies should be formulated in right earnest to reduce the wanton destruction of environment in the Himalayan region and beach resorts to prevent the repeated occurance of floods, landslides and earthquakes.

The first and foremost strategy should be the planned and controlled development of tourist places in the Himalayan regions. An upper limit on the growth of the sites should be made as has been done in Bhutan (Jenkins, 1992). In order to reduce the number of tourists visiting particular place during the peak season alternative sites around the major sites should be developed. This will reduce the occurance of problems like water, power and food articles shortages at a particular tourist spot during the peak season. Not only his, it will also reduce the tension between the local populace and tourists for essential commodities.

No hotel in a particular tourist spot should be allowed to be constructed, unless its architectural design is well integrated with the natural environment. The accommodation, recreational building facilities etc., should be in tune with the natural landscape surrounding them. For achieving this task the municipal and local authorities should be invested with power to implement the building laws in such areas. The local administration should see to it that other appropriate infrastructure standards pertaining to water supply system, sanitary and sewage disposal systems, telecommunication network, health care facilities have been developed and maintained.

In order to reduce traffic congestion, air pollution and water pollution, entry of automobiles should be restricted at the tourist sites. In order to reduce the behavioural changes among the animal within the sanctuaries the entry of automobiles like motor cars, buses, jeeps may be banned. Instead of motor cars and jeeps, elephant rides and battery charged noiseless cars should be given the permission to operate inside the wildlife parks.

The destruction of forests, flora and fauna can not be stopped only with the promulgation of laws, but with the active support of the law enforcing agencies like the police force, forest guards, residents of the areas concerned. If the residents of the areas can be convinced about the negative impact of tourism on their environment, which gives them economic prosperity; the battle against pollution is won.

The trekkers and mountaineers in these regions should be banned from carrying plastic bags or container the littering of which leads to the congestion of water streams and destruction of rare species of flora and fauna when thrown upon them after use. In most cases packets made of leaves which are easily soluble in water or marshy lands can be used by them. Even in the absence of a substitute for plastic bags and cans, the trekkers and mountaineers should be asked to take the used packs back during their return journey. Those violating such instructions should be heavily fined.

In order to check the flight of hill farmers from their traditional economic activities to tourism related activities, from tourism should be developed in the Himalayan regions. Dr. Tej Vir Singh writes, "The concept of farm tourism is integrative to craft tourism when the farmer takes up small operations viz. homestays, bed and breakfast, home made liquor, fruit juice and dairy products. This works as a defensive tourism promoting local economy and conserving heritage and rural charms of the valley". (Singh, 1989).

Ecological balance in an area can not be maintained without the support of the people of the area. Hence, groups of educated young men and women from the hills orate beach resorts should be mobilised to form 'environmental protection groups'. The main task of the members of the group will be to keep a strict vigil on the tourists, hotels, restaurants and resorts that the environmental laws are followed by the latter. In case of violation of the laws, they should inform the law enforcing agencies of the area concerned.

Finally, while marketing hill or beach resorts, the tourism planners should take extra care to inform the tourists about the hazards of environment pollution, and request them through print as well as audio-visuals media, not to violate the ecological balance of the region.

Conclusion

The hazardous impact of tourism in polluting the rivers of and seas India has long been overlooked by the environmentalists. Now a time has come to take a fresh stock of the situation. Many of the worst effects of the tourism on the environmental of the these regions can be controlled and prevented altogether through intelligent planning for tourism development and sensible management of tourists and tourists facilities. Participation of the scientists, technocrats, bureaucrats, tourism planners, environmentalists and people of the region is essential for formulating remedial strategies for reducing the conflict between tourism and environment.

BIBLIOGRAPHY

1. Bagri, Dr. S.C., Peaks of Faith (1990), Asian Panorama; pp. 18-19, New Delhi.
2. Bhasin, Raja (1992), Ringing in the destruction of the Himalayas, Sunday 13 December—The Economic Times, p.-14, New Delhi.
3. Bhatia, Ashima Kaul (1992); Just how golden is the goose? Sunday 28 November; The Telegraph Weekend, p.-5, Calcutta.
4. Bhatt, Chandi Prasad (1991); The Hug That Saves, The Hindu Survey of the Environment, p.-17, Kasturi & Sons Ltd. Madras.
5. Davidson, Rob (1989), Tourism pp. 129-39. Pitman Publishing, London.
6. Hussain, Abid (1989), Text of Fourth Somnath Chilbe Memorial Lecture at the Indian International Centre, Asian Panorama, p.-14, New Delhi.
7. Jenkins, Professor C.L. (1992), Environmental Considerations in Tourism Development, in the Approach to Tourism Management edited by Dr. Navin Mathur (et al); p.-147, Jodhpur.
8. Kothari, Ashish, (1992) in the just how golden is the goose? 1992, Sunday 28 November; The Telegraph Weekend, p.-5, Calcutta.
9. Lea, John (1988), Tourism and Development in the third world, pp. 65-69, Toutledge, London and New York.
10. Misra S.K. (1989). The Challenges of Tourism, Destination Traveller, p.-32, No. 151, Cross Section Publications (P.) Ltd. New Delhi.
11. Singh, Dr. Tej Vir (1989), The Kulu Valley : Impact of Tourism Development in the Mountain Areas p.-166 & pp. 1-90, Himalyan Books, New Delhi.
12. Sudhir, T.K. (1992), Alas, their tiger never roared that Monday; The Economic Times, Sunday 6 December, New Delhi.
13. Swaminathan, M.S. (1991), Maladies and Remedies; The Hindu Survey of the Environment, pp. 5-8, Kasturi and Sons Ltd. Madras.
14. Tangi, Mohamamed (1979), Tourism and the Environment p.-80, in Further case studies in Tourism (ed.) Roger Doswell, Barrie & Jenkins Ltd. Essex, U.K.

3

Strategic Management of International Business : Recent Trends

Narinder Kaur*
K.C. Singhal**

Introduction

There is growing realisation of the part of the Government that instead of doing some business, it should concentrate on creating an environment in which business prospers and entrepreneurial instincts are aroused so that the investors may get maximum output and reward from the efforts. Radical liberalisation has been ushered to make the Indian economy progressively market oriented and integrate it with the emerging global economic structure in a more meaningful way.

Recently, deregulation and the liberalisation initiatives have been undertaken with a view to increase production, improve quality and market the products and services abroad in competition with other multinationals. This resolve has found cosistency in the last three budgets of the Government of India.

New economic reforms, recently introduced by the Indian Government, led to more openness of Indian economic environment. These reforms have started to yield positive results in different economic areas. Even then we are far away from target of globalisation of Indian economy. The author is of the view that the Strategic Export Management can lead Indian economy to make it global economy. This paper

* Faculty Member, Deptt. of Economics, P.G. Govt. College (Punjabi University) Nabha, Patiala-147 001 (INDIA).

** Reader, Deptt. of Business Management, Punjabi University, Patiala, Patiala-147 001 (INDIA).

analysis the emerging trends in India's export markets. Recent trade policy reforms have also been critically evaluated in this paper.

In an otherwise promising outlook for the Indian economy a major factor for concern is the country's external payment situation. The external payment situation has continued to remain difficult on account of several medium-term factors such as :

(a) Deceleration in the rate of growth of domestic oil production.

(b) The bunching of repayment obligations to I.M.F.

(c) The liberalisation of imports which has led to massive trade imbalance.

(d) The economic survey has also stressed the role of high fiscal deficits leading to a continuous dose of money creation and consequent inflation to be contributing towards the current account deficit.

India's Export Performance

The need for augmenting exports is adequately recognised by the planning authority in India. The status and growth of Indian economy largely depend upon foreign exchange resources. Weak export capacity strains the economy and vitiates the climate of recovery. Economic growth rate of India is significantly retarded when foreign exchange position becomes adverse due to the depressed level of exports and abnormally high level of imports.

An analysis of export trends brings out an alarming picture of India's adverse balance of trade. The balance of payments situation in India has undergone a puzzling transition since the early fifties. During the quarter century that followed independence, trade deficits and payment difficulties were almost chronic. The first decade of planned economic development in India witnessed a stagnation in export earnings. The 1960's exhibit India's deep concern with self-reliance and its emphasis on import substitution. During the mild 1970's the balance of payments adjustment in response to the first round of oil price increase was unexpectedly smooth in India. It was based on a larger inflow of external resources, a dramatic increase in net invisible other than transfer payments, a phenomenal growth inremittances and above all, a management of the balance of trade situation which transformed a large deficit into a modest surplus within three years. In early 1980's the adjustments process has turned out to be much more difficult, following the second round of oil price increases. The worsening in the current account deficit in early 1990's was partly on account of the Gulf War and the higher price of POL imports. However, the trade deficit was exacerbated by deterioration in the invisible account because of lower remittances and higher interest payments.

Table-I presents the value of India's exports, imports and balance of trade position since 1970-71. The growth rate of exports (percentage change over the previous year) increased to 23.1 per cent in 1992-93 from 4.8 per cent in 1971-72 whereas the growth rate of imports increased to 38.7 per cent in 1992-93 from 11.6 per cent in 1971-72. This table also shows that India's exports have shown a sluggish tendency and imports have outpaced them resulting in a unfavorable balance of trade, which increased to Rs. 10,151 crore in 1992-93 from Rs. 99.04 crore in 1970-71. Thus, imports increased more rapidly than exports, particularly from 1973-74 onwards. Besides, the growth was observed more in imports than in exports accept in the year 1972-73, 1975-76 and 1976-77 during the period 1970-71 to 1979-80. But the growth rate of imports is less than exports which was observed during 1981-82 to 1984-85, and 1986-87 to 1989-90 and again in 1991-92. Since 1970's India faced an unfavourable balance of trade except in 1972-73 and 1976-77. Thus, India's trade balance had been highly unfavourable since 1973-74. The deficit assumed serious proportions towards the end of 1980's and early 1990s. Although India experienced a substantial rise in its exports, yet its share in total world exports declined from 0.70 per cent in 1970 to 0.54 per cent in 1990. Moreover, the ratio of exports to imports has been on the decline since 1970-71. Exports financed 93.9 per cent of imports in 1970-71 and 78.6 per cent in 1992-93.

Thus, export-earnings provide resources to finance imports. Table-I also indicates that imports are following as expanding path. Adequate earnings will be required to avert a foreign exchange crisis. Cut back in imports would only mean slackening the process of development which is against India's goal. More developmental imports means greater development and still more exports.

Extent of Export Diversification

For the purpose of empirical analysis of India's export performance, we need a method that explores in greater details the casual factors to which changes in export earnings over a period of time can be attributed. An immensely simplified model that has been frequently used in studies on the export performance of individual countries is the constant market share analysis of export growth. This paper examines the export performance in terms of changes in world demand, commodity composition and market distribution.

The study analyses these components by dividing the time period in 1970-71 to 1979-80, 1980-81 to 1990-91 and time period into 1970-71 to 1990-91, due to unfavourable balance of payments and oil price shock in 1970s and 1980s. In order to know the actual performance of exports, data have been converted into constant prices. The outlined approach provides a framework for an empirical investigation into the trends in India's major exports.

India's Share in International Business

Although world trade grew at a phenomenal pace. India's share in world exports declined continuously throughout the period from about 2 per cent in 1950 to 1 per cent in 1960 and 0.65 per cent in 1970. The value of India's exports in 1990 was about 20.5 times to its value in 1970. Table-II gives India's share of exports. It may be seen that it did not keep pace with the increase in world exports, rather India's share in world exports declined. It fell from 0.70 per cent in 1970 to 0.45 per cent in 1980 and rose to 0.54 per cent in 1990. Undoubtedly, a large increase in world exports was attributable to increased exports from developed countries. Thus, it might be argued that a developing country like India could not have maintained its share in the world trade. India's exports did not keep pace with the general growth in exports even from less developed countries (LDC).

The relative slow growth is often explained in terms of the fact that the bulk of India's exports were still concentrated in commodities like jute manufactures, tea, cotton-textiles, the world demand for which was growing very slowly. This is shown in Table-III

Tea and spices occupied first and second place respectively in world exports in 1970 and 1980. These two exports commodities taken together constituted 29.45, 22.49 and 10.35 per cent in 1970, 1980 and 1990 respectively of world exports, thus, showing a declining trend. These export categories, even taken individually, recorded a decrease in their shares during the period 1970-90. Cotton fabrics woven exports registered a shrinkage in its share from 6.82 per cent in 1970 to 5.29 per cent in 1980 which further declined to 2.41 per cent in 1990. India's share in world exports of iron-ore and concentrates also recorded a fall from 6.66 pre cent in 1970 to 6.31 per cent in 1980. However, it went up to 8.16 per cent in 1990.

The traditional export categories of coffee and substitutes and tobacco unmanufactured which registered an increase in their share in world exports during 1970-80 fell down in 1990. The rankings of these export categories present a composite picture. Leather manufactures was the most significant export commodity whose share in world exports went up from 0.76 per cent in 1970 to 6.36 per cent in 1980 and fell down to 5.58 per cent in 1990. Leather manufactures, however, went up in ranking from 15th place in 1970 to 6th place in 1990.

India's share in world exports of non-traditionals like electric machinery apparatus and appliances; transport-equipment; metal manufactures; fish; and chemicals in 1980 remained almost at the level of 1970 and fell down in 1990. However, share of iron and steel exports declined from 0.91 per cent in 1970 to 0.13 per cent in 1980 and 0.12 per cent in 1990.

Another important new export category-pearls, precious and semi-precious stones whose share in world exports in 1970 was 2.18 per cent, recorded an increase and it went upto the level of 3.12 per cent in 1980. This export category further registered an increase and its share went up to level of 11.23 per cent in 1990.

In 1980s, the share of coffee and substitutes; tea and mete; tobacco unmanufactured; cotton fabrics; non-cotton fabrics; fruits and vegetables 'sugar and honey' animal feeding stuff; leather manufactures; electric machinery apparatus and appliances; and transport equipment fell down. There is an improvement in machinery other than electric, iron-ore and concentrates; and rice.

Briefly, we observe that India's traditional exports which still constituted the bulk of world exports registered a decline in their shares. Even other exports did not perform well. The reason for this is the high domestic cost leading to reduced competitiveness of India's exports.

Trends in Commodity Composition

India's exports did not rise steadily although the rate of growth of exports during the 1970s and 1980s had gained momentum. Between 1950-51 and 1960-61, the amount and composition of India's exports changed little. Towards the end of 1950s, three initially dominant categories, i.e., jute manufactures; tea and cotton-textiles accounted for 49 per cent of exports. The process of change started with the decade of 1960s resulting in the fall of above three dominant categories of exports to a level of 28 per cent. The decades of 1970s and 1980s however, noticed substantial structural changes with regard to composition of exports.

Table-IV indicate the trends of the major exports in terms of their value, share, ranking and growth from 1970-71 to 1990-91. The striking features that emerges from this table is the declining importance of traditional export categories, the share of traditional export commodities recorded a fall during 1970-71 to 1990-91. It came down to 30 per cent in 1981 from 50 per cent in 1970-71. There was a dramatic fall in the share of jute manufactures and tea from 1970-71 to 1990-91, the share of these two export categories in India's total export earnings fell to 4.2 per cent in 1990-91 from 22 per cent in 1970-71. Similarly, the share of other traditional export categories like tobacco, cashew kernels, spices and oil cakes went down. Coffee whose share recorded an increase in 1970s, fell down in 1980s. The share of ironore also witnessed a contraction from 7.64 per cent in 1970-71 to 4.52 per cent in 1980-81 and which further declined to 3.22 per cent in 1990-91.

In contrast, the share of the relatively new items of exports or the non-traditional export categories such as handicrafts, raw cotton, and chemical and allied products registered a significant increase. The share of engineering goods increase in 1970s but fell down in 1980s. Cotton textiles and leather manufactures whose share fell down in 1970s, increased in 1980s. The share of non-traditional exports rose to a level of 55 per cent in 1990-91 from 28 per cent in 1970-71, which is a sufficient indication of the fact that these non-traditional, exports categories have shown dynamism in their behaviour.

During the decades of 1970s and 1980, some non-traditional exports have shown marvellous changes in their rankings as indicated in table-IV. Raw cotton which was at the bottom in 1970-71 occupies the eleventh position in 1980-81 and tenth position in 1990-91. Handicrafts, which did not figure among the principal export categories in 1960s occupied the first position in 1980-81 and 1990-91 whereas it was placed at the seventh place in 1970-71. Similarly, the other non-traditional exports like the chemical and allied products, leather manufactures and engineering goods also went up the ladder.

On the other side, the traditional export categories, on the whole, registered lower rankings in 1980-81 and 1990-91 as compared to 1970-71. For example, jute manufactures exports which were at the top in 1970-71, occupied sixth place in 1980-81 and seventh place in 1990-91.

The trend growth rates of valued of various exports categories also indicate the comparative importance of traditional and non-traditional exports during the period 1970-71 to 1990-91. Jute exports recorded a significant negative rate of growth during 1970s, 1980s and during the over all period of 1970-71 to 1990-91. The 1970s, coffee, spices, fish and fish preparations, engineering goods and leather manufactures had a significant rate of growth where as leather manufactures, cotton textiles and oil-cakes had a significant rate of growth in 1980s as well as from 1970-71 to 1990-91. Moreever, Leather manufactures in 1970s, fish and fish preparations, iron-ore in 1980s have significant but less than the overall exports growth rate. Similarly, during 1970-71to 1990-91, engineering goods, iron-ore, cotton textiles and coffee had a significant but less than overall exports growth rate. Cashew, raw cotton in 1970s, tea, sugar, coffee and raw cotton in 1980s had a negative rate of growth. Tobacco, oil cakes and sugar recorded a negative growth while the growth rates for export categories like the tea, cashew kernels, raw cotton and spices were not statistically significant during 1970-71 to 1990-91. Coffee was the only exception, which registered positive-significant growth rate. So on the whole, the traditional exports categories had become stagnant. All non-traditional export categories, on the other hand, witnessed positive growth rates. The highest rate was observed in case of handicrafts followed by chemicals and allied products and others during the entire period under study. All these export categories had growth rates higher than overall growth rate of India's exports (5.13 per cent).

Trends in Internationalisation of Indian Economy

Directional changes in India's exports provide us a deeper insight into the pattern of growth of many categories of exports. During the decade of 1960s, more than 40 per cent of the increase in India's exports in current prices went to the East European Countries. This may be because of the problems India faced in expansion of its trade with multilateral trade countries. Indeed, bilateral trade with East European Countries and expanded iron-ore exports to Japan were the saving factors of 1960s for export growth. Another point is whether concentration is upon a relatively stagnant commodities. Just as in the case of commodities, however, many opportunities in both old and new markets were not fully exploited. In fact, during 1950s and 1960s India failed to exploit to significant extent the immensely dynamic markets of Western Europe and other industrial countries. Further, just as overall export performance improved somewhat during the 1970s and 1980s, so did India's ability to exploit new market opportunities, even in the most competitive environment.

Table-V summaries the trends in the directions of India's exports during the period 1970-71 to 1990-91 for major countries. The table shows that there was no change in the rankings of the countries in 1970s and 1980s, so far as the first five places were concerned. There was also no change in the ranking of the countries so far as the first three places were concerned from 1970-71 to 1990-91. Among the first four major markets, former USSR and USA evidenced increase in their shares whereas shares of Japan and UK declined from 1970-71 to 1990-91 India's trade with these countries has been affected mainly under bilateral trade and payment agreements. The share of former F.R.G. increased whereas Canada, Iran, Australia witnessed decline in their respective shares during the overall period. Australia got a lower rank. In terms of growth during the period under study, the highest growth was that of former F.R.G. followed by former USSR, USA, France, Japan, Australia, Canada whereas Iraq witnessed significant negative rates of growth.

Table-VI shows the trend in the direction of India's exports during the period 1970-71 to 1990-91 for major regions. This table shows that the shares of North America and EEC countries in India's exports registered an increase while those of the Asia and Oceania, OPEC and East European Countries and EEC countries have gone up the ladder while North America, Asia and Oceania went down. The highest growth was observed in EEC countries in 1980s whereas it was highest for OPEC in 1970s. The trend growth rate of value of exports to these regions for the period 1970-71 to 1990-91 did show highest growth in North America followed by EEC countries, East European countries and Asia and Oceania. OPEC, however, exhibited a growth rate which was not significant.

This largely represents India's lost opportunity in the world market. In fact, India failed to exploit the fast expanding market of OPEC and remained content with its traditional markets. India's failure is largely due to internal factors like development strategy, internal demand and limited export surplus. To achieve a major breakthrough in the world market, much needs to be done at the level of policy.

Inspite of statistically significant growth rates of handicrafts and chemicals and allied products, India's overall growth rate remained low during the decades of 1970s and 1980s. The analysis shows that jute-manufactures, tobacco, oil cakes and sugar have insignificant role in or exports. The need is to stabilize the production of these commodities, and find new markets for them. Furthermore, engineering goods, cotton-textiles, coffee, iron-ore, fish and fish preparations and leather manufactures are the commodities for which attempts should be made to increase production. In order to boost the exports especially those of engineering goods, India has to offer heavy discount.

Moreover, the process of export expansion was accompanied by structural changes in the commodity composition. The study shows that the share of traditional commodities declined and that of non-traditional commodities increased during the period under study. Whatever diversification of exports took place, was mainly on account of rise in exports of iron and steel, engineering goods, chemical and allied products.

Globalisation Strategy and Export Business Diversification

The balance of payments crisis which emerged in the first quarter of 1991-92 was overcome by the concerted policy reforms initiated by the Government in July 1991. As a result of these policy reforms and successful mobilisation of exceptional financing, there was marked improvement in the external payments situation. This was reflected in the build-up of foreign exchange reserves by an additional amount of US $ 3.57 billion during 1991-92. The increase in reserves combined with establisation and structural reforms resorted international confidence and also provided the basis for further liberalisation trade, tariff, export credit and foreign investment polices during 1992-93. The 1992-93 saw the introduction of LERMS which constituted a dual exchange rate mechanism.

As a result of these measures, foreign currency assets which had decreased to US $ 1.1 billion in June 1991 rose to US $ 6.9 billion in the middle of July 1992 and were US $ 5.0 billion on 12 February 1993. Net inflows to the FCNR accounts have again become positive and there has been an acceleration in direct foreign investment proposals and approvals in the current financial year.

Exports have also increased at 3.4 per cent compared to a decline of 3.7 per cent in 1991. Hence, a faster rate of growth at 11.4 per cent to the general currency area because exports to the Rupee payment area declined by 64.4 per cent in doller terms.

The balance of payments continued to be under pressure in 1992-93. By the end of 1991-92, foreign exchange reserves had been built up to a respectable level of $ 5.63 billion from a low of $ 1.29 billion at the end of July 1991.

The trade policy regime was substantially changed in March 1992 when the liberalised exchange rate management system (LERMS) was introduced. Under LERMS, 40 per cent of foreign exchange earnings of exports of goods and services are required to be surrendered at the official exchange rate; this supply of foreign exchange finances import of essential items such as Petroleum, fertilisers or life-saving drugs. The remaining 60 per cent is to be sold in the market and finances all other imports. Along with this change in the exchange rate regime, the import licensing mechanism was virtually abolished, almost all capital goods, raw materials, inter-mediates and components being made freely importable, subject only to tariff protection. The peak tariff was also lowered in the Budget 1992-93 with the objective of gradually reducing protection to levels comparable with those in other developing countries.

Hence such a state of affairs could not be allowed to persist any longer. The first priority had to be on crisis management and this has been a major focus of policy in the past two years. However, efforts at short term stabilisation were also accompanied by measures of structural reforms and macro economic adjustments. Starting with a two step devaluation of the rupee by about 20 per cent, the structural adjustment programme embraced among others the industrial and fiscal polices, in early July 1991. A package of trade policy reforms was announced. The industrial policy liberalisation process was aimed at stepping up industrial growth promoting modernisation and technological upgradation to make industry competitive and cost effective. Raja Chelliah Committee report has been accepted by the Government and its recommendations for major corporate tax modifications are to be implemented in a phased manner. Monetary reforms have been initiated in the light of the Narasimham Committee Report.

Liberalised Exchange Rate Management System (LERMS)

A new system of exchange rate management was introduced in the Budget for 1992-93. The foreign exchange surrendered at official exchange rate is utilised to import essential items. All other imports of raw materials, components and also capital goods have been made freely importable on OGL foreign exchange for these imports has to be obtained from the market. There is a specified negative list of items which continue to be importable against licences. Foreign exchange required for other payments on private account including travel, debt service payments, dividends, royalties and other remittances has to be obtained at the market rate.

The system of eximscrips was itself abolished and was replaced by LERMS under which virtually all capital goods and raw materials and components were made freely importable subject to tariff protection as long as the foreign exchange to pay for those imports was obtained from the market.

Import Licensing

The import licensing system developed over the years was characterised by bureaucratic delays and arbitrariness and was also vulnerable to charges of corruption and misuse. The system operated to the dis-advantage of smaller enterprised which typically found it much more difficult and costlier to obtain licences. A step towards the simplification of the system was taken in July 1991 with the introduction of eximscrips, which were essentially tradable import licences issued to exporters for 30 per cent of the value of exports.

Conclusion

As the economy opens up and liberalisation picks up momentum, international competition will increase. Indian business needs to define for itself a global vision and develop strategies coherent with this vision, New Markets, new alliances and new customers are emerging everyday.. With changing environment, we must continually realign with the evolving world stage.

The globalisation of our economy is a compulsion under prevailing circumstances. Stability of policy is to be ensured for becoming an effective global player. It would be necessary to create a congential environment to woo foreign investment.

International trading environment is undergoing a rapid transformation. Protectionism is growing and multilateralism is under pressure. The equality of the present international trading system from the view point of India is an important factor. New linkages are sought to be enforced through the multilateral trade negotiations under aegis of GATT as symbolised by Dunkel draft proposals.

Keeping in view India's development, trade and financial needs,

India should prepare to play an active role in the international trading system, consistent with the national objectives. India's resistance to the introducing of new linkages intended to circumscribe the autonomy of development policies must continue with a renewed vigour. Hence, the export promotion measures should be adopted in the light of broader economic and social needs of the country and the changing global environment.

BIBLIOGRAPHY

1. Bhagwati, J.N., Foreign Trade Regimes and Economic Development Anatomy and Consequences of Exchange Control Regimes, Cambridge Massachusetts, Ballinger Publishing Company for the National Bureau for Economic Research, 1978.
2. Coppock, J.D., International Economic Instability, McGraw Hill, New York, 1962.
3. Foomkin, Joseph N., The Migration of Capital, People and Technology in Economic Development: Principles and Patterns, Williamson and Buttrick, 1954.
4. Ball, R.J., J.R. Eaton, M.D. Steuer, "The Relationship Between United Kingdom Export Performance in Manufactures and the Internal Pressure of Demand," Economic Journal, Volume LXXVI, No. 303. September 1966.
5. Bieda, K.,"The Causes of the Export lag of the Industrialising Countries," Kyklos, Volume XV, 1962.
6. Cross, A.K., "International Trade and Economic Development," Kyklos, Volume XIII, 1960.
7. Chenery, H.B. and A.M. Strout, "Foreign Assistance and Economic Development," American Economic Review, Volume LVI, No. 4, September 1966.
8. Grb, G.F., and Schiavo Campo, "Export Instability, Level of Development and Economic Size of LDCs," Oxford Bulletin of Economics and Statistics, Volume XIII, No 4, November 1969.
9. Ghos, Arun, "State of the Economy and 1993-94 Budget," Economic and Political Weekly, Volume XXVIII, No. 15, April 10, 1993.
10. Glezakos, C., "Export Instability and Economic Growth: A Statistical Verification," Economic Development and Cultural Change, Volume XXI, No. 4, 1973.
11. Gill, Sucha Singh and Ranjit Singh Ghuman, "India's Agricultural

Exports: Performance and some Policy Issues," Indian Journal of Agricultural Economics, Volume XXXVIII, No. 3, July-September 1982.

12. Houthakkar, H.S., and S.P. Magee, "Income and Price Elasticities in World Trade," The Review of Economics and Statistics, Volume LI, No. 2, May 1969.

13. Junz, H.B. and R.R. Rhomberg, "Price Competitiveness in Export Trade Among Industrial Countries," American Economic Review, Volume LXIII, No. 2, May 1973.

14. Kaur, Narinder and K.C. Singhal, "India's Agricultural Exports: Performance and Policy Perspectives," Indian Management Studies Journal, Volume I, No. I, October 1989.

15. Lancieri, Elio, "Export Instability and Economic Development, A Reappraisal," Banca Nazional Del Lavoro Quarterly Review, June 1978.

16. Panchamukhi, V.R., Trade Policies of India-Quantitative Analysis, Concept Publishers, Delhi, 1978.

17. Singh, Manmohan, India's Export Trends and the Prospects for Self-sustained Growth, Clarendon Press, Oxford, London, 1964.

18. Wolf, Martin, India's Exports, Oxford University Press, New York, 1982.

19. Balassa, B and M. Sharpston, "Export Subsidies by Developing Countries: Issues of Policy," Commercial Policy, Issue No. 2, Graduate Institute of International Studies, Geneva and the Trade Policy Research Centre, London, 1977.

20. Halder, Animesh, India's Export Pattern, Minerva Associates Publications Pvt. Ltd., Calcutta, 1976.

21. Helleiner, G.K., International Trade and Economic Development, Penguin, 1972.

22. Hirschman, Albert O., The Strategy of Economic Development, Yale University Press, New Have, 1958.

23. McBean, A.I., Export Instability and Economic Development, George Allen and Unwin Ltd., London, 1966.

24. Massell, B.F., "Export Concentration and Fluctuations in Export Earnings: A Cross Section Analysis," American Economic Review, Volume LIV, No. 2, March 1964.

25. Nayyar, Deepak, "India's Export Performance, 1970-85", Economic and Political Weekly, Volume XXII, Nos. 19, 20, and 21, Annual Number 1987.

26. Sarkar Prabirjit, "Rupee Depreciation and India's External Trade and

Payments Since 1971," Economic and Political Weekly, Volume XXVIII, Nos. 24 and 25, June 13-20, 1992.

27. Shetty, S. Vasudeva, "India's Trade with the Socialist Countries of East Europe Under Bilateral Trade and Payment Agreements," Indian Economic Journal, October-December 1976.

28. Singh, Ajit, and Jayati Ghosh, "Import Liberalisation and the New Industrial Strategy: An Analysis of Their Impact on Output and Employment," Economic and Political weekly, Volume XXIII, Nos. 45, 46 and 47, Annual Number 1988.

29. Smriti Mukherjee, "Export Instability and Economic Development (1950-51 to 1980-81): The Indian Case," Indian Journal of Economics, Volume LXVII, No. 266, January 1987.

30. Trivedi, H.K., "Export Strategy for India," ed. In N.S. Gupta, and et al, Export Strategies of 90's, Anmol Publications, New Delhi.

31. Government of India, Economic Survey, New Delhi, Various Annual Issues.

32. Government of India, Planning Commission, Eighth Five Year Plan, 1992-97, New Delhi.

33. International Monetary Fund, Annual Report, 1991, Washington, D.C.

34. International Monetary Fund, International Financial Statistics, Washington, D.C., Yearbook 1991, 1992.

35. United Nations, Yearbook of International Trade Statistics, New York, Various Issues.

36. United Nations, Economics Commission for Asia and far East (ECAFE), Economic Survey of Asia and Far East 1959, Bangkok, 1960.

37. United Nations, F.A.O., Trade Commerce, Yearbook, Rome, Various Issues.

38. United Nations Conference on Trade and Development (U.N.C.T.A.D.) Trade and Development Report, Geneva, Various Issues.

39. World Bank, World Bank Atlas, Washington, D.C. 1991.

40. World Bank, World Bank Report 1980, Oxford University Press, New York.

41. World Bank, World Tables, Washington, D.C., 1991.

Table I
Trends In India's Trade 1970-71 to 1990-91

(Rs. Crore)

Year	*Exports*	*Growth rate**	*Imports*	*Growth rate**	*Balance of trade*	*Exports as % of Imports*
1970-71	1535.16	—	1634.20	—	-99.04	93.9
1971-72	1608.82	+4.8	1824.54	+11.6	-215.72	88.18
1972-73	1970.83	+22.5	1867.44	+2.4	+103.39	105.5
1973-74	2483.20	+26.0	2920.90	+56.4	-437.70	85.0
1974-75	3328.83	+34.1	4518.78	+54.7	-1189.95	73.7
1975-76	4042.25	+21.4	5265.20	+16.5	-1222.95	76.8
1976-77	5142.25	+27.2	5073.79	-3.6	+68.46	101.3
1977-78	5407.90	+5.2	6020.20	+18.7	-612.30	89.8
1978-79	5726.26	+5.9	6814.30	+13.2	-1088.04	84.0
1979-80	6418.40	+12.1	9142.60	+34.2	-2724.20	70.2
1980-81	6710.70	+4.6	12523.90	+37.0	-5813.20	53.6
1981-82	7805.90	+16.3	13608.00	+8.7	-5802.10	57.4
1982-83	8803.30	+12.8	14293.00	+5.0	-5489.70	61.6
1983-84	9770.70	+11.0	15831.00	+10.8	-6060.30	61.7
1984-85	11855.20	+21.3	17134.00	+8.2	-5278.80	69.2
1985-86	10895.00	-8.4	19658.00	+14.7	-8763.00	55.4
1986-87	12452.00	+14.3	20096.00	+2.2	-7644.00	62.0
1987-88	15674.00	+25.9	22240.00	+10.7	-6570.00	70.5
1988-89	20232.00	+29.1	28235.00	+26.9	-800.00	71.7
1989-90 (P)	27681.00	+36.8	35416.00	+25.4	-7735.00	78.2
1990-91	32553.00	+17.6	43193.00	+22.00	-10640.00	75.4
1991-92	44042.00	+35.3	47851.00	+10.8	-3809.00	92.00
1992-93 (P)	37329.00	+23.1	47480.00	+38.7	-10151.00	78.6

Source : Government of India, Economic Survey, various issues, New Delhi.
Note : *Growth rate is the percentage change over the previous year.
(P) : Provisional.

Table II
World Trade and India's Exports

(Rs. Crores)

Year	*World Exports*	*India's Exports*	*India's exports as a Percentage of World Exports*
1970	219489.65	1532.87	0.70
1971	246142.75	1530.58	0.62
1972	296697.58	1859.01	0.63
1973	419461.56	2258.34	0.54
1974	657315.26	3180.84	0.48
1975	699563.52	3647.75	0.52
1976	84300.80	4971.90	0.59
1977	931839.57	5573.73	0.60
1978	1010688.50	5465.55	0.54
1979	1287402.20	6343.16	0.49
1980	1502304.80	6751.18	0.45
1981	1626593.20	7182.64	0.44
1982	1635147.70	8847.99	0.54
1983	1712689.40	9238.56	0.54
1984	2055794.00	11267.55	0.55
1985	2251281.70	11305.27	0.50
1986	2526109.40	11853.08	0.47
1987	3052939.96	14644.47	0.48
1988	3748544.00	18544.40	0.49
1989	4716249.20	25711.72	0.55
1990	5793649.00	31463.44	0.54

Source : International Monetary Fund, <u>International Financial Statistics,</u> Washington D.C., Year Book 1991.

Table III

India's Share in World Exports of Principal Commodities

(Rs. Crore)

Commodity	*1970*			
	World	*India*	*India's Share*	
			%	*Rank*
Meat and Meat Preparations	2711.65	3.02	0.11	(22)
Rice	699.85	4.54	0.65	(17)
Vegetables and Fruits	1112.96	12.86	1.16	(11)
Sugar and Honey	2042.82	19.67	0.96	(13)
Coffee and Substitutes	2424.90	23.45	0.97	(12)
Tea and Mate	444.12	148.29	33.39	(1)
Spices	192.93	39.34	20.39	(2)
Animal Feeding Stuff	1579.78	57.50	3.64	(8)
Tobacco	800.48	31.78	3.97	(7)
Unmanufactured Leather	530.38	71.12	13.41	(3)
Leather, Manufactures	99.87	0.08	0.76	(15)
Furskins, tanned or dressed	161.91	0.01	0.01	(24)
Fish	1604.75	31.02	1.93	(10)
Machinery other than Electric	25720.62	28.75	0.11	(22)
Electrical Machinery Apparatus and appliances	12287.18	16.64	0.14	(20)
Cotton fabrics woven	1086.48	74.15	6.82	(4)
Pearls Precious Semi-precious stones	1839.29	40.10	2.18	(9)
Fabrics woven of man made fibres	3001.43	143.00	4.76	(6)
Textile fabrics woven other than of cotton or man made fibres	204.28	1.51	0.74	(16)
Transport equipment	22607.21	25.72	0.11	(22)
Metal Manufactures	3274.56	20.43	0.62	(18)
Iron and Concentrates	1795.41	119.54	6.66	(5)
Iron and Steel	11000.96	99.87	0.91	(14)
Chemicals	8977.82	28.75	0.32	(19)

Table III (Contd.)
India's Share in World Exports of Principal Commodities

(Rs. Crore)

Commodity	*1980*			
	World	*India*	*India's Share*	
			%	*Rank*
Meat and Meat Preparations	14021.30	52.68	0.38	(17)
Rice	3424.34	125.81	3.67	(9)
Vegetables and Fruits	1888.53	203.65	1.08	(14)
Sugar and Honey	12724.69	36.17	0.28	(18)
Coffee and Substitutes	10205.39	213.09	2.09	(11)
Tea and Mate	1282.45	355.41	27.71	(1)
Spices	842.93	122.66	14.55	(2)
Animal Feeding Stuff	8116.19	128.95	1.59	(13)
Tobacco	2691.50	118.73	4.41	(8)
Unmanufactured Leather	2685.21	268.91	10.01	(3)
Leather, Manufactures	766.64	48.75	6.36	(5)
Furskins, tanned or dressed	1240.00	0.79	0.06	(24)
Fish	9638.47	190.28	1.97	(12)
Machinery other than Electric	181216.20	209.16	0.12	(23)
Electrical Machinery Apparatus and appliances	47922.63	89.64	0.19	(20)
Cotton fabrics woven	5214.74	275.99	5.29	(7)
Pearls Precious Semi-precious stones	14596.09	455.27	3.12	(10)
Fabrics woven of man made fibres	7332.25	34.60	0.47	(16)
Textile fabrics woven other than of cotton or man made fibres	2506.72	160.40	6.40	(4)
Transport equipment	13330.46	191.07	0.14	(21)
Metal Manufactures	28967.29	173.77	0.60	(15)
Iron and Concentrates	5122.74	323.17	6.31	(6)
Iron and Steel	53650.03	68.41	0.13	(22)
Chemicals	94903.26	247.68	0.26	(19)

Table III (Contd.)
India's Share in World Exports of Principal Commodities

(Rs. Crore)

Commodity	*1990*			
	World	*India*	*India's Share*	
			%	*Rank*
Meat and Meat Preparations	55016.82	75.27	0.14	(19)
Rice	5961.86	360.58	6.05	(5)
Vegetables and Fruits	83226.27	551.38	0.66	(14)
Sugar and Honey	25422.81	0.00	0.00	(23.5)
Coffee and Substitutes	17731.55	215.23	1.21	(11)
Tea and Mate	3176.98	348.33	10.96	(2)
Spices	2165.24	204.80	9.46	(3)
Animal Feeding Stuff	24946.70	236.30	0.95	(13)
Tobacco	7887.30	87.52	1.11	(12)
Unmanufactured Leather	16248.96	701.92	4.32	(7)
Leather, Manufactures	4325.24	241.55	5.58	(6)
Furskins, tanned or dressed	1794.16	0.00	0.00	(23.5)
Fish	53838.80	929.46	1.73	(10)
Machinery other than Electric	112724.71	507.62	0.45	(15)
Electrical Machinery Apparatus and appliances	318518.54	113.78	0.04	(21)
Cotton fabrics woven	23845.70	574.13	2.41	(8)
Pearls Precious Semi-precious stones	49704.36	5583.78	11.23	(1)
Fabrics woven of man made fibres	34980.00	61.26	0.17	(17)
Textile fabrics woven other than of cotton or man made fibres	12513.61	267.81	2.14	(9)
Transport equipment	690828.62	201.30	0.03	(22)
Metal Manufactures	110926.35	448.10	0.40	(16)
Iron and Concentrates	12529.36	1022.23	8.16	(4)
Iron and Steel	177891.40	206.55	0.12	(20)
Chemicals	460262.43	726.42	0.16	(18)

Source : Government of India, ***Economic Survey,*** various annual issues, New Delhi.

Note : Figures in parenthesis are ranks of shares.

Table IV
Trends in the Value of India's Exports at Constant Prices, 1970-71 to 1990-91
(Base 1978-79 = 100)

Commodity	*1970-71*		
	Value (Rs. Crore)	*Share %*	*Rank*
1. Jute Manufacturers	423.22	12.40	1
2. Tea	329.11	12.40	2
3. Engineering Goods	289.78	8.49	3
4. Iron-ore	260.67	7.64	4
5. Cotton-textiles	206.89	6.06	5
6. Leather Manufactures (Excluding footwear)	194.22	5.69	6
7. Handicrafts	178.44	5.23	7
8. Cashew Kernels	126.89	3.72	8
9. Oilcakes	123.11	3.61	9
10. Spices	86.22	2.53	10
11. Tobacco	69.78	2.05	11
12. Fish and fish preparations	67.78	1.99	12
13. Chemical and allied products	65.33	1.92	13
14. Sugar	61.33	1.80	14
15. Coffee	55.78	1.64	15
16. Raw-cotton	31.11	0.91	16
Total Exports (including others)	341.56	100.00	16

Table IV (Contd.)
Trends in the Value of India's Exports at Constant Prices, 1970-71 to 1990-91
(Base 1978-79 = 100)

Commodity	*1980-81* Value (Rs. Crore)	Share %	Rank
1. Jute Manufacturers	304.15	4.92	6
2. Tea	391.98	6.34	3
3. Engineering Goods	805.44	13.02	2
4. Iron-ore	279.54	4.52	7
5. Cotton-textiles	336.22	5.44	5
6. Leather Manufactures (Excluding footwear)	348.29	5.63	4
7. Handicrafts	890.66	14.40	1
8. Cashew Kernels	129.12	2.08	12
9. Oilcakes	115.30	1.86	13
10. Spices	102.67	1.66	15
11. Tobacco	114.65	1.85	14
12. Fish and fish preparations	200.00	3.23	9
13. Chemical and allied products	207.19	3.35	8
14. Sugar	33.18	0.54	16
15. Coffee	197.42	3.19	10
16. Raw-cotton	151.98	2.46	11
Total Exports (including others)	6184.98	100.00	16

Table IV (Contd.)
Trends in the Value of India's Exports at Constant Prices, 1970-71 to 1990-91
(Base 1978-79 = 100)

Commodity	*1990-91* Value (Rs. Crore)	Share %	Rank
1. Jute Manufacturers	101.88	4.92	7
2. Tea	365.81	6.3	6
3. Engineering Goods	1111.11	9.98	2
4. Iron-ore	358.63	3.22	8
5. Cotton-textiles	717.94	6.45	5
6. Leather Manufactures (Excluding footwear)	877.26	7.88	3
7. Handicrafts	2249.57	20.21	1
8. Cashew Kernels	152.82	1.37	12
9. Oilcakes	208.21	1.87	11
10. Spices	80.0	0.72	15
11. Tobacco	89.91	0.81	13
12. Fish and fish preparations	338.21	2.95	9
13. Chemical and allied products	869.74	7.81	4
14. Sugar	12.99	0.12	16
15. Coffee	86.15	0.77	14
16. Raw-cotton	289.23	2.60	10
Total Exports (including others)	1129.23	100.00	16

Table IV (Contd.)

Trends in the Value of India's Exports at Constant Prices, 1970-71 to 1990-91

(Base 1978-79 = 100)

Commodity	*Growth Rate* 1970-71 to 1979-80	1980-81 to 1990-91	1970-71 to 1990-91
1. Jute Manufacturers	-10.39**	-8.42**	-7.72**
2. Tea	3.01	-0.85	0.42
3. Engineering Goods	13.11**	0.56	5.05**
4. Iron-ore	1.18	2.00*	2.06**
5. Cotton-textiles	4.69	8.82**	4.41**
6. Leather Manufactures (Excluding footwear)	6.64**	10.58**	5.87**
7. Handicrafts	21.27*	11.02**	13.89**
8. Cashew Kernels	-2.67	2.21	0.50
9. Oilcakes	0.38	7.64*	-0.04
10. Spices	8.30*	2.79	2.22
11. Tobacco	2.46	-7.85**	-1.38
12. Fish and fish preparations	14.25**	3.02*	6.51**
13. Chemical and allied products	12.12**	14.52**	12.96**
14. Sugar	9.44	-22.07	-13.81
15. Coffee	16.02**	-3.34	3.86*
16. Raw-cotton	-11.03	-1.48	5.40
Total Exports (including others)	7.27**	5.62**	5.13**

Source : DGCIS, Calcutta.

Notes : All growth rates are semi-logarithmic least squares trends.

* Satistically significant at 5 per cent level.

** Satistically significant at 1 per cent level.

Table V
Value and Growth of India's Exports to Major Countries
(Base 1978-79 = 100)

Commodity	1970-71		
	Value (Rs. Crore)	*Share %*	*Rank*
1. Former U.S.S.R.	466.33	13.67	1
2. U.S.A.	460.76	13.51	2
3. Japan	452.18	13.25	3
4. U.K.	378.76	11.10	4
5. Former F.R.G.	71.80	2.10	5
6. Canada	62.13	1.82	6
7. Iran	59.22	1.74	7
8. Australia	54.36	1.59	8
9. France	39.96	1.17	9
10. Kuwait	34.98	1.03	10
11. Romania	30.44	0.89	11
12. Iraq	21.40	0.63	12
Total Exports (including others)	3411.56	100.00	12

Table V (Contd.)
Value and Growth of India's Exports to Major Countries
(Base 1978-79 = 100)

Commodity	*1980-81*		
	Value (Rs. Crore)	*Share %*	*Rank*
1. Former U.S.S.R.	1130.22	18.27	1
2. U.S.A.	685.11	11.08	2
3. Japan	550.98	8.91	3
4. U.K.	363.95	5.88	4
5. Former F.R.G.	354.61	5.73	5
6. Canada	57.46	0.93	10
7. Iran	113.58	1.84	7
8. Australia	84.44	1.37	9
9. France	135.48	2.19	6
10. Kuwait	89.49	1.45	8
11. Romania	53.82	0.87	11
12. Iraq	47.91	0.77	12
Total Exports (including others)	6184.98	100.00	12

Table V (Contd.)
Value and Growth of India's Exports to Major Countries
(Base 1978-79 = 100)

Commodity	*1990-91*		
	Value (Rs. Crore)	*Share %*	*Rank*
1. Former U.S.S.R.	1796.58	16.14	1
2. U.S.A.	1640.00	14.74	2
3. Japan	1038.97	9.34	3
4. U.K.	727.52	6.54	4
5. Former F.R.G.	871.45	7.83	4
6. Canada	96.07	0.86	8
7. Iran	48.21	0.43	9
8. Australia	109.74	0.99	7
9. France	261.88	2.35	6
10. Kuwait	25.30	0.23	11
11. Romania	32.82	0.29	10
12. Iraq	15.04	0.14	12
Total Exports (including others)	11129.23	100.00	12

Table V (Contd.)
Value and Growth of India's Exports to Major Countries
(Base 1978-79 = 100)

Commodity	Growth Rate 1970-71 to 1979-80	1980-81 to 1990-91	1970-71 to 1990-91
1. Former U.S.S.R.	1.43	2.71	6.80**
2. U.S.A.	5.33**	10.66**	6.63**
3. Japan	4.29**	7.20**	4.10**
4. U.K.	5.12**	7.24**	1.07
5. Former F.R.G.	18.78**	11.38**	10.30**
6. Canada	-2.98	7.03**	2.37**
7. Iran	10.44	-8.40**	-3.93
8. Australia	5.99**	4.32**	2.75**
9. France	18.13**	8.52**	5.60**
10. Kuwait	25.20**	-8.67**	-0.63
11. Romania	3.79	-8.56*	-0.37
12. Iraq	11.00	-11.16*	-5.85*
Total Exports (including others)	7.29**	5.62**	5.13**

Source : DGCIS, Calcutta.

Notes : All growth rates are semi-logarithmic least squares trends.
* Satistically significant at 5 per cent level.
** Satistically significant at 1 per cent level.

Table VI
Value and Growth of India's Exports to Major Regions
(1978-79 = 100 base)

Region	*1970-71*		
	Value (Rs. Crore)	*Share %*	*Rank*
North America	522.89	15.33	3
E.E.C.	621.36	18.21	2
Asia and Oceania	519.80	15.24	4
O.P.E.C.	228.89	6.71	5
East European Countries	805.40	23.61	1
Others	713.22	20.90	-
Total Exports (including others)	3411.56	100.00	5

Table VI (Contd.)
Value and Growth of India's Exports to Major Regions
(1978-79 = 100 base)

Region	*1980-81*		
	Value (Rs. Crore)	*Share %*	*Rank*
North America	742.57	12.0	3
E.E.C.	1334.01	21.57	2
Asia and Oceania	652.53	10.55	5
O.P.E.C.	701.61	11.34	4
East European Countries	1369.89	22.16	1
Others	1384.37	22.38	-
Total Exports (including others)	6184.98	100.00	5

Table VI (Contd.)
Value and Growth of India's Exports to Major Regions
(1978-79 = 100 base)

Region	1990-91		
	Value (Rs. Crore)	*Share %*	*Rank*
North America	1736.07	15.60	3
E.E.C.	3060.17	27.50	1
Asia and Oceania	1162.73	10.45	4
O.P.E.C.	625.98	5.62	5
East European Countries	1989.40	17.88	2
Others	2554.88	22.95	-
Total Exports (including others)	11129.23	100.00	5

Table IV (Contd.)

Value and Growth of India's Exports to Major Regions

(1978-79 = 100 base)

Regions	Growth Rate		
	1970-71 to 1979-80	1980-81 to 1990-91	1970-71 to 1990-91
North America	6.29**	4.56**	10.43**
E.E.C.	15.36**	10.01**	5.58**
Asia and Oceania	7.27	6.79**	4.63**
O.P.E.C.	19.96*	-2.03	1.85
East European Countries	-1.71	2.67	4.80**
Others	9.74**	3.69	4.94**
Total Exports (including others)	7.27**	5.62**	5.13**

Source : DGCIS, Calcutta.

Notes : (i) All growth rates are semi-logarithmic least square trends.

: (ii) Others include developing countries of Africa, Asia and Latin America and Carribean excluding members of OPEC

* Satistically significant at 5 per cent level.

** Satistically significant at 1 per cent level.

4

Performance Evaluation of State Financial Corporations (A Case Study)

B.S. Bhatia* K.C. Singhal*
Pervinder Kaur**

Intı oduction

The IFC confines itself to the financing of the public limited companies and co-operative societies, it is debarred by its statutes to assist private limited companies, partnerships and firms owned and managed by individuals. Therefore, it was envisaged to diversify the activities of the IFC to meet the needs of different regions and small scale sector. In the light of this, a battery of regional development banks was set up at the state level. It was in this background that the PFC was set up in 1953 to fill up the gap left by other term lending institutions in meeting the requirements of medium and small scale industrial units in the state.

The Punjab Financial Corporation, the primery term lending institution in the state, was reconstituted under the Punjab Reorganisation Act. 1966, on the 1st April 1967. It was split up into four corporation of Punjab, Haryana, Himachal Pradesh and Delhi. It is managed by a Board of Directors constituted under the SFC's act and the day-to-day working is looked after by the Managing Director, who is appointed by the State Government in consultation with the Industrial Development Bank of India, and Board of Directors of the Corporation.

---

* Professor and Reader respectively, Deptt. of Business Management, Punjabi University, Patiala, Punjab, INDIA.

** Research Scholar, Deptt. of Business Management, Punjabi University, Patiala, Punjab, INDIA.

Rationale of Institutional Finance

The financial institutions in the developing countries are appropriately referred to as development banks, implying that their task goes far beyond the conventional function of providing term finance to qualifying entrepreneurs and mobilising resources via their lending operations. But these institutions just cannot be an instrument growth. They can act as the growth-inducing sector in desirable directions and can make the task of entrepreneurs easier by providing finance in time and even before that by information on market and other related services. The development banks have to adopt their lending strategy and activities towards realisation of the socio-economic objectives of the country. It is quite a Complex task to work towards simultaneous achievement of what may sometimes turn out to conflicting objectives. A project to be established in a less developed region may be more expensive than in some other region. The entrepreneurs who are willing to take advantage of incentives for development of less developed regions may lead to further concentration of production assets in the hands of top few. These are complex issues, a development bank has to face and it has to decide various trade-offs between the likely benefits and costs involved and must prepare a happy mix of objectives.

Although profit is a criterion of efficiency of management of a corporation, a financial corporation, however, should not be judged only in terms of its financial record. Of greater significance to the economy is the corporation's contribution in terms of its impact on the thinking, work ethos and the attitude of its clients and of the business community. Financial corporations are channels through which society achieves modernity, and entrepreneurial and institutional growth. Thus, its true profitability can be found in and flows from an enhanced sense of business ethics, innovation in techniques and improvement in management practices. Hence, the purpose of this study is to analyse and evaluate the financial performance of PFC.

Objectives and Methodology

The study aims at analysing the financial performance of Punjab Financial Corporation. The main source of secondary data for evaluating the performance of the Punjab Financial Corporation are its annual reports and reports of Bureau of Public Enterprises, Punjab.

Financial analysis is the process of determining the significant operating and financial characteristics of a company/corporation from accounting data and financial statements. The goal of such analysis is to determine the efficiency and performance of the corporation's/company's management, as reflected in the financial records and reports.

To evaluate the financial performance of a financial corporation, the financial analyst needs certain yardsticks. The yardstick frequently used is ration analysis, since analysis and interpretation of various ratios gives a better understanding of the financial condition and performance of the organisation as compared to the analysis of financial data. To make a meaningful comparison, it is desirable to compare ratios over a period of time.

Performance of PFC has also been evaluated on the basis of ratios used by IDBI for evaluating the performance of SFC's which explained in this paper. Besides this some other well known ratios have also been used for this purpose.

IDBI Ratios

IDBI as an apex institution evaluates the financial performance of SFCs through select indicators, given as under :

Debt to Equity Ratio

Debt equity ratio is calculated to measure the relative claim of outsiders (i.e. shareholders against the firm's assets) which shows the extent to which debt has been used in the capital structure. The high debt equity increases the financial leverage, which results in increased earning per share because of its fixed interest obligations, being an admissible expense while computing profits for tax purpose resulting in tax saving and issue of debt does not result in dilution of control.

Analysis of table-I reveals that the debt to equity ratio of PFC has been increasing almost every year except the year 1988-89 when it went down to 3.84:1 and further increased to 4.21:1 in year 1989-90. This shows that PFC is making increasing use of financial leverage.

Debt Service Coverage Ratio

The debt service coverage ratio indicates the capacity of the PFC to repay the borrowings from IDBI availed in the form of refinance and interest on bonds, deposits and other borrowings. Debt service coverage norm is considered most vital in determining the financial worthiness of the project. The norm is between 1.5 to 2.0; i.e. the project cash flow should be such that profit after tax but before depreciation and interest

Table I
Debt Equity Ratio of PFC

(Rs. in lakhs)

Year	*Debt*	*Equity*	*Ratio of Debt to Equity*
(1)	(2)	(3)	(2/3)
1980-81	2703.98	974.47	1.77:1
1981-82	2987.42	1098.56	2.71:1
1982-83	3840.32	1289.11	2.97:1
1983-84	4449.92	1532.43	2.90:1
1984-85	5010.99	1638.84	3.05:1
1985-86	5354.74	1717.21	3.11:1
1986-87	7116.61	1870.97	3.80:1
1987-88	9354.52	1917.42	4.87:1
1988-89	11898.07	3092.08	3.84:1
1989-90	14801.21	3513.24	4.21:1

Source : Annual Reports of PFC, 1980-81 to 1989-90.

on borrowings should be 1.5 tó 2.0 times the sum of interest on borrowings and capital repayment installments.

The average Debt Service coverage ratio of PFC from 1980-81 to 1987-88 comes out to be 1.14 times where as it varied from minimum of 0.867 in 1984-85 to maximum of 1.66 in 1989-90. Comparison of debt service coverage ratio of PFC with all SFCs in India over a period of 5 years from 1980-81 to 1984-85 depicts that PFC is better placed in terms of servicing of its debts.

Return on Capital Employed

Return on capital employed establishes relationship between profits and the capital employed. It is the primary ratio and is most widely used to measure the overall profitability and efficiency of a business.

The return on net capital employed indicates how well management has used the funds supplied by IDBI, RBI, State Government and deposits from Public. The higher the ratio, the more efficient the PFC is using funds entrusted to it.

Table II reveals the return on capital employed of PFC during the period. It has gone down from 6.52% in 1980-81 to 0.12% in 1989-90. It is because of increase in cost of borrowings, administrative expenses and switch over from accrual system to cash accounting system w.e.f. 1.4.1984.

Cost of Borrowings

The cost of capital is an important concept in forming a firm's capital structure. It is one of the basic cornerstone of the theory of financial management. The primary purpose of measuring the cost of capital is its use as a decision criterion in capital budgeting decisions. Thus, cost of capital is simply the rate of return the funds used should produce to justify their use within the firm in the light of wealth maximisation.

Cost of debt (Kd) is the interest rate specified at the time of debt issue. The interest paid on debt is tax deductible. As a result, the effective cost of debt, i.e. the after tax cost of debt would be substantially less than the before tax cost.

After tax cost of debt = (i - t) Kd

Table III reveals the cost of borrowings over a period of 10 years from 1980-81 to 1989-90. The cost of borrowing is increasing from 6.23%

Table II

PFC : Return on Capital Employed

(Rs. in lakhs)

Year (1)	*Profit after tax interest* (2)	*Capital employed* (3)	*Return on Capital employed*
1980-81	253.63	3920.34	6.52
1981-82	345.34	4403.19	7.84
1982-83	375.12	5589.37	6.71
1983-84	472.70	6652.29	7.10
1984-85	254.04	7096.34	3.57
1985-86	458.04	7516.20	6.09
1986-87	522.16	9705.52	5.38
1987-88	774.78	12295.05	6.30
1988-89	30.788	15520.10	0.19
1989-90	-23.10	18900.29	0.12

Source : Annual Reports of PFC, 1980-81 to 1989-90.

Table III
PFC : Cost of Borrowings

Year *(1)*	*Interest* *(2)*	*Funded debt* *(3)*	*PFC* *(2 to 3)*
1980-81	168.63	2703.98	6.23
1981-82	191.43	2987.41	6.49
1982-83	241.66	3840.32	6.29
1983-84	323.04	4450.42	7.25
1984-85	272.80	5010.99	5.44
1985-86	429.68	5354.74	8.02
1986-87	493.70	7216.61	6.84
1987-88	697.41	9354.52	7.45
1988-89	943.31	11898.07	7.92
1989-90	1199.23	14801.29	8.10

Source : Annual Reports of PFC.

in 1980-81 to 8.10% in 1989-90. This is because of old bonds being redeemed and fresh bonds being issued at higher rate of interest. The cost of borrowing of PFC remained on the lower side except for the year 1981-82 during the sixth year plan. It was lowest in 1984-85 because of conversion of accounting system from accrual to cash accounting.

Administrative Cost as a Percentage of Average Total Assets

Expense ratios are calculated to explain the change in profitability position of concern. Administrative cost as a percentage of average total assets is shown in Table IV.

Arrears as a Per cent of Loan Outstanding

The ratio of overdues to loan outstanding gives an idea to what extent there is default in payment, i.e., delayed payment of suit filed cases. It reflects the efficiency of project appraisal exercise of SFC.

Table-V reveals the position of PFC with respect to overdues as a % of loan outstanding as presented in annual reports. The overdues amount do not include overdues against suit filed cases. It has deteriorated from 22.6% in 1981-82 to 17.82% in 1987-88 and further to 15.34% in 1988-89 and to 12.14% in 1990. This ratio remained between 25% to 29% for all SFC's during sixth plan period. The performance of PFC is below average in this regard.

It reflects the quality of project appraisal and follow-up and monetary system of PFC. The regular post sanction inspection of borrowing

Table IV

PFC : Administration Cost as a %age of Average Total Assets

Year	*Admn. Cost.*	*Average Total assets*	*Admn. Cost as a % of assets*
(1)	*(2)*	*(3)*	*(2/3)*
1980-81	37.96	3920.34	0.96
1981-82	43.01	4303.19	1.02
1982-83	63.73	5589.37	1.14
1983-84	72.33	6652.29	1.09
1984-85	74.72	7096.34	1.05
1985-86	98.76	7516.20	1.31
1986-87	119.12	9705.52	1.22
1987-88	140.21	12295.05	1.14
1988-89	150.92	15526.03	0.97
1989-90	191.76	18900.09	1.04

Source : Annual Reports of PFC, 1980-81 to 1989-90.
Ratios of PFC has been calculated by Author.

units are conducted by PFC through its branch officers at district level. Follow up inspection in fully disbursed cases other than court cases and transport cases were carried out in 1166 units in 1987-88 as compared to 882 units in 1986-87. The percentage of default at the close of year is 12.92% as compared to 15.03% in 1986-87 and 16.48% in 1985-86 as per Table VI. Percentage of default at the close of the year is increasing. Constantly from 4.65% in 1981-82 to 16.4% in 1985-86 and then decreased to 15.03% in 1986-87, 12.92% in 1987-88 and to 8.6% in 1989-90.

Recovery Against Total Demand

The financial performance of PFC can also be judged by looking at the recovery position during the year. Recovery of principal and interest constitutes substantial share in the source of PFC which constituted 52.3% in 1987-88 as against 44.4% in 1986-87.

Table VII shows the recovery performance of PFC from 1980-81 to 1989-90 as represented in their annual reports. .

Table V

PFC : Overdues as a Percent of Loan Outstanding

(Rs. in lakhs)

Year	Overdues at the end of the year	Overdues against suit filed cases at the end of the year	Total outstanding	Loan Disbursed	Overdues as a outstanding PFC	% of loan All SFCs
(1)	(2)	(3)	(2+3)=4	(5)	(4 to 5)	(6)
1981-82	191.50	739.34	930.84	4116.19	22.6	25.30
1982-83	209.83	703.49	913.32	5146.37	17.7	26.10
1983-84	376.53	727.34	1103.87	6216.35	17.75	25.50
1984-85	751.77	841.38	1593.15	6768.06	23.53	26.70
1985-86	1172.25	884.00	2056.25	7111.28	28.91	29.10
1986-87	1351.70	762.48	2114.18	8985.87	23.52	N.A.
1987-88	1471.66	557.82	2029.48	11385.01	17.82	N.A.
1988.89	1698.68	508.63	2207.31	14382.57	15.34	N.A.
1989-90	1500.04	643.19	2113.95	17404.11	12.14	N.A

Source : Annual Reports of PFC (1980-81 to 1989-90).

Table VI

PFC : Per cent of Default at the Close of Years

(Rs. in lakhs)

Year	*Overdues at the end of year*	*Loan Outstanding*	*%of default at the close of the year*
1981-82	191.50	4116.19	4.65%
1982-83	209.83	5146.37	4.07%
1983-84	376.53	6216.35	6.05%
1984-85	751.77	6768.06	11.01%
1985-86	1172.25	7111.28	16.48%
1986-87	1351.70	8987.87	15.03%
1987-88	1471.66	11388.01	12.92%
1988-89	1698.68	14382.57	11.81%
1989-90	1500.04	17404.11	8.06%

Source : Annual Reports of PFC, 1980-81 to 1989-90.

It shows the better position than what it was envisaged. The corporation has been able to exceed the recovery targets for the year 1981-82 fixed at Rs. 20 crores as against the targets for Rs. 16 crores in the previous years. The recovery performance was increasing upto 1988-89 (53.89%) but slightly decreased to 50.74% in 1989-90.

During the year 1989-90 the corporation has been able to achieve all time high recovery due to following additional measures.

1. Effective utilisation of branch network for recovery purpose.
2. Effective utilisation of the provision of Section 29 of SFC Act, 1951.
3. Regular monitoring of default cases and recovery position, and
4. The suit filed cases were also an encouraging factor to enter into compromise with corporation.

Table-VIII shows recovery performance of PFC under individual heading. Recovery of current dues increased form 60.58% in 1980-81 to 81.5% in 1987-88 but started decreasing to 79.37% in 1988-89 and 65.61% in 1989.90. The percentage of recovery of current dues was lowest in 1984-85 during the period under consideration.

For arrears under other than suit filed cases percentage of recovery decreased from 31.23% in 1980-81 to 23.6% in 1987-88. It was lowest in the year 1985-86 (15.61%) and highest in the year 1983-84 (51.03%).

Table VII
PFC : Recovery Performance

(Rs. in lakhs)

Year	*Current dues*	*Arears in other than suit filed cases*	*Arears in suit filed cases*	*Total re-coverables*	*Total recovery*	*Percentage*
1980-81	690.16	159.71	591.54	1441.41	690.85	47.93
1981-82	714.39	173.63	813.66	1701.68	770.84	45.30
1982-83	895.51	191.52	739.63	1826.66	913.34	50.00
1983-84	1226.34	209.83	703.54	2139.71	1035.84	48.41
1984-85	1447.01	376.53	727.34	2550.88	957.73	37.6
1985-86	1735.90	751.77	841.38	3329.05	1272.80	38.2
1986-87	1744.90	1172.25	884.00	3801.15	1686.97	44.4
1987.88	2142.30	1351.78	762.48	4256.56	2227.00	52.3
1988-89	2758.14	1471.66	557.82	4787.62	2580.31	53.89
1989-90	3977.87	1698.68	508.63	6185.18	3138.44	50.74

Source : Annual Reports of PFC (1980-81 to 1989-90).

Table VIII

PFC : Recovery Performance (Individual head wise)

Year	*Current Dues*			*Other than suit filed cases*			*Suit filed cases*		
	Collectable	*Collected*	*%*	*Collectable*	*Collected*	*%*	*Collectable*	*Collected*	*%*
1980-81	690.16	418.13	60.51	159.71	49.89	31.23	591.54	93.54	15.8
1981-82	714.39	494.64	63.29	173.63	55.31	31.85	813.66	116.19	14.27
1982-83	895.51	746.96	83.38	191.52	63.51	33.16	739.63	177.04	23.95
1983-84	1226.34	908.97	74.12	209.83	107.08	51.03	703.54	96.84	13.77
1984-85	1441.01	845.28	58.40	376.53	65.52	17.40	727.34	46.53	6.50
1985-86	1735.90	1091.03	62.90	751.37	117.09	15.60	841.38	64.68	7.70
1986-87	1744.90	1341.30	76.90	1172.25	252.31	21.00	884.00	93.86	10.60
1987-88	2142.30	1745.04	81.50	1351.78	318.83	23.60	762.48	163.23	21.40
1988-89	2758.14	2189.03	79.37	1471.66	293.29	19.93	557.82	97.99	17.57
1989-90	3977.87	2605.84	65.61	1698.68	493.48	29.05	508.63	39.22	7.69

Source : Punjab Financial Corporation, **Annual Reports** (1980-81 to 1989-90).

It increased from 19.93% in 1988-89 to 29.05% in 1989-90. For arrears of suit filed cases percentage of recovery is quite fluctuating, it is 21.41% in 1987-88 as compared to 15.8% in 1980-81 and 76.9% in 1988-89. It is maximum in the year 1982-83 (23.95%) and minimum in the year 1984-85 (6.5%).

Other Ratios

A fairly long experience on evaluation of financial performance of a concern is available. See for example, Hampten (1983), Vanhorne (1983), Chandra (1986), Pandey (1983), Kuchal (1988). In addition to the above IDBI ratios, following ratios have been selected, computed and analysed for PFC and in comparison with all SFC's in this section. These are :

Funded Debt to Total Captialisation

This ratio establishes a links between the long-tern raised from the outsiders and total long-term funds available in the business. This ratio is a variation of debt to equity ratio and shows the extent of debt in the capital structure of an organisation.

$$\text{Funded debts to total capitalisation} = \frac{\text{Debt}}{\text{Debt + Equity}} \times 100$$

Table IX shows the funded debt to total capitalisation ratio of PFC from 1980-81 to 1989-90. The share of funded debts, has increased from 68.97% in 1980-81 to 78.31% in 1989-90. This shows that long-term fund from outside sources are constantly increasing.

Administrative Cost as a Per cent of Total Income

Administration cost a percentage of total income explains the extent of admn. expenses in the profitability position of PFC.

Table X reveals that it has increased from 10.03% in 1980-81 to 12.3% in 1989-90. However, it was maximum in the year 1985-86 (16.9%) and then starting decreasing to 12.3% each in 1988-89 and 1989-90.

Earning Per Share

The profitableness of the common shareholder investment can be measured in many other ways. One such measure is to calculate the earning per share. The earning per share calculations made over years indicate whether or not the SFC's earning power, on per share basis has changed over period.

Table IX

PFC : Funded debt to total capitalisation

Year	*Funded debt*	*Total capitalisation*	*Percentage*
(1)	*(2)*	*(3)*	*(2 to 3)*
1980-81	2703.98	8920.34	68.97
1981-82	2987.41	4404.19	67.84
1982-83	3840.00	5589.37	68.70
1983-84	4450.42	6652.29	66.90
1984-85	5010.99	7096.34	70.61
1985-86	5354.74	7576.20	71.24
1986-87	7216.61	9705.52	74.35
1987-88	9354.52	12295.05	76.08
1988-89	11898.07	15526.03	76.63
1989-90	14801.29	18900.09	78.31

Source : Annual Reports of PFC, 1980-81 to 1989-90.

Table X

PFC : Administrative Cost as per cent of Total Income

(Rs. in lakhs)

Year	*Administrative cost*	*Total income*	*Percentage*
(1)	*(2)*	*(3)*	*(2 to 3)*
1980-81	37.96	378.42	10.03%
1981-82	45.01	449.98	10.00%
1982-83	63.73	551.33	11.05%
1983-84	72.33	674.81	10.07%
1984-85	74.72	371.10	20.10%
1985-86	98.76	597.93	16.05%
1986-87	119.12	700.75	16.09%
1987-88	140.21	966.48	14.50%
1988-89	150.92	1225.10	12.03%
1989-90	191.76	1550.62	12.03%

Source : Annual Reports of PFC, 1980-81 to 1989-90.

Table-XI shows earnings per share of PFC over a period of 10 years from 1980-81 to 1989-90. It has deteriorated from 17.17 in 1980-81 to 1.46 in 1989-90. the main factors responsible for it are employment of huge debt, increased cost of borrowings, increase in administrative and other financial expenses, high default ratio and social objectives of PFC.

Dividend Per Share

The net profits after tax belongs to shareholders. They are interested in real sense in the earning distributed and paid to them as cash dividends. Therefore, a large number of present and potential investors are more interested in the dividend per share rather than earning per share.

Table XII shows the average dividend paid to the shareholders. The dividend paid per share almost remained at the same level. In the year 1980-81, it was 3.19 per share whereas in 1987-88 it was 3.17. There are four classes of shares (including State Govt.). It can be concluded that PFC, as a financial corporation, is contributing also towards state exchequer despite its multi facted socio-economic role in the industrial development of Punjab.

Return on Shareholder's Equity

The common shareholders are the residual owners in the real sense of the word. The assume the maximum risk, and have the higher stake in the organisation. There are four classes of shares of PFC as on 31.3.1990.

1. 4,49,000 shares of 100 each fully paid up guaranteed by the Government of Punjab under Section 4(3) of state financial corporation Act, 1951.
2. 44.900 shares of 100 each fully paid up from IDBI under section 4(3) of state financial corporation Act, 1951.
3. 74,390 shares of other financial institutions like scheduled banks, co-operative banks and Insurance company, and
4. 1535 shares of other private shareholders.

The authorised capital of PFC is Rs 50 crores, with a view to strengthening the equity base, the paid up capital of PFC was enhanced from Rs. 973.92 lakhs in 1987-88 to Rs. 2498.92 lakhs in 1989-90. Government of Punjab and IDBI has an equal contribution to the share capital of PFC i.e. 46.10% each during the year 1987-88, whereas share of scheduled banks, insurance company's and co-operative banks is 7.64% and private shareholders have 0.16% share in the share capital of PFC.

Table XI

PFC : Earning Per Share

Year	*Profit after Tax*	*No. of equity shares*	*Earning per share*
(1)	*(2)*	*(3)*	*(2 to 3)*
1980-81	87.00	5.066	17.17
1981-82	96.30	5.366	17.94
1982-83	133.46	5.966	22.37
1983-84	149.61	6.966	21.48
1984-85	—18.76	7.986	
1985-86	28.36	8.426	3.36
1986-87	28.46	9.739	2.92
1987-88	77.37	9.739	7.94
1988-89	30.92	21.059	1.46
1989-90	—23.191	24.989	—

Source : Annual Reports of PFC, 1980-81 to 1989-90.

Table XII

PFC : Average Dividend Per Share

(Rs. in lakhs)

Year	*No. of Shares*	*Dividend Paid*	*Dividend Per Share*
(1)	*(2)*	*(3)*	*(2 to 3)*
1980-81	5016	16.20	3.19
1981-82	5366	16.53	3.08
1982-83	5966	18.87	3.16
1983-84	6966	24.28	3.48
1984-85	7986	26.82	3.35
1985-86	6426	26.91	3.19
1986-87	9739	29.72	3.05
1987-88	9789	30.93	3.17
1988-89	21.059	N.A.	N.A.
1989-90	24.989	N.A.	N.A.

Source : Annual Reports of PFC, 1980-81 to 1989-90.
Ratio has been calculated by Author.

Table XIII depicts return on equity shareholders of PFC. It is showing a declining trend. The return on shareholders equity has deteriorated from 8.92% in 1980-81 to 0.99% in 1988-89 and NIL in 1989-90. The main factors responsible for this are :

(a) increased cost of borrowings, increased administrative and other financial expenses and high default ratio.

Table XIII

PFC : Return on Shareholder's Equity

(Rs. in lakhs)

Year (1)	*Profit after Tax* (2)	*Net worth* (3)	*Percentage* (2 to 3)
1980-81	87.00	974.47	8.92
1981-82	96.30	1098.56	8.76
1982-83	133.46	1289.11	10.35
1983-84	149.68	1532.43	9.76
1984-85	—18.76	1638.84	—
1985-86	28.36	1717.21	1.65
1986-87	28.46	1870.97	1.52
1987-88	71.37	1917.42	4.03
1988-89	30.92	3092.08	0.99
1989-90	—23.10	3513.25	—

Source : Annual Reports of PFC, 1980-81 to 1989-90.

Conclusion

The study of financial performance of PFC reveals that PFC is making increasing use of financial leverage as indicated by its debt equity ratio during the period under study. The recovery performance of PFC is better than what it was earlier. The corporation has been able to achieve all time high recovery as shown by recovery against total demand ratio. The earnings per share of PFC deteriorated from 17.17 in 1980-81 to 1.46 in 1989-90. The main factors responsible is employment of huge debt, increased cost of borrowings, increase in administrative and other financial expenses etc.

BIBLIOGRAPHY

1. Berarwalla, B.L., 1987. "State Financial Corporations : Legal Remedies for Recovery of Loans". The Economic Times, August 20, pp. 6-8.

2. Chari, VV. 1976. "Performance and Problems of State Financial

Corporations" in Financial Institutions of India : Commerce—Economics studies. Vol. XII, Vora and Co., Bombay.

3. Diamond, William, 1974 "Interplay between Financial Institutions and Economic Development" in Financial Institutions of India : Commerce Economic Studies, 1976, Vol. XII, Vora and Co., Bombay.

4. Hampton, John, J., 1983 "Financial Decision Making", (Third Edition,) Prentice Hall, New Delhi.

5. Khan M.Y. 1981, "Development Banking—The Indian Experience" Lok Udyog. July.

6. Vanhorne, James, C., 1983, "Financial Management and Policy". (Sixth Edition), Prentice Hall, New Delhi.

7. Kuiper, E.T., 1972 "The Promotional Role and Management Responsibilities of a Development Finance Company" Development Digest. Vol. X, No.4, Oct. pp. 14-24.

8. Johnston, J., 1972. "Econometric Methods (2nd Edition) Mc-Graw-Hill. International Book Company.

9. Akram, S., 1987. "State Financial Corporation Striving for a dynamic development financing of small enterprises". Indian Journal of Commerce, (40) (1-2). Jan.-June, pp. 29-33.

10. Appa Rao, B. and Sujatha, A., 1985. Recovery Performance of SFC's: An Analysis". Lok Udyog, 19 (5), August, pp.-21-27.

11. Batra, Vinod, 1986. "Development Baking in India". Print Well Publishers, Jaipur.

12. Bhatt. V.V. 1976. "Structure of Financial Institutions : Legal Remedies for Recovery of Loan." The Economic Times. August 20, pp. 6-8.

13. Bhattacharya S.N. 1981 "Development of industrially Backward Areas' The Indian Style", New Delhi, Metropolitan.

14. S.A., 1984. "Challenges of Development Banking". Development News Consultency and Development No. 5.

15. Development Banking Centre, 1982. "Selected Readings in Development Banking" MDI, New Delhi.

16. Gupta, Rakesh, 1986. "State Financial Corporation Need for performance indicators". The Economic Time, 15th Sept., pp. 3-6.

17. Joshi, S., 1987. "Financial Institutions : Role in industrialisation of Backward Regions" Indian Management, Jan.

5

Emerging Dimensions in Services Management (A Case of India's Financial Services)

G.S. Batra*

At present in many industrialised countries more than 45 per cent of the national income is being derived from personal and industrial services and about 70 per cent of jobs are being offered by the service sector of the economy Numerous types of services are markted to customers, some of the most notable are food (hotels and restaurants), personal care (beauty parlours, laundries), automotive, entertainment, communication, lodging, transport, insurance, finance (Telephone and Postal), advertising and promotion engineering, consultancy, office services, tourist and travel and many other professional services. The service market consists of providers of personal and professional services as well as providers of industrial service.

Since 1950 services of infinite variety have grown up in importance. In a buyer's market, no organisation can survive long if it fails to recognise the significance of customers and it can earn profits only through customer service and satisfaction. Business exists to serve customers and it can earn profits only through customer service and satisfaction. This is equally true even in the case of marketing of services.

There is a regular market for services represented by activities, benefits and satisfactions offered for sale by providers of services. These services may be labour services (domestic, office, factory, workers),

* Faculty Member, Deptt. of Business Management, Punjabi University, Patiala.

personal services (hand laundry, photographers, barber), professional services (lawyer, accountant, musician, engineer), or institutional services such as offered by transport, banking, insurance, warehousing, advertising and such other service organisations. Above all we have government services also.

When a customer buys a service in the service market, he buys the time, knowledge, skill or resources of someone else who is the provider or supplier of a service. The buyer receives satisfaction or benefits from the activities of the provider who may be an individual, a firm or a company, i.e., an institution specialising in selling certain benefits or satisfactions.

Scope and Types of Services

Services can be classified according to the market to which they are offered : 1. Services sold in the consumer market, 2. Services sold in the industrial market. We have many services common to both the markets, e.g., financial, insurance, transport, and communication services.

Consumer Service

In the modern society, we come across many types of services sold to the consumer. Most important common services are :

Food Services

Restaurants, cafeterias and hotels are offering food services to numerous individuals and families who have firmly developed the habit of eating out. These eating places are ever growing as the service they sell is definitely wanted by the public. Small eating places offer simple and cheaper meals. Five Star hotels offer elegant and costly food but with superb services and royal comforts. Increasing tourism has also boosted the development of hotel industry. Then we have also caterers who specialise in supplying food and service for dinner and parties at our residence on ceremonial occasions.

McDonald's (Nationwide chain of Hemberger Stands selling food article in the U.S.A.) is a supreme example of application of manufacturing and managerial approaches to solve the problems of customer services in food industry. Modern scientific methods of production and marketing are applied in supplying food products to millions of people. The customer services are planned, controlled, automated, audited for quality control and regularly reviewed for performance improvement and customer reaction. McDonald service organisations are the best examples of scientific commercialisation of marketing of customer service.

Hotel and Motels

Lakhs of people every day use lodging and boarding services all over the country. Tourism is growing and hotels and motels are growing in numbers every year. Modern hotels provide luxurious life to travellers and tourist population. Tourism is now considered as a source of foreign exchange in all countries. Modern hotels provide numerous amenities, comforts and refined services.

Personal Care Service

Rising standards of living brought about development in the personal care services (helping a customer to be well groomed). These services are offered by beauty parlours, barber shops, laundries, dry cleaners, garment repair shops, shoe-repair shops, and so on. People have money and are prepared to spend money on themselves.

Entertainment Services

Rising purchasing power and more leisure time are responsible for the steady growth of entertainment services. Movies, sports, amusement parks, circuses, car racing, cricket, billiards, music, dancing and drama are such popular forms of organised entertainment today.

Transport Services

Railways, buses, ships, and aeroplanes provide transport services for moving people and goods. Fastest growth has taken place in air transport. A person can have round the world trip just in one fortnight. Air transport has become very popular in international tourism.

Communication Services

We have now at our disposal latest means of communication such as telephone, telegraphs, telex and postal service. Now we have radio, television and also satellite communications all over the world. Within a few minutes we can talk on phone with any person in Europe and America through satellite communication system.

Insurance Services

Insurance gives protection against risks, i.e., fire, accident, death, theft, sickness, unemployment and so on. People can save for their children's education, daughters marriage, or for their retirement. Security of life and property provided by insurance gives us freedom from anxiety, and peace of mind.

Industrial Services

In the industrial market, many services are offered to facilitate the process of production, finance and marketing. Manufacturers, wholesalers and retailers also sell some services along with the sale of goods. They also buy many services in the conduct of their business. There are also specialised services firms selling their services to industry.

Industry wants the services of transport, storage, finance, insurance and communication services as these facilitate the business operations. Business also purchases specialised services such as merchant banking, advertising and sale promotion services, engineering and office services. Some of the most important industrial services are :

Transport and Warehousing Services

Marketers need these services for physical distribution of commodities. Flow of goods in the process of marketing is facilitated through transport and warehousing services. Transport provides equalisation of supplies of physical products placewise, whereas warehousing assures equalisation of supplies timewise. These two wings of physical distribution offer maximum customer service and satisfaction.

Financial Services

Banks, investment companies, accounting firms, financial institutions offer numerous financial services to business concerns. Finance is the life blood of business, Long-term finance is required for working capital. Merchant banking services are required for promoting new enterprises and floatation and marketing of new capital issues. Investment companies guide business about the purchase of shares bonds and property to ensure sound investment portfolio. Accounting firms help in the maintenance of accounts, planning for profit, taxation and auditing of annual accounts.

Insurance Services

Risk of loss in business is inevitable. Business risks are numerous. Many of them cannot be eliminated or avoided. But they can certainly be transferred or shifted. Insurance companies enable businesses to transfer many business risks conveniently. They voluntarily assume the risk of loss due to accidents in the factories. We have transportation insurance, unemployment and health insurance schemes to provide social security to employees. Insurance facilitates smooth running of business.

Management Consultancy Services

Consultancy services firms offer numerous services to business enterprises. They advise top management on all managerial problems of production, marketing, finance, personal and office administration. Merchant banking services to new businesses at the time of project formulation and public issue of prospectus are also consultancy services. It is said that management and technical consultancy are really a boon or a blessing to the small and medium-size businesses as these enterprises cannot afford to employ many specialists on very high salaries to solve their managerial and technical problems. Consultancy service organisations have a very bright future in India.

Vital industrial services mentioned above clearly point out that mass production of numerous goods and their equitable distribution or marketing to satisfy ever-growing and ever-changing consumer demand will be impossible without these facilitating services provided to modern economy.

The phenomenal growth of business or industrial services particularly since 1950s is due to following reasons :

1. Modern business has become much more complex and specialised. Specialisation demands the services of specialists. It is preferable to use outside experts rather than employ them on a permanent basis.
2. Modern business has become more competitive. Marketing specialists are necessary to guide a firm in planning marketing strategies and preparing marketing programmes to meet keen competition. Almost in all areas of business, we have now consultants to guide management in solving managerial problems.

Objectives of the Study

The main objects of the study are :

1. to examine the growth and extent of financial services being provided in the country;
2. to evaluate the performance of financial services; and
3. to suggest measures to strengthen the financial services.

Research Methodology

It is concerned with the identification of universe, sample design, justification of sample, period of reference, sources of data and the data processing. The frame work of the study adopted is one that seek to combine relevance (to the research purpose) with the economy in procedure.

An exploaratory research design has been followed for the purpose of study. This type of approach is required to find out the most likely explanation. Since an exploaratory study largely interprets already available information, it makes use of the secondary data and the emphasis is more on the analysis and interpretation of the existing and available information.

Besides the data collected through questionnaire, it was necessary to use many other sources of information, both recorded and unrecorded. Reports, official records, books, journals, memeographs and unpublished works were used extensively. Interviews with prominent industrialists in the area, both old guards and young enthusiasts, helped in eliciting certain vital information that did not find any place in the records anywhere so far.

Managing the Financial Services

Any activity that facilitates individual economic agents to exchange resources to be available at different points in time and firms to acquire investible resources, can be called a financial service. Obviously, management of financial service is crucially important for a modern society.

India is one of the foremost countries of the world as regards number and size of institutions that produce and market financial services — commercial banks, development banks, and investing institution in public sector and many private sector organisations.

Many of the services rendered by these institutions developmental or otherwise can be called traditional. However, some important innovations in financial service have recently taken place, or are in offing. Particularly, these are : leasing, Venture capital, Merchant banking, Mutual funds and factoring. This not makes certain observations on the current state and suggests some measures for improving the management of these services.

Leasing Services

Recently the tendency of the commercial banks and other financial institutions to act as a leasing intermediary[1] and to dominate the lessors' market is increasing dramatically. The important reason, perhaps, is the ability of the financial institutions (because of their high profitability and relatively high tax brackets) to exploit the attractive tax concessions in the form of depreciation allowance and investment allowance,[2] allowance for investment deposit account[3] granted by the Income Tax Act, 1961. Proper consideration of these tax concessions will help the leasing intermediaries to lower the lease rent and offer the same to the lessees who are unable to take full advantage of tax benefits because of their low profitability and in this way their dominance is evident in the competitive market.

In the Western countries, industrial equipment leasing boom began in the mid 1950s and experienced its most rapid growth during 1960s, when leasing entered almost all the areas. Today, in those countries the use of equipment from aircrafts to the hospitals beds is obtained through leasing. Leasing Companies have grown from a few lessors, twenty years age, to thousands of public, private and bank subsidiary leasing companies, today, leasing expanded into areas namely aircrafts, autos, computers, communication equipment, earth moving equipment, office equipment, hotels, vehicles, etc.

Leasing plays an important role in capital formation in the developing countries like India. Leases come in all sizes, varieties and modes. The rapid growth of equipment leasing in India is obvious, even to the casual observer. During the last seven years, literally six hundred odd leasing companies have been formed. A survey made by the author regarding the lessees' (users of the equipment on lease) industry reveals that most leading industrial organisations are taking the equipment on lease either in a big or small way.

In the last 4 to 5 years, leasing has come in a big way to India. This is evidenced by the mushroom growth of leasing companies as well as volume of business in the last 4 years. It is estimated that there are about 600 small and big companies on register but only one-fifth of these are actively engaged in the business. A large number of companies including public sector organisations such as Air India, ONGC, SAIL, HMT, ISRO, BHEL, Coal India etc. are looking for leasing as a means of financing for on going capital expenditure.

Leasing as a Source of Finance

Leasing is very important source of finance from the point of view of the leasee to finance:

(a) Vehicles,
(b) Balancing Equipments,
(c) Modernisation upto moderate amount related to existing business operation.
(d) Cars, Scooters, and other Vehicles and other durables required for business of the assessee or for providing the same to employees/directors,
(e) Items entitled to 100% or 50% depreciation, and
(f) Assets which are not being financed by banks/institutions.

However, the leasing is not a good source of finance to meet the cost of a new project or expansion, diversification of relatively larger amounts.

Leasing Industry in India

First leasing company of India Ltd. was the first company, which commenced industrial lease business in the country in 1973 at Madras. Followed by 20th century leasing Ltd. which commenced its activities from Bombay in 1980. The excellent and solid performance of these companies led others to enter the field. All-hire-purchase and investment companies added leasing to the Memorandum of Association as one of the objectives of the companies from 1980 onwards. The following table shows the growth of leasing companies in India during the period 1980 through 1987.

Table I
Growth of Leasing Industry

Year	*No. of Companies**	*Growth Rate (%)*
1973	1	***
1980	8	.....
1981	20	150
1982	70	250
1983	160	130
1984	400	150
1985	480	20
1986	530	10
1987	600	13

*Number of companies includes the private limited companies.

Source : Various Govt. Publications and Annual Reports of Leasing Companies.

But the growth in leased assets by the industry is lower than that of the industry. Table -II explains the assets leased from 1985 through 1989, the cumulative assets and its growth during the same period.

Table II
Assets Leased by Industry

Year (January December)	*Assets leased during the year (Rs. in crores)*	*Cumulative assets leased (Rs. in crores)*	*Growth Rate %*
1985	80	250	.....
1986	180	430	125
1987	220	650	22
1988	270	920	23
July 1988	250	1170	85

Source : Annual reports of leasing companies.

The growth can also be seen through the funds mobilised by the leasing industry. The leasing industry has mobilised through all the sources of the tune of Rs. 3,160 crore as on 31-3-1988. The details of funds mobilised are given in the Table - III.

Table III
Funds Mobilised by Leasing Industry

Source of Funds	*As on March, 1988 (Rs. in crores)*	
Net owned funds	340	(11%)
Public Deposits and intercorporate deposits	2350	(74%)
Bank Borrowings	390	(12%)
Debentures	80	(3%)
Total	3160	100

Source : Reserve Bank of India Bulletin, June 1988.

During the last two decades, leasing has emerged as an important instrument to finance long-term capital requirements of Industries. ICICI was the first financial institution to establish leasing as a financial product in 1983.

Table IV reveals amount sanctioned, asset capitalised and income from leasing business to ICICI from 1986-87 to 1990-91. During the year 1990-91, lease sanctions and disbursements were highest of Rs. 172.89 and Rs. 111.75 crore as compared with Rs. 103.70 crore and Rs. 26 crores respectively in 1986-87. Cumulatively upto 31st March, 1991, gross leased assets were Rs. 344.68 crore. The income from leasing business is also showing an increasing trend.

During the year 1988-89, leasing division of ICICI introduced the 'Instalment Sale Scheme' to cater for clients who prefer ownership of equipment. Under this scheme sanctions were Rs. 38.30 crore as against sanctions of Rs. 32.47 crore in last year. Due to certain administrative constraints, of this scheme, a new scheme "Asset Credit Scheme" was introduced during the year 1989-90. Sanctions were amounted Rs. 342.08 crore and disbursements were Rs. 180.72 crores against sanctions of Rs. 213.97 crore and disbursement of Rs. 57.78 crore last year. This indicates the importance given by the clients to this scheme.

Table IV
Leasing Activities Performed by ICICI

(Rs. in Crores)

Year	*Sanctions*	*Assets Capitalised*	*Income from Leasing*
1986-87	103.70	26.00	8.36
1987-88	145.56	54.12	23.03
1988-89	152.52	52.53	33.94
1989-90	103.13	69.82	49.80
1990-91	172.89	111.75	69.60

Source : Annual Reports of ICICI.

Role and Performance of Mutual Funds Services

Mutual Funds are essentially portfolios, which co-mingle the savings of a large number of individuals in a large diversified investment portfolio. Mutual funds claim to offer professional management of funds to diversify and thus to reduce the unsystematic risk, while offering good returns. Mutual funds have long been popular in the developed economies. In India the first Mutual fund to be established was the Unit Trust of India. State Bank of India established a Mutual fund in 1987, and since then a number of public sector banks and other public sector corporations have established mutual funds. The regulatory framework in India does not permit establishment of mutual funds in joint/private sector till date. However, private companies offer portfolio management services outside the ambit of mutual funds. A few foreign and Indian banks have established funds which are based abroad for non-resident Indians and for investment in Indian stock-markets. The rapid growth that mutual funds have witnessed point to increasingly important role that mutual funds are slated to play in future.

A mutual fund combines the capital of many investors with employment of an experienced agent in purchasing securities of various companies, thereby providing diversification and supervision which the investors may not be in a position to afford individually. Mutual fund also combines in one stock certificate the convenience and satisfaction of owing shares in many industries.

Mutual funds have taken many turns and now the profile of this financial institution is assuming new shape. With the renaissance of mutual funds a change is taking place in the composition of investors. The traditional investors who used to invest in mutual funds, keeping in view the college education for children and retirement age are giving way to younger generation with shorter time horizon and greater expectations. There is a growth in the number of young people with growing expectations which has stated causing strains in mutual fund structure. While expectations are increasing, the industry is working with old software. The six mutual funds of U.S.A. which recorded high growth rates in 1983 provide some glimpse into the working of successful mutual funds. These mutual funds are being managed by professionals graduating from the colleges of management. Their approach to investment is more in terms of looking for companies with strong management, promising products, sound financial and marketing strategies. Few of them rely on market tips or mere hunches. Most of these managers are very young and almost all of them are achievement-oriented. The striking features in the domination of youth in the industry. While the managers are young, ambitious and dynamic, the investors' profile is becoming more and more young and sophisticated. Thus industry is getting dominated by the youth.

The realisation that no single investment product could meet all the financial needs of investors has led the mutual funds to develop a wide variety of products. There is mutual fund for every investor need. In seventies, almost 94 per cent of all mutual fund assets were associated with equity mutual funds but in early eighties they accounted for only 17 per cent. During this period the mutual fund business experienced a big change. Investor emphasis on yield and relative safety moved mutual funds in the direction of income oriented portfolio as against growth oriented investment. The industry introduced money market funds, municipal bond funds and bond funds.

Performance of Mutual Funds

The past decade has witnessed a phenomenal growth of the capital market in India. The changes made in FERA i.e., dilution of equity holdings by a number of foreign companies in the late 70s and important policy initiatives like 'Investment Policy statement in 1980, Technology Policy statement in 1983, Portfolio Investment Policy in 1983. Broad Banking of Industry in 1984, delicensing of industries (1992-93), increasing the assets threshold limit of MRTP companies, exempting export earning from tax, re-endorsing of the capacity for all industries, raising the limit to Rs. one crore in capital exemption order, setting up of Securities Exchange Board of India (SEBI) etc. provided a boost to the primary and secondary market. The number of individual share holders are increasing at a very fast rate. No doubt the primary and secondary market made a good progress after 1990 in terms of capital raised, number of listed companies, amount of capital of listed companies underwriting, turnover in various stock exchanges. Still there is a urgent need to activate the capital market as the general public is hesitant to invest in industrial securities because of uncertainties, pitfalls, price manipulation in the stock market by the interested parties, insider trading, kerb trading, option dealings etc. The introduction of mutual funds, a new financial instrument can help in solving this problem as mutual funds are managed by full time professional money-managers who make all the investment decisions on behalf of investors.

The Public sector mutual funds (Promoted by banks, L.I.C. and G.I.C.) other than those of UTI have achieved phenomenal growth in the preceding four and a half years. The UTI has already been there since 1964 and has been playing a crucial role in the Indian Capital Market. These newly created funds have been collectively able to mobilise savings of the magnitude of more than Rs. 10,000 crores. According to Dr. S.A. Dave the number of mutual funds, which was now about eight, would rise to anything between 20 and 25 in the next two to three years. At this rate of growth, these funds are most likely poised to out perform the UTI as far as the availability of total investible funds with these institutions are concerned. Further, according to the RBI Governor, the scope for various mutual funds to mobilise household savings is not going to be exhausted as currently these funds are on the average, just generating Rs. 5,000 crores per annum as against the total availability of Rs. 20,00,000 crores per annum from the savings of the household sector.

Future Prospects of Mutual Funds

The success of mutual fund depends essentially on the buoyancy of capital market in the country. The number of investors in corporate securities has increased to more than 7 million as against 2 million in the recent past and now constitute one per cent of the population as against 30 per cent of population in U.S. taking interest in corporate securities. The dilution of equity ownership by FERA companies has generated a keen public interest in corporate securities. The suspicion, misgivings and apprehensions associated with the shares and other securities seem to be gradually declining. This is supported by the oversubscription of number of issues and also by an active response to debentures and deposits.

There has been a significant increase in the number of listed companies, share-holders and stock exchange in the last few years. The rapid industrialisation of the country being envisaged under the Five Year Plans would further create the demand for additional funds. The management in the corporate sector is inclined more to raise funds from the individual investors as against financial institutions and institutional investors after seeing the episode of Escorts and L.I.C. The saving rate in India of 23% of G.D.P. provides an excellent opportunity for tapping the savings for investment in the organized corporate sector.

UTI can hardly meet the increasing requirements of funds of our corporate sector. There is need for the systematic growth of mutual funds in the private sector by providing the necessary fiscal incentives and facilities. There is need for organizing publicity to create interest of the investors in corporate securities not only in urban but also in rural areas.

Merchant Banking Service

The banking services scenario of the ninties will be dominated by tough competition among banks/financial institutions/public and private investment companies. The expectation of ordinary customers in the wake of consumerism, equity cult, high technology, new economic policy and marketing strategies adopted by foreign banks will be on the rise, compelling the banks to excel for customer allegiance. Banks have to offer various types of services and execute them with speed and quality. During current decade the fittest will survive. To attain the first seat, to maintain the present market share and to increase it further, banks have to go in for aggressive marketing. The banks have to realise that they have to operate in a market driven environment. Days are gone when it was felt that the customers would accept whatever service is offered to them.

Merchant banks are neither merchants nor are they necessary banks. Merchant banking originated through the entering of London merchants in financing of foreign trade through acceptance of bills. Later the merchants also assisted the governments of undeveloped countries in raising long-term funds through floatation of bonds in the London market and obtaining their quotation on the London Stock Exchange. Over a period merchant banks extended their activities to domestic business of syndication of short-term and long-term finance, underwriting of new issues, acting as registrars and share transfer agents, debenture trustees, portfolio managers, negotiating agents for mergers and take-over, etc.

The post-war period has witnessed the rapid growth of merchant banking through the innovation of instruments such as "Euro-Dollars" and the growth of various financial centres like Singapore, Hong Kong, Bahamas and more recently Bahrain, Kuwait, Dubai, etc.

Growth of Merchant Banking in India

Merchant banking in India is of recent origin. It had its beginning in India in 1967. When Grindlays Bank established a division, followed by Citibank in 1970 (it has now cease to provide merchant banking services) and State Bank of India in 1972. Later on the ICICI set up their merchant banking division followed by a few other banks like Syndicate Bank, Bank of India, Bank of Baroda, Chartered Bank, Mercantile Bank, etc. Some leading brokers have also entered the field.

Role of Merchant Banking in India

As the merchant banking is an essential function in project counselling and credit syndication/management, it acts as a catalyst in the process of floating project ideas into industrial ventures. The functions of merchant banking have to expand a lot. The scope is extremely wide. Merchant banking today is a protective and promoting force to entrepreneurs, corporate sector and investors. The role can be enlarged both in domestic and international market. The operations have to expand both horizontally and vertically so that merchant banking can evolve itself into a powerful subsidiary organ of the parent organization.

The setting up of a separate merchant banking division by leading share brokers, commercial banks and other reported financial institutions is a very encouraging development. The growing popularity of the services of the merchant banker is a clear indication of the vast scope that lies ahead. In the context of the massive investment that is envisaged in the various sectors of the economy and industry in particular, merchant banking expertise is likely to be in a much greater demand in the coming years.

India has built up a wide base of industrial structure. With acceleration of the process of industrialisation, the demand both for financial and other services rendered by merchant banking institutions and required by the industrial sector will grow.

Table V reveals the merchant banking activities undertaken by ICICI since its inception. Cumulatively upto 1985, this division has completed 204 assignments and assisted in raising a total amount of Rs. 1446 crore whereas this figure raised to 845 and a total amount of Rs. 14,906 crore (including Rs. 10031 crore from the capital market) by the end of 31st March 1991. This reflects the importance of MBD division.

Table V
Merchant Banking Activities By ICICI

Year	*Assignments Completed*	*Amount (Rs. Crore)*
Upto 1985	204	1,446
1985-86	49	1,106
1986-87	67	1,882
1987-88	105	2,165
1988-89	117	2,033
1989-90	170	3,662
1990-91	122	2,515
Cumulative	845	14,906

Source : Compiled from Annual Reports of ICICI.

Evaluation of the Working of Merchant Banks

Many merchant bankers have not shown much entrepreneurial ability. Their phenomenal growth has really coincided with a period in which a lot of money was lying around probably in banking deposits. What they have succeeded in doing is to draw existing investors' preference in favour of one instrument against the other. They have not succeeded in broad-basing the corporate sector's search for funds by channelising rural funds into productive investment. Further, they have failed to develop an independent rating agency like standard and poor in the U.S.

Merchant banking in India is still based on personalised business contacts. There is a drive towards professionalism. Each merchant banking house boasts of professional talent. Some of them have drawn young talent from management schools and accounting firms but still these merchant banking houses require a professionalised profile in the coming year.

Merchant banking have more often than not been guilty of over-doing in pushing the sale of new issues. They would be appreciated much more if they looked upon their role as that of an impartial adviser rather than merely looking to their own and their clients gains. A credibility gap has been created in the minds of the investing public regarding their usefulness.

Venture Capital Service

Venture capital is the response of investible funds to capitalize on an opportunity to earn very high returns as compared to conventional security-backed lending, by enabling high risk but high promise projects to realise their full potential.

The growth of venture capital is typically the response to the demand created for more risk-bearing funds, to finance commercialisation of new technologies and innovative market solutions.

In the US, this industry is almost 4 decades old and grew rapidly in the 60s and 70s. Currently there are almost 700 players in the US venture capital market an investment of around three billion US dollars annually. The total investment pool in the US alone is around 30 billion US dollars.

Venture capital has varied conception. In India, venture capital comprises seed capital finance for high technology and funds to turn R & D into commercial production. Quite a few institutions finance venture capital. For example TDICI (UTI and ICICI), RCTE (IFCI), IDBI's Venture Capital Fund, SBI capital markets, Can Bank Financial Services in public sector and CVF in private sector. All these institutions have their beginning only in late eighties. Venture capital finance is an innovation in that the traditional profitability criteria for investment may not permit it in view of high risks, involved.

In India, the venture capital companies have made investments of around Rs. 100 crores in over 200 companies. This is a modest beginning considering that total term lending amounts to Rs. 20,000 crores every year. However, in the years to come, such assistance is expected to increase substantially.

Factoring Service

Factoring is not a new concept to the business community of the Western World. Its origin can be traced during the fifteenth century in England and France. For exporting their goods to their colonies these countries required the services of specialised agents which later came to be known as factoring organisations. Initially these organisations, were called upon to distribute goods, provide funds and collect debts. Later on they restricted their activities to provision of funds and collection of debts. Factoring is very popular in Western countries, but in India it has started gaining in the recent past only.

Factoring may be defined as a continuing arrangement between the financial institutions or banks (factor) and a business concern (the supplier) selling goods or providing services in credit, wherein the factor undertakes the task of recording, collecting, controlling and protecting the book debts and also **purchasing** the bills receivables of the supplier.

Under factoring between a supplier and his customer there enters a factor who performs a variety of financing services including credit management. The charge for the services is in the form of a discount or a rebate deducted from the individual debts. The factor may also release 80 to 85 per cent of uncollected and not due accounts as advance and the balance minus his charges on the maturity of the debts. For this facility the factor charges interest varying between one to two per cent over the prevalent bank rate. Factoring, therefore, is a modern service which puts at the disposal of a business enterprise an operative instrument, specially conceived for a synthesis of financial, administrative and gurantee services.

Conclusion

The number of financial institutions in public sector that provide financial services is rather large. Overlap and duplicity reduces cost affectiveness and output efficiency. There is a need for allocative planning regarding 'who should do what'. The selection should be based on some past performance linked efficiency criteria. These then should compete with private sector freely under minimal government control to check only illegal/unethical practices.

Marketing persons know very well that products have a life cycle (PLC) and passes through four stages. Introduction, growth, maturity and decline. Clearly all the financial services are still at the introduction or growth stage and marketing, financial manufacturing (service package), purchasing and personnel strategies should be accordingly formulated. Often, in case of large public sector organization the focus of attention becomes the employees of the organization (e.g., unions and pressure groups). The simple lesson of marketing concept-customer satisfaction or social interest (in case of societal marketing) should always be kept in mind.

Much of the existing finance theory is based on the assumption of perfect capital market (with or without uncertainty). But the existence of a few large agencies of financial services in India characterises an oligopolistic market structure. This opens up new opportunities and challenges to finance professional to devise new theory of finance which will be relevant in the different countries of the world.

Development Banks have been doing a commendable task in the field of merchant Banking services specially for medium & large size units. These agency can also provide services to bigger projects for entering in joint ventures abroad besides promotion and syndication of projects, investment management and advising services. The merchant Banking activities may change in description on coverage in line with changing need, pattern of the enterprise attunting the changing economic environment in the country.. Demand will change subject to the changes in other environmental factors, particularly under the influence of technological developments taking place. The coverage of rural areas and small business is the present day need of the environment and the shift in demand of merchant banking services is bound to occur. The merchant Banking professionalism requires new response in education and training confirming to the dynamism of the change. Professional development programmes have got to be reshaped to enable Merchant Banks to render more specialised services. Financial Institutions in India should actively contribute towards venture capital facilities for accelerating economic activity, particularly by the small corporate firms having assessed prospects for their future growth potential.

REFERENCES

1. Leasing intermediary is the lessor who purchased the asset from the manufacturer (or vendor) and in turn, leases it to the lesses. In 1984, the Research Bank of India permitted the banks to set up subsidiaries to transact business in equipment leasing and associated activities.
2. Investment allowance is granted in respect of some eligible assets u/s 32A of the Income Tax Act, 1961. However, the deduction is withdrawn if the eligible asset is acquired or installed after 31-3-90 vide Notification No. : S.O. 233E, dated 19th March 1990. Some controversies exist regrading the availability of the benefit by the lessor.
3. Allowance for investment deposit granted under section 32 AB of the Income Tax Act, 1961 is withdrawn from the assessment year 1991-92.

BIBLIOGRAPHY

1. Brick, Ivan E., Fung, W. and Subrahmanyam M. Leasing & Financial Intermediation : Comparative Tax Advantages, Financial management, Spring. 1987.
2. Gupta, K.G., Financing — An Analytical Evaluation, The Chartered Accountant, December 1986.
3. Kajaria, U.N., Tax Planning Through Leasing, The Chartered Accountant, June 1989.
4. Annual Reports, First Leasing Company of India.
5. Annual Reports, 20th Century Leasing Company Ltd.
6. Gupta, N.K., Lease Financing, Deep & Deep, Delhi, 1991.
7. Hanson, G.D., Merchant Banking, Service Bankes (ed), Institute of Bankers, London, 1982, pp. 252-53.
8. Verma, J.C., Organisation and Management of Merchant Banking, Tata Mcgraw, Delhi, 1992.
9. Batra, G.S., Management of Financial Services, Finance India, Sept. 1983, Vol. VII, No. 3.

6

Strategic Management of Indian Financial Markets: Taking Shape for Turbulent Times

A.S. Chawla and G.S. Batra*

The rapid growth and globalisation of financial markets is perhaps one of the most significant developments at international level, India too has initiated the process of liberalisation of the financial sector. As a result of that many changes has been brought in primary and secondary markets and efforts have also been made to woo the foreign investor through FDI and portfolio investments. However, there are doubts with regard to the results we may obtain from these measures. There are opinions that the concept of welfare state which India has pursued for decades and is of utmost importance will be pushed in the background, the consequences of which may not be favourable for the economy. The present working paper discusses some of these aspects emerging from the structural changes in the financial markets.

With the objective of bringing about a highly competitive system and promoting efficiency in the real sectors of the Indian economy, recent economic reforms in the areas of trade, industry and exchange rate system have been taken to correct the macro-economic imbalances and bring about the structural adjustments. The liberalisation and supportive policies of the Government have gained momentum in the last few years with major plans of diversification, expansion and modernisation of industrial sector in the country. This has led to an increased demand for funds and encouraged authorities to find out alternative sources of finance for the industry. Since the conventional

* Reader and Faculty Member respectively, Department of Business Management, Punjabi University, Patiala.

budgetary support cannot be of any positive help to the public sector and the private corporate sector which used to depend heavily on banks and financial institutions in the past, now collects funds from the capital markets.

The Indian financial markets plays a crucial role in economic development through saving-investment process, also known as capital formation. A vibrant and competitive financial markets is necessary concomitant of trade and industrial policy liberalisation to sustain the ongoing reform in the structural aspects of the real economy. Many financial reforms were taken to improve the efficiency and stability of the financial system, internal and external developments which made it increasingly difficult to maintain a tightly regulated financial system.

The process of liberalisation initiated by the Government has not been new, but prior piecemeal efforts were not stable and widespread. The structural reforms initiated during last three years have had a positive impact on the investment climate in the country. The new economic policies aimed at liberalisation and globalisation are all embracing, consistent and appear to be irreversible. The country has pursued conservative, inward looking policies for almost four decades. The positive effect of these policies may be many but they are outweighed by their negative impact of inefficiency, corruption, delays and non-competitive nature of industrial/economic environment. Many mighty socialist economies have crumbled under their dead weight and India could very well imagine what is in store for it, if it does not change the course. The whole nation is in a mood for change and manmohanomics is getting a fair trial inspite of scams and corruption charges.

Capital market which is concerned with the supply of long-term funds in response to gradual liberalisation of economic and industrial policies since the beginning of eighties resulted in a virtual capital market revolution.

In its bid to open up the country's economy, the government of India has geared up the financial sector to meet the challenges, which economy is likely to face. As such Indian financial markets are undergoing a process of rapid change which has transformed the entire complexion of financial system. The government of India during last three years have announced a number of measures to make the Indian financial markets more potent and capable of raising vast resources from the domestic market and abroad.

The purpose of this working paper is to examine the developments in the Indian financial markets, as a result of liberaslised policy of the government. The developments in the Indian financial market be studied from the following angles.

1. examine the policy changes initiated in the domestic capital market and their implications for the economy.
2. to review the policy changes initiated to tap the international resources for the development of the economy.

Section I

Capital Market Reforms

The need for reforms in the capital market has been evident for some time. Over the last couple of years, there has been a determined shift to equity financing. From 1990 onwards, growth in listings (now over 65000), market capitalisation (above Rs. 205000 crores), trading volumes (approximately Rs 370 billion a year), and investors' interest (probably more than 15 million share-holders), have all attained new heights as per Table I.

Table I
Recent Trends in the Stock Markets in India

Sr. No.	*Particulars*	*1983*	*1993*
1.	No. of stock exchanges	10	21+1 (OTC)
2.	No. of listed companies	3118 (on Dec. 31)	6800 (on March 31)
3.	Amount of capital raised	Rs. 706 crores (1982-83)	Rs. 1600 crores 1992-93)
4.	Number of investors	3 million	25 million
5.	Total capital listed	Rs. 6533 crores (on Dec. 31)	Rs. 55000 crores (on Dec. 31)
6.	Average daily turnover	Rs. 22.69 crores (1982-83)	Rs. 238 crores 1992-93)
7.	Total market capitalisation	Rs. 8706 crores (on Dec. 31)	Rs. 205000 crores (on March 31)

Source : The Stock Exchange Review, Sept. 1993.

The functioning of stock exchanges shows many shortcoming with long delays, lack of transparency in procedures and vulnerability to price rigging and insider trading. The reforms measures initiated in the capital market over the past two years, starting with the conferring of statutory status on the SEBI, repeal of capital issue control act and the abolition of the office of the controller of capital issues, have brought about significant improvement in the functioning and regulatory efficiency of the market. Steps taken by SEBI for establishing a fair transparent and a strong regulatory framework for the efficiency functioning of the capital market and investors interest have helped in developing the capital market on healthy lines and will help in bringing the functioning of capital market upto international standards.

The intermediaries in the securities market such as merchant banking, brokers and portfolio managers and registrars have been brought into the regulatory framework of SEBI and would have to adhere to capital adequacy norms, meet certain eligibility criteria and abide by a code of conduct which envisage a sense of responsibility towards investors.

Emerging Trends in Capital Markets

SEBI has taken a number of steps to bring transparency, check malpractices, and protect the interests of the investors. A few have already been implemented to set the things right and in the proper perspective.

To overcome the problem of overtrading, SEBI has prescribed the minimum capital need norms. The minimum capital prescribed by SEBI for each broker is Rs. 5 lac each for Bombay and Calcutta, Rs. 3.5 lac each for Delhi and Ahmedabad, and Rs. 2 lac each for all other exchanges. In addition, SEBI has decided that the additional capital together with the minimum capital should not at any point be less than 8 per cent of the gross outstanding business in any exchange. The SEBI has further decided that this 8 per cent requirement can be achieved in a phased manner - 3 per cent from December 1993, 5.1 per cent from June 1994, and the full 8 per cent by December 1994.

In a bid to ensure greater transparency and to check malpractices, stock brokers would now be required to divulge details of all transactions, the exact price at which they were transacted, and the brokerage involved. This will reveal a much better picture of volumes and actual turnover of the script. The SEBI has further finalised the norms for regulating the transactions between clients and brokers. In future, every member broker may have to keep books of accounts to show and distinguish in connection with ones business as a member, money received from or on account of, and money paid to a or on account of each of his client, and the money received and paid on the member's own account.

Governing boards of the most of the stock exchanges have been given enough powers to control excessive speculation and other malfunctioning, foreseeing the emerging crisis and averting the same in time, establishing effective reporting and audit system, and taking disciplinary action against the stock brokers who flout the rules and bye-laws.

The Government has announced the proposal to set up a National Stock exchange which would serve as a model for other stock markets in the country.

In order to provide liquidity to stock markets, it has been proposed to introduce market making in a phased manner in a few big stock exchanges of Bombay, Calcutta, Delhi and Madras. Each market maker should market for a minimum of 10 scrips of which not more than 5 should be scrips from the ones included in the BSE National Index. Each market maker shall be required to acquire and make a market for at least 2 lac shares in each of the scrips. The buying and selling spread would be determined by the supply and demand conditions prevailing in the market. The commercial banks would provide suitable bank credit to market makers approved by SEBI with a margin of 25 per cent on the scrips for which they make the market.

Primary Market Reforms

SEBI has also initiated reforms in the primary market. The objective is to strengthen the standards of disclosure, introduce certain prudential norms for the issues and inter-mediaries, and remove the inadequacies and systematic deficiencies in the issue procedures. Among the steps taken are the following:

(a) The minimum percentage of securities to be issued to the public for the purpose of listing of securities, was reduced from 60 per cent to 25 per cent through an amendment of the securities contract (Regulation) Rules, 1957;

(b) An advertisement code was laid down to ensure that the advertisements are fair and do not contain statements to mislead the investors;

(c) Allotment procedures were revised to introduce the requirement that shares be alloted on a pro-rata basis, raise the minimum amount of application money for public and rights issues to Rs. 5,000 and on par issues from 100 to 500 shares, allow mutual funds and Foreign Institutional Investors (FIIs) to apply for firm allotment in public issues and reduce the number of collection centres to a minimum of 30;

(d) A system of appointing SEBI representatives to supervise the allotment process was introduced to minimise malpractices in allotment of over-subscribed public issues;

(e) Prudential norms were introduced for right issues; and

(f) Public sector bonds were brought under the regulatory authority of SEBI as per Box-I.

Mutual Funds

For the first time mutual funds are governed by a uniform set of regulations which require them to be formed as trusts and managed by a separate asset management company (AMC) and supervised by a board of trustees or trustee company. SEBI (Mutual Fund) regulations provide for arms length relationship between the various constituents of the mutual fund and thus bring about a structural change which will ensure qualitative improvement in the functioning of the mutual funds. The regulations lay down certain eligibility criteria for the sponsors of mutual funds and require that the AMCs have a minimum net worth of Rs. 6 crores of which the sponsors must contribute at least 40 per cent. The SEBI (Mutual Fund) Regulations also provide for an approval of the offer documents of schemes by SEBI. The regulations prescribe minimum amount to be raised by each scheme. A close ended scheme with a fixed size of mutual fund must raise a minimum of Rs. 20 crore and open ended scheme of Rs. 50 crore. The entire subscription amount must be refunded within six weeks of the closure of the scheme in case the amount collected by the scheme falls short of the prescribed amount. There will also be certain investment restrictions for ANCs. The advertisement code prescribes norms for fair and truthful disclosure by the mutual funds in advertisements and publicity materials. The Regulations are intended to ensure that the mutual funds grow on healthy lines and investors' interests are protected.

Twenty private sector sponsors have been given approval by SEBI to set up mutual funds. In accordance with the regulations, these sponsors are now in the process of setting up separate asset management companies, trustee companies, and appointing independent custodians. Some of them have completed these formalities and set up the mutual funds and also launched schemes after approval of the offer documents by SEBI. The existing mutual funds have also restructured the funds in accordance with the regulations. Since the notification of the Regulations by SEBI, there has been visible improvement in the disclosure standards of the mutual funds.

Credit Rating Agencies

Credit rating has assumed great importance for individual investors, brokers and financial advisers with the expansion of money, Government security and equity markets, Credit Rating and Information Services of India Limited (CRISIL) has rated over 750 debt instruments issued by 557 companies. It has started rating the debt instruments of banks, and has already rated four public sector banks and one private sector bank, and of IDBI, EXIM-Bank, SIDBI and SFCs. This is being extended to rating of debentures, fixed deposits and commercial paper. Investment Information and Credit Rating Agency of India Limited (ICRA) also rates long-term (e.g., debentures, bonds and preference shares), medium term (e.g., fixed deposit) and short-term (e.g., commercial paper) instruments. Cumulatively till end December 1993, ICRA has rated 236 debt instruments of manufacturing and finance companies involving Rs. 11049 crores.

Over the Counter-Exchange

The Over the Counter Exchange of India (OTCEI), Bombay started its operations in September, 1993 and sixteen companies have already been listed with it. Regional windows have been opened at Delhi and Madras, besides representative offices have been opened in 18 major cities throughout the country.

Evaluation of the Working of SEBI

The stock exchanges have come into conflict with SEBI regarding exercise of powers relating to calling for periodical returns, prescribing maintenance of certain documents, approving bye-laws, and licensing of dealers in securities in certain areas. As a matter of fact, Central Government has the authority to exercise these powers under the securities contracts regulation act, 1956. These are now sought to be transferred to SEBI through the new legislation.

It is true that SEBI has had tussle with almost every participating institution in the capital market in respect of one or the other issue. Instead of taking up the entire work with such a great speed, it should have implemented its policies in a sequential manner allowing the participant institutions to learn the art of compliance. More so, SEBI should have taken atleast public financial institutions and governing boards of stock exchanges into confidence, while formulating the guidelines for different issues.

Number of steps have been initiated by SEBI to check these multiple irregularities. The effectiveness of the regulations would largely depend in their effective enforcement. The SEBI has made a significant contribution towards shaping and disciplining the Indian securities market.

Indian financial sector has succeeded in ensuring the following:

(1) Mobilisation of resources;

(2) large percentage of savings passing through financial markets;

(3) integration of rural population into the formal financial system;

(4) intermediation of sizeable financial savings in rural areas;

(5) loan for investments to all levels of industry and agriculture; and

(6) availability of equity funds from the capital market to medium and large scale industries.

Insurance Sector Reforms

A committee was appointed in April 1993 by the Ministry of Finance under the Chairmanship of Sh. R.N. Malhotra, former Governor of Reserve Bank of India to study the working of Life Insurance Corporation of India (LIC), General Insurance of Corporation of India (GIC) and its four subsidiaries and the insurance business as a whole and to make recommendations for reforms in the insurance sector in line with on going reforms in other parts of the financial sector viz., banking and capital market. Some important recommendations made by the Committee in this respect are given in Box-II.

Section II

The foreign resources flows to India in two ways:

(1) The Foreign Direct Investment,

(2) Portfolio Investment.

  (a) Foreign Institutional Investors,

  (b) Euro-equities.

Foreign Direct Investment

The urgency to ensure a steady flow of foreign direct investment is very essential and of strategic nature because aid commitments are gradually dwindling and borrowing abroad have become scarce. The inflow of equity will have advantages of reducing repayment burden. Foreign Direct Investment, thus has a great potential in the years of nineties.

In the decades of the eighties, foreign investment policy had played a very limited role in the process of growth and development. During the period 1986-90, there has been 900 crore foreign direct investment flow to India which comes to Rs. 180 crore per annum. This reveals that during the decade of eighties, India followed a restrictive foreign investment policy. Foreign Direct Investment, moreover, was permitted in areas of high-tech sophisticated technologies and substantial exports. Foreign equity participation was restricted to 40 per cent of the total capital.

From July 1991 onwards, Government of India, initiated a more liberal and productive foreign investment policy so that more and more foreign direct investment could be attracted and utilised for rapid industrial growth. Under the new foreign investment policy, there has been automatic approval of FDI upto 51 per cent equity holding in 34 specified high priority, capital intensive, high tech units. Government is open to bring in the list some areas considering the priorities of the nation.

51 per cent financial institutions was also allowed to trading companies for exporting world markets for Indian goods. These policy guidelines shall allow royalty upto 5 per cent on domestic sales and 8 per cent of export sales alongwith lumpsum technology payment upto Rs. 7 crores.

A special board known as Foreign Investment Promotion Board was also established to look after the regulation and monitoring of large foreign investment projects where higher foreign equity limit of more than 51 per cent may be allowed, keeping in mind interest of the nation.

Since the adoption of new foreign direct investment policy FDI flows to India has recorded 25 times increase. The approvals of direct foreign investment proposals rose from US $ 73 million (Rs. 128 crore) in 1990 to US $ 235 million (Rs. 535 crore) in 1991, to US $ 1318 million (Rs. 3888 crore) in 1992 and To US $ 2091 million (Rs. 6577 crore) during Jan-Oct. 1993 of which 90 per cent has gone to high priority areas as indicated in Table-II.

In the area of technical collaboration more than 88 per cent foreign investment are confined to high priority areas. The bigger chunk of FDI is allowed in the vital sectors of the economy namely, power, oil, food processing, chemicals, electrical and electronic equipment, telecommunication, transportation, industrial machinery and hotel and tourism industry.

Industry-wise FDI Flows

Till the end of March 1993, the power and oil refinery units have attracted maximum foreign direct investment. Table-III reveals that nearly 47 per cent of the total amount till March 1993 flows in power and oil refinery sector. On the other side, services sector and Hotel and Tourism got the least attention getting only 2.35 per cent and 2.36 per cent FDI flows. In fact the focus of the government has been to develop power and infrastructure sector for overall development of the economy.

The industry ministry has decided to go ahead with its proposal to give automatic clearance for foreign equity investment upto 75 per cent against the level of 51 per cent permitted earlier. It has also plan to abolish the condition of balancing capital goods import with foreign equity.

Besides increasing the limit of automatic clearance, the government has also decided to enlarge the list of 34 industries where foreign investment proposal will receive automatic clearance.

Portfolio Investment

The process of globalisation has opened the ways for foreign institutions to participate in the capital market. With a view to facilitating the entry of FIIs into the country, SEBI has simplified the procedures. The entry of FIIs is also facilitated by increasing the role of foreign brokers in the transactions of FIIs. Foreign brokers are allowed to assist FII's and operate on their behalf by transacting orders to buy or sell securities to members of the Indian stock exchanges. The foreign brokers have been permitted to open bank and custodial accounts for this purpose. Government have also allowed some firms to set up joint ventures in the financial sector.

Table III
Industry wise F.D.I. Flows

Industry	*Amount of F.D.I. (Rs. in Million)*
Power	17393
Oil Refinery	16172
Food Processing	8794
Chemicals	6119
Electrical Equipments	5026
Hotel and Tourism	2159
Service Sector	1772
Textile	1719
Transportation	1714
Tele-communication	1337
Others	10514
Total	72719

Source : Hindustan Times, New Delhi, June 22, 1993.

There has been continuous increase in the number of FII's registered with SEBI and in the volume of investments effected by them in India. Till the middle of the January 1994, SEBI had registered 134 FII's who have 175 broad based institutional fund under them, about US $ one billion dollars have already been invested by them. The size of the inflow of investment funds and the increase in FIIs is indicative of the growing confidence of the international investing community in Indian markets and their regulatory mechanism.

During 1992-93, portfolio investment in the country was $ 241.5 million which went upto 1.120 billion dollars till the end of December 1993, aggregate total FIIs stood at $ 1.36 billion at the end of December 1993, which is 1/3 of the total domestic market inflow in the stock market. This clearly indicate that market has been attracting the attention of FII's. Indian companies too have been accessing Euro issues, 12 companies have entered the capital market till December 1993.

Implications

In the liberalised industrial environment, the new entrepreneur will launch capital issues. With the abolition of restrictions on premia and fixation of issue price will boost the morale of established units to raise additional resources from the capital market. With the increased rate of interest the cost of capital is increasing. The capital is becoming more scarce due to the competition from public sector financial institutions. The financial institutions and the development banks now find themselves strapped for cash and will not be in a position to satisfy all the capital needs of the private sector. In the changing scenario, the financial sector will have to act as a catalyst to mobilise the necessary resources from the capital market and put it to most optimum use.

The immediate impact of liberalisation measures is imbalance between the supply and demand in the market. There is a shortage of good scrips and with the boom in the market, the demand has increased and the shortage of floating stocks has skyrocketed the prices : The existing legal system and methods of operation of companies are not changed. The present disclosures as per Schedule II of Compnies Act are inadequate. There are delays in settlements, allotments and refund orders and rigging up the premiums in the grey markets. The present system of allotment is defective leading to around 20 per cent of total shares to be in odd lots, which quote at 15-20 per cent discount over the normal rates for marketable lots. The insider trading on confidential information and cornering of shares are the other malpractices. Recent liberalisation has accentuated these problems.

Right issues have grown due to companies preference for keeping the costs low and shareholders and company managements also preferred to keep the benefits of growth and appreciation to themselves rather than share with others. The main problems of capital market are the malpractices of companies, defective practices of brokers and infrastructural weaknesses which have not been changed by the recent reforms.

As money becomes scarce and an important resource, the corporate sector, will have to look more towards the capital markets. This requires creative thinking to innovate products, so that more funds are attracted. A lot of market research will have to go into this. Investors' preferences will have to be studied and the product will have to be designed, which would meet his requirement. Emergence of a growing body of investors looking for the right kinds of assets in the market place, facilitating innovation will have to be taken into consideration.

The interest rate on new debenture issues may stabilise at high level as 20 per cent. Non-convertible debentures will become the principal instrument in the corporate debt market. It is likely that innovative instrument like junk bonds, deep discount bonds and pay in kind bonds may be introduced. The convertible debentures will no longer be attractive. The convertible debentures will be seen where there is a genuine option to convert the debentures into equity or to retain it as a debenture. Due to increase in the interest rate on debentures the demand for equity is likely to be affected. However, this adverse effect may be offset by the impact of the new industrial policy, price decontrol of selected industries.

The liberalisation of the financial sector throws up the need for several financial markets and services. The Indian financial services companies are expected to provide fund based services such as leasing, hire purchase, financing for take over and loan syndication and non fund based services, such as portfolio management, investment advice, financial engineering and restructuring and issue management.

Foreign investment flows has drastically changed the Indian financial market scenario. Till the end of eighties Indian industry had been facing severe foreign currency crunch resulting in incapacity to import sophisticated technology as such competitive environment for the industry could not be created. Industry was dependent on foreign currency loans which were marked by a number of limitations including heavy repayment burden.

Due to liberalisation, foreign investments have increased. It is for more easy for more Indian industry to meet the foreign currency requirements and to import sophisticated technology and cheap raw material.

There is no denying the fact, with the foreign direct investments and portfolio investment, industrial sector is in very comfortable position, but the implications may not be as brighter as they look like or are being projected by the government.

One of the basic objective of planning effort during last four decades has been balanced regional development which is likely to be reversed. It is amply clear from MOU signed till the end of March 1993 that FDI are flowing to the states which have been industrially prosperous, fact foreign investor, like any other prudent entrepreneur, would primarily like to invest in the sectors and states where benefit would accrue to them whereas the priorities of our country may be secondary consideration it is pertinent to mention that the problems of Indian economy are different from that of earstwhile U.S.S.R. or majority of the South East Asian countries. The concept of welfare state in country, where vast majority of population is poor, can not be pushed to the background. As such policies pursued in the past can not be disregarded. But government shall have to make compromises in view of luring/attracting foreign investments.

The fast pace with which transition in the economy is taking place may not be judicious for the domestic industry which has been protected for years and needs time for preparing themselves for competitive environment.

Our government shall also keep in mind the lessons which we learnt from broad banding done by Rajiv Government in 1985. Many collaboration were allowed with specific objective but the results have not been forthcoming. The pepsi foods had entered the Indian market in 1989 with huge promises to farmers and export obligations, but today we find that they are concentrating only on soft drink market which perhaps is no priority for our country. The entry of Coco-cola in no way can be justified but one has to bear with as it is due to liberalisation.

Four LCV manufacturers were granted licences in 1985 when broad banding was done and we find that experiment has not been successful. In one of the cases, foreign collaborator has gone to the extent of reducing its equity stake simply because quick gains are not forthcoming leaving the Indian partner in a dismal condition.

Recent report in the Tribune* amptly describes how the domestic industry has suffered due to entry of the Foreign Investors and TNC's Kamla dies is one such glaring example. It is feared that foreign investors will eat away even the efficient industrial units.

The mergers and acquisitions which are taking place due to liberalised policy is likely to restrict competition. The Hindustan Levers and Tomco merger looks to be strategic but it will lead to oligopoly/monopolistic conditions.

On the other hand FII's seems to be under full control of Indian stock market it is observed during last few months that any sharp rise or fall in the share price index is dependent upon the entry/exit of FII's. It is therefore feared that a small investor who has insufficient knowledge of the market may suffer due to erratic movements in the market. The boom of 1985 and 1992 is the evidence that when few persons are in control of the market, vast majority of investors suffer. So far the policy of the government has been to encourage small investors, but with liberalisation there are tendencies to discourage the small investor. This may adversely affect the investment environment in country.

---

* *The Tribune,* May 9, 1994.

Conclusion

The process of reforms in the capital market has only just begun. It needs to be deepened to bring about speedier conclusion of transactions, greater transparency in operations, improved services to investors, and greater investor protection while at the same time encouraging the corporate sector to raise resources directly from the market on an increasing scale. Major modernisation of the stock exchanges to bring them in line with world standards in terms of transparency and reliability is also necessary if foreign capital is to be attracted on any significant scale.

The capital market requires reforms in many areas and many of these areas are inter-connected. As a result, SEBI has to proceed simultaneously on several fronts like companies, brokers, merchant bankers, mutual funds, various market players etc. SEBI powers need to be enhanced to ensure strict compliance with the rules and regulations. Stringent action should be taken against those who violate the rules and heavy penalties should be levied.

The promotion of foreign investment by government through various measures like allowing foreign equity participation even upto 100 per cent in specified cases, raising of ceilings on equity holding of NRI's and overseas corporate bodies in Indian companies and throwing open the Indian bourses to foreign institutional investor is an indication that our country no longer wants to isolate itself from the rest of the world. Infact, India may not have any other option also. But there is need for caution, any step taken in this direction shall not completely disregard the policies pursued in the past. The lessons we have learnt from the past shall form a base for any changes likely to take in future.

Gradualism which permits the setting up of only those industries which are globaly competitive while permitting the existing industries to slowly adjust themselves to new competitive environment, is preferable to sudden exposure to competition. The quick transition may once again lead us to failure. Thus, Indian financial markets are taking shape for turbulent times.

Box - I

Capital Market Reforms in 1993-94

* Capital Issues (Control) Act, 1947 repealed and the office of the Controller of Capital Issues (CCI) abolished control over price and premium of shares removed. Companies are now free to approach capital market after clearance by SEBI.

* Securities and Exchange Board of India (SEBI) armed with necessary authority and powers for regulation and reform of capital market.
* Indian companies permitted to access international capital markets through Euro-equity shares.
* Companies required to disclose all material facts and specific risk factors associated with their projects while making public issues.
* Merchant banking statutorily brought under the regulatory framework of SEBI and merchant bankers required to abideby a code of conduct.
* Private mutual funds permitted and a few already set up. All mutual funds allowed to apply for firm allotment in public issues.
* Investment norms for NRIs liberalised allowing companies to accept capital contribution and issue shares of debentures to NRIs or overseas corporate bodies without prior permission of RBI.
* Foreign Institutional Investors (FII) permitted to invest in Indian capital market on registration with SEBI. Common application forms simplified for them and foreign brokers permitted to assist them.
* Over the Counter Exchange of India (OTCEI) commenced operations and a number of shares already listed with it.
* SEBI notified several regulations for intermediaries in the secondary market bringing these intermediaries within regulatory framework for the first time.
* SEBI introduced new reforms in the primary market for improving the disclosure standards, introducing prudential norms and simplifying issue procedures.
* The procedures for lodgement of securities for transfer was considerably eased for domestic and foreign institutional investors through the introduction of a 'Jumbo' transfer deeds and consolidated payment of stamp duty.
* SEBI introduced a code of advertisement for public issues for ensuring fair and truthful disclosure.

Source : *Economic Survey,* Government of India, 1993-94, p.-51.

Box - II

Recommendations of The Committee on the Reforms in the Insurance Sector

* Private sector be permitted to enter insurance industry with a minimum paid up capital of Rs. 100 crore.
* Foreign insurance companies be allowed to enter by floating an Indian company preferably a joint venture with Indian partners.
* State level cooperatives be enabled to set up cooperative societies

not more than one in a State for transacting Life Insurance business subject to regulation by the insurance regulatory authority. Their capital base should be appropriately lower.

* Postal Life Insurance be permitted to transact life insurance business in rural areas among the general public. It should be suitably strengthened.
* The Officer of Controller of Insurance be restored its full function under the Insurance Act and set up as a separate office.
* State be initiated to set a strong and effective insurance regulatory authority in the form of a statutory autonomous board on the lines of SEBI.
* Life Insurance Corporation of India (LIC) be converted into a company and its capital should be raised to Rs. 200 crore, 50 per cent to be owned by Government and the rest by public at large with suitable reservation for its employees.
* Capital of General Insurance Corporation of India (GIC) be also raised to Rs. 200 crore, 50 per cent to be owned by Government and the rest by public at large with suitable reservation for its employees.
* LIC be fully restructured its central office should be a compact and highly professional establishment concentrating on policy formulation, investment, product development actuarial valuation, personnel policy and accounts of the Corporation.
* Zonal Offices of LIC be converted into its Head Offices for insurance business and related matters in their jurisdictions and Zonal managers be made members of LIC Board.
* GIC to function exclusively as a reinsurance company and as Indian reinsurer under the Insurance Act.
* Four subsidiaries be fully delinked from GIC by acquisition of entire stock in each of them by the Government.
* Capital of each subsidiary be thereafter raised to Rs. 100 crore, with 50 per cent equity held by Government and rest by public at large with suitable reservation for concerned employees.
* Tariff Advisory Committee (TAC) be linked from GIC to function as separate statutory body under necessary supervision by the Insurance regulatory authority.

Source : *Economic Survey,* Government of India, 1992-93, p.-57.

Table II
Foreign Investment Flows

(US $ million)

	1991-92	1992-93	1993-94* April-June	1993-94* July-Sept.	1993-94* Oct.-Dec.	1993-94* April-Dec.
A. Direct Investment	148.0	343.5	161.4	137.5	126.4	425.3
(a) RBI Automatic Route	0.2	42.6	4.9	18.6	26.8	50.3
(b) SIA/FIPB route	85.4	239.9	89.6	75.9	50.2	215.7
(c) NRIs (40% and 100% Schemes)	62.4	61.0	66.9	43.0	49.4	159.3
B. Portfolio Investment	-	241.5	45.5	263.8	1050.7	1360.0
(a) FIIs	-	1.0	45.5	194.8	761.7*	1002.0*
(b) Euro equities	-	240.5	0.0	69.0	289.0	358.0
Total (A+B)	148.0	585.0	206.9	401.3	1177.1	1785.3

Source : Economic Survey, Government of India, 1993-94, p. 76.

*Provisional *Upto January 13, 1994.

BIBLIOGRAPHY

1. Henning N-Charles, William Pigotte, Robert Haney Scott, Financial Markets and the Economy, Prentice Hall, Inc. N.I., pp. 244-45.
2. Francis Jack Clark, Investment Analysis and Management, McGraw Hill International, pp. 26-30.
3. Pradumna B. Rana and J. Malcohn Dowling, Jr. "Foreign Capital and Asian Economic Growth" Asian Development Review, Vol. 8, No. 2, (1990), pp. 77-102.
4. Edward K.Y. Chen, "Changing Pattern of Financial Flows in the Asia-Pacific Region and Policy Responses" Asian Development Review, Vol. (1992), pp. 46-47.
5. "Growth and Prospects for Private Placement Market (PPM) in India", The Chartered Accountant, Jan. 1992 p. 575.
6. Ghansagi, B.D., "Investors Protection", The Stock Exchange Review, Sept. 1993, pp. 1-3.
7. "Secondary Market Trends, The Stock Exchange Review", Sept. 1993, pp. 14-15.
8. "Free Pricing of Capital Issues", The Chartered Accountant, March 1993, p. 749.
9. Institute of Chartered Financial Analyst of India, Chartered Financial Analyst, Various Issues.
10. Summary of the Report of the Committee on the Financial System (Narasimham Committee), Prajnan.
11. Vol. XX, No. 4, Oct-Dec. 1991, pp. 442-43. Ojha, P.D. Investors and the Capital Market, RBI Bulletin, Dec. 1987, pp. 1139-44.
12. Government of India, Ministry of Finance, Economic Survey, 1993-94.
13. Navin Chandra Joshi, Over the Counter Exchange: Will it Click? The Economic Times, April 29, 1992.
14. Rangmani, P.T., Companies Bill to Promote Immodernisation Equity Cult, The Hindu, May 27, 1993, p. 18.
15. Reserve Bank of India Bulletin, July 1992.
16. SEBI Guidelines for Investor Protection: Some Suggestions, The Economic Times, June 1992.

7

Managing Privatisation : Global Developments and Strategic Issues

G.S. Batra*
&
Narinder Kaur**

Introduction

The industrialisation is utmost essential for economic progress of a country. To fulfil this gigantic task, the Government of India made its Industrial Policy more flexible one by allowing both public and private sector for rapid and balanced industrialisation with a view to benefiting the common man. At present, although India has been able to stand in a commanding position, nevertheless the performance of the public sector is not all satisfactory due to various reasons.

State intervention in the economic or business activities is no longer an economic anathema or political taboo as in the past. Increasing intervention by the state in the economic field has been the characteristic feature of this country, particularly during the recent past. The extent of this increased state activity is tremendous. Its influence on the social, political and economic life of the community has been far-reaching. The gospel of laissez-faire is dead, and will never revive much as the so-called "Liberal" thinking or the old "Liberal" attitude may still hanker after it.

* Deptt. of Business Management, Punjabi University, Patiala, Punjab (INDIA).

** Deptt. of Economics, Post Graduate Govt. College (Nabha), Punjabi University, Patiala, Punjab (INDIA).

Conceptual Framework

The concept of privatisation has been the subject of considerable discussion and debate in recent years in our country. In recent times, the concept of privatisation as an instrument of greater economic prosperity, is sweeping across global economies regardless of their dimensions, status, divergent economic policy and legal environment.

Privatisation Signifies that the management culture and expertise of private sector should be induced into public sector undertakings and area reserved for public sector should be vacated for the entry of private enterprises or at least opportunities should be opened up for private sector to compete on equal footing with public sector enterprises in these areas.

Privatisation also means any policy change that restricts the involvement of State or Public Sector in the economic activities of the nation-be it divestiture, de-nationalisation de-reservation of industries exclusively reserved for public sector, closure, liquidation, leasing or transfer of Management of the Public Sector Enterprises etc. Thus, the scope of privatisation is not confined to the enterprise sector ownership transfer alone, rather allocation leading to substitution of private for public provision of goods and services falling within the purview of privatisation .

Recent Developments

In recent times governments have come under severe pressure to reduce tax without reducing services offered to public. Invariably governments have run into deficit budgeting. The U.S government wanted to reverse the trend. The congress passed the Gramm-Rudman-Hollings Amendment in 1985. It aimed at restricting the federal spendings and balancing the federal budget. The friction between competing demands for lower taxes and for expanded services has led governments to innovative new methods of financing and providing the service. One of these methods has come to be called 'Privatisation '.

Privatisation refers to the transfer of functions previously performed exclusively by government, usually at zero or full cost prices, to the private sector at prices that clear the market and reflect the full cost of production. 'Kolderie' identifies at least two different ideas that are encompassed by the term privatisation . He says government performs two functions, either or both could be privatised. One is the policy decision (provision) the actual provision of goods and services. The second administrative act of production of goods and services.' There could be a wide variety and types and forms of privatisation. Since 1970s the idea has gained popularity in U.S.A. and Western Europe. Some economists claim that "the cost of public supply is approximately twice that of private supply" (S. Hanke). John Naisbitt says that privatisation is sweeping the U.S.A. and has public support. He further claims that "Privatisation is part of the process of rethinking the welfare state. Society is searching for new ways of delivering services because of our collective sense of efficiency. The entrepreneur, not the bureaucrat, is the hier of society. While we can't be sure how it will all turn out, privatisation will be part of the emerging post-welfare state.

Until recently the federal government (US) has been the most reluctant to privatize. Of course, it has relatively few enterprises to sell in comparison to European nations. In spite of that the then president proposed in fiscal year 1987 that government divest itself of some of its property. This move was done more on political than economic grounds as the sales would raise only about 8.5 billion, or 1% of government's anticipated revenues for that year.

Butler has contended that the great failure of supply side economics has been the assumption that government could cut spending to live within its income. He views privatisation as the most feasible method to achieve a balanced budget. All the proposed privatisation efforts are providing to the highly controversial. Notwithstanding the controversy 'privatisation' has been prescribed as a patent remedy to all less developed countries via the conditionality of loans or assistance granted by IMF, World Bank or U.S. to these countries.

The Rationale and Strategies of Privatisation

The ideas that propel privatisation are :

(i) Those who want cheap and efficient goods should turn to private sector (supposedly efficient and cheaper).

(ii) Those who want wide choice must allow competition between private and public sector.

(iii) Those who want entrepreneurial development they must unlock opportunities and provide alternatives in private sector.

That means private sector would provide a wide variety of cheaper, more efficient goods and services and encourage new entrepreneurs. The strategies for achieving privatisation broadly comprise :

(a) Sale of government enterprises (Controlling interest/power of making decision; handing over sick units etc).

(b) Contracting out government services to private sector.

(c) Charging fees equal to full cost for services provided by government.

(d) Issuing vouchers to disadvantaged persons and reimburse the cost of service availed from private sector.

Is Privatisation Inevitable?

Privatisation allow governments on governing. It reduces government's time and resources in providing social security and welfare activities by replacing the welfare state system of collective provision and finance with more privatised system. These includes introduction of private insurance, funding the health services, contracting out-hospital cleaning and catering, running public transport system on competitive basis, replacement of state redistribution by public charity, etc.

It is difficult to define the welfare state. Usually it is identified with social security system. The state can provide security in three ways :

(i) By making income transfer from tax payers to benefit recepients in the form of cash payments. These include sickness benefits, short-term unemployment benefits, retirements benefits, etc.

(ii) By providing free health care, education and various other social services, and

(iii) By providing subsidies to reduce the cost of certain commodities deemed socially desirable.

In the most general sense, privatisation involves the rolling back of activities of the state. There can be various kinds of privatisation :

(1) Privatisation may involve a reduction in state provision. It includes privasing the social security system by providing for private insurance companies, contracting out of hospital cleaning and catering etc.

(2) Privatisation can involve a reduction in state subsidy. For example, student grants may be replaced by student loan or there may be reduction in subsidy to public transport.

(3) Privatisation can imply reduction in state regulation. Government may lift certain restrictions on public transport or public housing

to provide adequate competition between private and public sector.

By privatisation we do not simply mean the replacement of the state by market. The kind of state intervention to be replaced has to be specified. It should also be specified which other institution will replace it. The arguments about the merits and demerits of privatisation will vary according to the type of activities involved.

The Case for Privatisation

The case for privatisation rests upon the weakness of the welfare state. To many scholars, welfare state has resulted in economic stagnation. It led to large-scale unemployment in some countries. It led to fiscal crisis in the form of economic recession. While the recession reduced government revenue, it added to public expenditure on welfare activities. Consequently, a decline in the resources available to social services followed. At the heart of the crisis is the general loss of confidence in the social services provided by the welfare state.

Privatisation has emerged as a major public policy issue is the eighties in many parts of the world, Programmes of privatisation are under way in several western countries such as U.K., U.S., Canada, France and Italy. A total of $ 10 billion was expected to be raised through divestiture by the French Government in 1987. The French privatisation plan covered 42 banks, 2 financial holding companies, 9 industrial and 3 insurance companies. By 1987, the U.K. had raised nearly $ 21 billion through the privatisation of public enterprises.

Most of the privatisation activities in the U.S. have so far been concerned with routine services. Privatisation of industrial and commercial public enterprises has been insignificant in the U.S. The basic reason is that public enterprises provide the infrastructure only. However, a poll conducted in May 1988 showed that 69% Canadians were in favour of privatising Air Canada. Canadian Government believes in privatising on pragmatic grounds rather than on ideological grounds. It believes in managing government assets better and selling those which no longer meet a public policy purpose or complete and grow in a commercial world."

Privatisation in Developed Economies

U.S.A. In the United State where public ownership play a relatively minor role in economic activity, proposals for sale of assets are fairly recent. In the U.S. growth of privatisation has been predominantly in the area of "Contracting-out" of public services. Urban services such as vaste water/sewage treatment, solid waste disposal fire protection, garbage collection, and public transportation have been contracted out by many state governments.

A number of local governments are now contracting out the management and operation of public hospitals to commercial hospital chains. A survey conducted in 1982 showed that 47 per cent of the cities and countries had sub-contracted emergency medical service to private operators. There is speculation that the technology of limited access high-way networks with electronic road pricing system might offer scope for the further privatisation in the transportation sector. Experimental programmes in Minnesota have been funded by the state for school districts to contract out to groups of teachers the task of teaching non-core subjects such as arts and science.

United Kingdom

In 1979, the U.K. set off the most aggressive and well known privatisation programme. The British Government realises regularly 7 billion pound sterling from the sale of nationalised industries primarily by stock floatation, the most notable example being the sale of Britain Telecom and British Gas.

More recently, the privatisation of state owned British Airways in 1987, followed by the privatisation of BAA plc (formerly the British Airport Authority) towards the summer of 1987 is the most significant events in U.K. civil aviation. Already the seven airports involved : Heathrow, Gatwick, Stansted, Glasgow, Edinburgh, Prestwick and Aberden—have been converted into companies and are now operating as entities in their own right, under over all authority of BAA plc itself.

Among other public enterprises which British Government has privatised are British Aero-space including defence equipment, British Petroleum. British Leyland, Cabler Wireless, British Oil, Enterprises oil and on shore oil, the hotel chain of British Railways, the seaports run by Associated British ports, the national freight company which ran a large road haulage business and the Jaguar Car Company.

France

The French Government also announced its plans to transfer to the private sector as many as 65 publicly controlled enterprises worth between French Franc 200-300 billion. The French privatisation plan covered 42 banks.

Japan

In Japan, in addition to the privatisation of Nippon Telegraph and Telephone (NTT) and the State Tobacco Corporation in April 1985, the Government of Japan has announced the division and privatisation of Japan Railways the biggest semi-state company.

Privatisation in Less Developed Countries

Following the path of rich industrialised countries, some other countries in the third world began to move towards the privatisation. Complete privatisation of public sector is not possible in less developed countries (LDCs) because :

1. Shortage of technical and entrepreneurial know-how and skill in LDCs.
2. The private sector is more interested in 'Under World Manoeuvers' or operated in an illegal manner, resorting to practices such as cornering and hoarding has resulted into the parallel economy, it is not correct to attempt privatisation at this stage.
3. Inter-government and International negotiations for funds and technology are greater with public sector.
4. Emergence of serious setbacks in functioning of private sector such as industrial sickness; and
5. Resource bottlenecks of private sector in a low saving economy like LDCs.

Argentina

From 1930-70s industries were developed under protectionist background in Argentina. In 1986 crisis developed for want of credit from banks. An export oriented policy with regional market arrangements with Brazil was followed. Custom duty was abolished. Privatisation of key companies was also carried out (selling off or reducing state holding). Inspite of privatisation in 1986 budget deficit rose to 7.5% of GDP in 1988. A major reorganisation of state sector through privatisation, tight financial control and management shake up was undertaken.

Brazil

In 1960s it encouraged large foreign investment and large development projects. US, Europe and Japan poured loans into Brazil (cheap imported oil and easy foreign capital). Import substitution industrialisation reigned supreme from 1950 to 1962 and 1968 to 1981 (profitable consumer industries out stripped basic industries). But frequent state intervention was alleged as the cause of deterring investment and technology. Strong state sector dominated but flawed for indiscipline, due to independent power of borrowings and rampant mismanagement. Country suffered from high foreign debts, (fair whether) and flight of capital. Its privatisation efforts were aimed at reducing "the public sector deficits". Privatisation was judicially inducted to improve efficiency of public sector.

Indonesia

The country suffered since 1974 from World recession and falling foreign exchange revenues resulting in rescheduling of projects. Inefficient monopoly, high transport and energy cost make industry non-competitive. Small size of market, high labour cost, corruption, red tape and lack of infrastructure repeal investors. Infrastructure building is not the field for private investors.

Indonesia has 215 state industries and now started privatisation. Foreigners equity can be up to 80% in export sector firms. It deregulated protected sector, relaxed capacity ceiling which can be exceeded by 30% without permission. Out of $ 35 billion only 25% are coming from private investors, Dept. servicing absorbed 38% of export income in 1988. Since 1985-86 export declined by 9.1%, oil receipts by 12.5%, non-oil exports by 0.7%. The official capital inflow was lower by 3.3 billion, but private investment increased by about $ 150 million only.

Nigeria

During 1973-80, the oil revenue of Nigeria was invested in public sector projects. The spending from high foreign exchange reserves resulted in high rates of inflation. Expenditure on infrastructure went to construction and services, but neglected manufacturing. The result was narrow Urban based production structure. The 1980s oil glut and losses were encountered with austerity measures. It failed to correct foreign payment crisis. Consumer imports, prestigious and wasteful projects, political patronage and personal enrichment were the causes of ill. The government adopted measures of devaluation, package of fiscal measures like abolition of import licences, price control and subsidies. The restructuring of economy was attempted via :

1. diversification and reduction of dependence on oil.
2. fiscal balance.

3. platform of sustainable non-oil, non-inflationary growth, and
4. reduced investment on and improved efficiency of the public sector.

The problem is however the fundamental restructuring of economy and diversifying the industry. The state-owned enterprises wholly or partly privatised in East and South-East Asian countries are shown in Table I.

International Comparison

Compared to the privatisation programmes in the industrially advanced countries, efforts are quite modest in scale. Liquidation and closure of firms rather than divestiture seem to be preferred policy in LDCs.

The availability of modalities of privatisation or divestiture are not the same in the advanced industrial societies and in the LDCs. In the industrial countries, once a political decision has been made to divest,

Table I

Privatised Public Enterprises in Asian Countries

Implemented in some Cases		*Name of Countries*
Tele-communication	:	Japan, South Korea, Thailand, Malaysia, Sri Lanka and Bangladesh.
Airlines	:	South Korea (Korea Air) Singapore (SAI) Thailand (Thai International) Malaysia (MAS) and Bangladesh (Bangladesh Bhavan).
Shipping and/or ship building	:	Singapore, Bangladesh and Sri Lanka.
Container terminals	:	Malaysia.
Transport (Railways & Bus Services)	:	Japan (Japan National Railways), Thailand (Bankok Bus Co.), & Sri Lanka (Ceylon Transport Board).
Highways	:	Malaysia
Banks	:	South Korea, Singapore, Bangladesh, Philippines & Taiwan.
Oil and Petro-Chemicals	:	South Korea, India, and Philippines.
Industrial enterprises including textiles engineerings. Chemical etc.	:	Philippines, Sri Lanka, India, and China.
Hotels	:	Singapore and Philippines.
Retail establishments	:	China

the major task is to fix the right merchant or investment banker to implement the decision, getting the correct valuation of assets and then putting the assets up for sale at the price using the facilities of well-developed capital market. In LDCs capital market infrastructure for consultancy, speedy communication etc. are partly developed and potential buyers few in number. In determining who be allowed to buy the divested assets, numerous political, social and cultural factors come into play.

Some of LDCs had to face the problem of private sector's resource crunch. For example the Government of Bangladesh came out with the new industrial policy in June' 82 and it decided to return the nationalised firms to their original owner. In many cases it was found that these owners do not have sufficient resources to buy their firms back.

Contracting out of public services which has been important feature of U.S. and U.K. privatisation programme is absent in LDCs and the focus and privatisation in LDCs has been exclusively on the divestiture of commercial and industrial enterprises.

Last factor is that the economic policy, environment and legal frameover in the two sets of countries is very different. In the industrial countries a state enterprise that is introduced to the private sector, finds itself in a well developed corporate system and a legal system that is well structured. This is not the case in LDCs where environment is characterised by a stringent legal framework for companies to operate in and a high degree of protection in the industrial sector.

Public Sector Vs. Privatisation — Indian Case

The reasons starting public sector undertakings were to control the commanding heights of the economy, promote critical development in terms of social gain or strategic value rather than primarily on considerations of profit and provide commercial surpluses with which to finance further economic development. Accordingly, the government entered into various activities like manufacturing, agriculture, banking, insurance, transport, warehousing and the like.

Over the last 42 years since independence, the growth of the public sector enterprises has been phenomenal. From an investment of Rs. 29 crores in five enterprises in 1951, the total investment increased to Rs. 1,10,000 crores in 250 enterprises as on 31 March, 1992.

The basic features of Public Enterprise in India are :

(i) Investment of national resources to the extent of Rs. 1,10,000 crores (31-3-1992).

(ii) Gigantic size of its Public Enterprises.

(iii) Its pervasiveness in all the sectors of the economy.

(iv) Poor returns.

(v) Bureaucratic management.

(vi) Emphasis on social returns and upliftment of backward regions.

Public enterprise presents a mixed picture and it can not be privatised in a wholesale manner. The economic, political and social systems, of which Public Enterprise is a sub-system, which were touched briefly in the proceeding paras will also permit the wholesale privatisation. India is not Europe, therefore, the lessons of privatisation learnt in those countries cannot be applied here in toto. Here the decision about privatisation has to be made on case to case basis.

Emerging Dimension of Privatisation

The important question here is to identify the prospective candidates for privatisation .Public enterprise have entered into non-essential, non-basic and non-strategic areas. In their enthusiasm of attaining the commanding heights, Public enterprise has been ushered in those areas, where it should not have been pushed into. Public enterprises should not be treated as a sacred cow, which cannot be touched upon. Public enterprise in these spheres should be privatised by outright sale (in whole or parts) or lease to the private sector. The Maruti Udyog, Hindustan Aeronautics and the like fall in this category.

What is non-essential and non-basic, can be decided with reference to the category of consumers. If it is a class goods (as opposed to mass goods), it can be treated as non-essential. Even mass goods can be treated as non-essentials for the purpose of privatisation. If their sources of supply (production) are multiple (d.e. there is no monopoly) and the supplies are reliable (quality) and uninterrupted (quantity). Drugs, Pharmaceuticals, Hotels, production of TV, textiles, cycles and cement belong to this category. The mode of privatisation can be their outright sale/lease to private sector entrepreneurs.

These steps will help the Pubic Enterprise and the government both. It will enable the Public Enterprise to concentrate on the basics and essential entorproces and help the government by generating cash incomes, so urgently needed to tide over resource crunch.

Another category, where selective and cautious approach of privatisation can be adopted, is that of enterprises engaged directly in the foreign trade. Private sector, with the help of Public enterprise infrastructure in the form of financial institutions and insurance organisation, export promotion councils etc. has come up of age in the exports of a number of items. Public enterprise can be withdrawn from those areas through privatisation, adopting the mode of sales to private sector. Public enterprise should avoid duplication of national efforts. But at the same time it should stay where new grounds are being broken, where trade with socialist countries is being carried on and where the Public enterprise withdrawl is likely to create private sector monopolies. Acceptance of this recommendation will reduce the role of State trading corporation and similar other organisatinons such as the Cashew corporation of India the Mica Trading Corporation and commodity Boards etc.

There is fourth category and this encompasses the various undertakings under the administrative control of union Ministry of Agriculture, Co-operation and Food and Civil supplies. The undertakings are National Seed Corporation, State Farm Corporation of India, Central Warehousing Corporation. All these undertakings can be privatised by transferring (through sale) them to the user's cooperative societies. If for some known or undisclosed (political consideration) reasons Public Enterprise stake in these undertakings is considered essential, Public Enterprise can be a minor stake-holder.

Privatisation, can also be done by accelerating the process of ancillarisation and associating the small and medium private sector undertakings in the process. Even the defence industries, which normally have a veil of secrecy around them, can be opened (within limits) for the purpose.

State Electricity Board without any exception, are in a bad shape. The Boards, generate and distribute electricity (generation and distribution of electricity is the exclusive responsibility of the state and it billongs to schedule A, of the industrial policy resolution, 1956). In the field of power generation, there are three resources viz., atomic power, hydro-electric power and lastly the thermal power. The first two sources of power generation will continue to be the state monopoly for reasons of defence in the case of former and state ownership of river valley projects in the later case. In the thermal power generation private sector can be associated either through participation in its equity capital or the private sector can be allowed to establish their own power generating station on a selective basis. The power generated by state electricity board and the private sector power generating stations can be fed into the national power grid. Such privatisation in the field of power generation will inject competition, which in turn may lead to efficiency.

Conclusion and Recommendations

As compared to the developed countries, privatisation has been very modest in developing countries. The developing countries prefer liquidation and closure of firms to divestiture. They contemplate slow-death for those enterprises which incur heavy losses year after year. It will attract less public attention and create less nuisance for the government.

In developing countries, most of the private enterprises are in consumer goods. Most of the public utility services are in public sector. They are monopolistic in nature. There is no system of contracting out public services in these countries. Contracting out public services is bound to lead to decentralisation. Most of the governments in developing countries are not in a position to lessen their grip on public enterprises for various socio-economic and political reasons. That's why, we find the focus on industrial and commercial enterprises only as far as privatisation is concerned in these countries.

While the governments in the developed countries are in a position to offer attractive concessions to potential buyers, the governments in developing countries cannot do so. Divestiture can cause distortions to the economy. It can also lead to potential revenue losses to the exchequer.

This explains why the pace of privatisation has been very slow in developing countries. In countries where the private sector is underdeveloped, it is difficult to find potential buyers. Again, due to political hostilities, it is neither feasible nor desirable to depend on foreign buyers.

Resistance to privatisation is also likely from the trade unions in the public sector. The political leaders and bureaucrats also consider privatisation as a threat to their power and patronage. Intellectuals may also challenge privatisation on the grounds of social cost involved in the process. Powerful combination of these forces creates an atmosphere hostile to privatisation. Therefore, privatisation should not be attempted in such countries unless and until proper analysis has been made of the economic and political situation prevalent. It may also require an ideological shift in most of countries.

The third world countries should not follow the path of privatisation blindly. Profound economic changes cannot occur with pari pasu or prior transformation of the ideological climate. In this set of affairs, a set of economic policies is of little relevance if in the absence of a determined political movement bound together by a cohesive and dynamic ideology, the will is lacking to implement them.

BIBLIOGRAPHY

1. Calvin, A. Kent (Ed.) Privatisation of Public Enterprises, Quorum Books, London, p.-2.
2. T. Kolderie, Two different concept of privatisation, Public Administration Review, Aug. 1986, pp. 285-90.
3. S. Honke, The user of Free Illusion, Reason, August 1983, p.-33.
4. S.M. Butler , Privatising Federal Spendings, New York Universal Books, 1985.
5. Samuel Paul, Privatisation, Economic and Political Weekly, Feb. 6, 1988, p.-273.
6. Batra, G.S. Emerging Dimension of Privatisation, Second World Business Congress, Finland, Turki, 1993.

8

Industrial Relations in Indian Corporate Sector : Challenges Ahead

B.S. Batia & G.S Batra *

Introduction

"Industrial Relations" refers to a dynamic and developing concept which is not limited to "the complex of relations between trade unions and management but also refers to the general web of relationships normally obtaining employers and employees—a web much more complex than the simple concept of labour-capital conflict.[1]

Under the heading, "Industrial Relations" the ILO has dealt with the relationships between the state on the one hand and the employers 'and employees' organisations on the other with the relationships among the occupational organisations themselves. The ILO has used the expression to denote such matters of freedom of association and the right to collective bargaining of collective agreements, of conciliation and arbitration proceedings and the machinery for co-operation between the authorities and the occupational organisations at various levels of the economy.

"Industrial relations are an integral aspect of social relations arising out of employer-employees interaction in modern industries, which are regulated by the State in varying degrees, in conjunction with organised social forces and influenced by the existing institutions. This involves a study of the State, the legal system, and the workers 'and employers' organisations at the institutional level and of the patterns of industrial organisation (including management), capital structure (including technology) compensation of the labour force,

---

* Professor and Faculty Member respectively, Deptt. of Business Management, Punjabi University, Patiala.

and a study of market forces—all at the economic level.[2]

Accelerated development of industries, diversification of Industrial structure as well as shifts in the technological and scientific base of industrial production have an intimate relationship with the work-environment in industry. Besides, ensuring efficient use of resources and raising productivity, stability in the growth of industrial produce is an obvious imperative. Industrial peace and harmonious labour-management relations are its essential prerequisites. Historical experience of the insdustrialised world shows that these are not obtained automatically. Labour force needs some protection against exploitation without, at the same time, vitiating the environment for industrial growth and diversification. Two distinct sources for the protection of labour force are statutory measures and unionisation of labour force as a countervailing power. Some of the legislative measures are a consequence of the political pressure from labour organisations.

Growth of modern industries in India since Independence is accompanied by a clear enunciation of industrial and labour policies of the government. Work-environment in industry has undergone noticeable changes since then. Legislative measures like the Industrial Disputes Act, 1947 (along with a series of amendments in it), Indian Factories Act, 1948, Employees' State Insurance Act, 1948, Minimum Wages Act, 1948, Payment of Bonus Act, 1965, Shops and Establishments Acts of various states etc., are all a testimony to the government's endeavour towards promoting harmonious industrial relations by monitoring the work-environment. Legislative enactments, however, are by themselves not enough; their effectiveness calls for a sensitive and vigilant machinery which can ensure the creation of conditions for avoidance/ prevention of disputes. Growth of trade unions received a fillip from the constitutional right of freedom of association to all citizens subject to the interest of public order. They promote and protect the interest of their members through a wide variety of functions. Figures show an eight-fold growth in the number of unions between 1951 and 1981. The increase in their number is, however, accompanied by multiplicity of unions with mutual rivalries which is hardly conductive to the promotion of industrial peace.

Dynamics of Industrial Relations

Harmonious industrial relations are an indispensable condition for rapid industrialisation, economic growth and social justice. Hence industrial peace is an urgent need of the hour. The relationship between management and labour has been changing, the world history explains the impact of freedom-struggle in different countries on labour-management relations. Now in the present context workers in organised form have become more important for industrial peace. Gone are the days when workers were unorganised, un-reorganised and un-educated, now they have recognition for their work and the overall condition of workers is improving day by day. Before independence the condition of workers in India was very poor. What independent India inherited was a legacy of under-development, a stagnant agriculture, a shrinking export market, low consumption of commercial and industrial energy and an infrastructure based on the needs of colonialism. The frontliners of Indian political by accepting socialistic pattern of society, have not only shown their keen interest and dedication for solving these vexed problems but by acceptance of planned economy they opened the doors of democracy for working class also. Enactment of labour laws played an important role for the identification of labourers image. Every industrial organisation has three major resources e.g., man, material and machine. But the man is the most important factor to generate the output. For a radical change in the concept, the management and labour has to realise their own mutual obligations, their own mutual roles without which no enterprise can really exist. Labour and management have to realise that none of them is made of bricks but are human beings, with human problems, human views and there can always be differences of view point. Every human being, has the desire for growth which finds expressions in his creativeness. A good labour-management relation can also top the vast resources that reside in human beings. Human beings are the greatest beings, much higher than all animals, all angles and none is greater than mankind. Man is the most versatile resource available to us because by his thoughts and action he can create, improve and affect the total system. Manpower is an asset which appreciates with time and can be effectively utilised only if better labour-management relation exists. It is more effective to consider, 'Human relations' approach in effective utilisation of manpower. This approach recognises human dignity as well as human productivity. In fact, the effective utilisation of all resources depends on the effective utilisation of human resources.

The two important areas in labour-management relations are conflict and co-operation. The industrial production is based on co-operation between Labour and Capital. Co-operation between the two is one of the basic requirements for the growth of industrialisation. Co-operation is the formal feature of Labour-Management Relations. The co-operation between the two is nothing more than the mere coming together of labour and capital or union and management and regarding each other as partners.

Industrial Relations Scene in India

The growth and development of the labour-movement with particular reference to trade union movement was the out-come of industrial revolution. Some of the worst features of industrialisation marked the history of early factory system in India. Industrial relations constitute one of the most delicate and complex problems of modern industrial society. In the absence of effectiveness in the working class, the poor conditions of labourers were not cared. In early days the workers who migrated from villages to industries were neither complete workers nor complete villagers. They joined the industries as part time jobs, thus they remain unorganised. The problem of unorganised workers is still prevailing in India. Simultaneously there is ad-hocism in the nature of trade unions in India. Anyhow, the condition and position of workers have now changed tremendously. The workers have now realised that most of their demands can be satisfied if they resort to collective action, while employers are aware of the fact that they can resist these demands. This denial or refusal to meet their genuine demands has often led to dissatisfaction on the part of workers, to their distress, and even to violent activities on their part, which have hindered production and harmed both the workers and the employers. Consequences of industrial disputes are very far-reaching as they paralyse the economic, social and political life of a country.

Trends in industrial unrest show that neither legislative measures, nor trade unions have been helpful in promoting industrial peace in India. The number of disputes, with occasional exception, has been on rise. The total number of man-days lost in some years, e.g., 1982 has been extremely high. Wide and violent fluctuations in the index of industrial unrest are an ample evidence of the failure of the existing mechanism in preventing disputes from arising or of its inability to settle them quickly once they arise. Over time, the proportion of disputes which lasted over a longer duration has tended to grow.

Emoluments of workers i.e., wages and allowances have continued to remain a predominant cause of industrial disputes, followed by personnel and retrenchment issues. Figures reveral that not more than half the disputes are successful, partially or wholly, in terms of their results. The huge proportion of unsuccessful disputes is a pointer to the possible accumulation of unrest among workers.

The state of industrial relations in the public sector industries is not distinctly different from that of the private sector industries. There is some evidence of the discrimination on the part of the government in implementing its labour policies in the two sectors by being indulgent to the public sector management. The rights of workers in the public sector departmental undertakings to organise themselves and the modes of expressing their grievances are curtailed by special legislative powers of the government.

The Table I gives an idea of the trends in industrial unrest.

Table I
Trends in Industrial Unrest

Year	*1961*	*1971*	*1976*	*1981*	*1985*	*1988*	*1989*	*1990*
Number of disputes								
Total............	1357	2752	1459	2589	1755	1746	1021	1149
Strikes............	1240	2478	1241	2245	1355	1304	750	897
Lockouts & others	117	274	218	344	400	442	271	252
Number of Workers involved ('000)								
Total...............	512	1615	737	1588	1079	1192	608	915
Strikes............	432	1476	550	1261	878	937	445	804
Lockouts & others	80	139	186	327	201	255	163	111
Number of Man-days lost (Lakhs)								
tal............	49	165	127	366	292	339	152	126
....	30	118	28	212	115	125	56	53
& others	19	47	99	159	177	92	96	73

nd Book of Labour Statistics, 1991.

From the above table it is clear that from 1971 number of dispute and number of mandays lost have been increasing. Number of mandays lost increased from 49 lakhs in 1961 to 126 lakhs in 1990. During the above period the number of workers involved were 5,12,000 and 9,15,000 respectively.

The Table II exhibits the index of industrial unrest in the manufacturing sector from 1974 to 1990 indicating severity rate of 197.3 in 1974 and 86.5 in 1990.

Table II
Index of Industrial Unrest in the Manufacturing Sector (1974-1990)

Year	*Index of man-days lost per 1000 workers (1961 = 100)*	*Severity rate**
1974	460	197.3
1975	354	143.7
1976	211	89.5
1977	324	149.3
1978	357	164.6
1979	577	269.9
1980	248	116.1
1981	424	208.0
1982	944	419.9
1983	564	291.0
1984	630	319.7
1985	316	165.4
1986	386	200.0
1987	405	224.0
1988	366	193.8
1989	195	104.1
1990	165	86.5

* Ratio of man-days lost to one million man-days scheduled to work.

Source : Hand Book of Labour Statistics, 1991.

The Table III indicates wages have been a major cause of dispute, followed by personnel and Retrenchment, i.e., if we exclude the cause mentioned as OTHERS. In table III there are two additional causes, namely Leave and Hours of Work and Indiscipline and Violence; out of these two causes 'Indiscipline and Violence' has been a very important cause of dispute in the recent years. In the last three years, i.e., 1987, 1988, 1989, it has shown an increasing trend and it is very clear that if we want to cut down the percentage of disputes in the country, a congenial atmosphere has to be created so that indiscipline and violence may be avoided. It is very necessary that the root cause of indiscipline and violence be pointed by the management and steps are taken to eradicate it.

Apart from the above given causes, there are two problems which have become chronic to our industrial relation, viz., trade union recognition and the related issue of trade union rivalry and they lead to various industrial disputes.

Even though the given table shows a trend in all sectors we can safely conclude that the same (of almost the same) trend is followed in both the public and private sector individually also.

Table III

Percentage Distribution of Disputes by Causes for Both Public and Private Sector during the period 1986-89

Year	*Wages & Allowance* *1*	*Bonus* *2*	*Personnel Retrench ment* *3*	*Leave & Hours of Work* *4*	*Indisci pline Violence* *5*	*Others* *6*	*4 5 6* *7*
1986	25.7	9.7	23.3	1.3	15.1	24.9	41.3
1987	27.6	7.7	17.1	1.2	14.0	32.4	47.6
1988	27.8	6.9	17.0	1.6	15.8	30.9	48.3
1989	23.4	4.1	19.9	1.1	17.1	34.4	52.5

Source : Pocket Book of Labour Statistics, 1990, p-81, Labour Bureau, Simla, Ministry of Labour, Government of India.

The Table IV shows the industrial disputes by sectors in four years. It is evident from the table that the number of dispute in public enterprises have been less than those in the private sector. The workers involved have been more in the public enterprises than in the private sector, except in the year 1986, when mandays lost have been more in the private sector.

A very unique feature of disputes in public sector is that the employees of public enterprises sometimes resort to various forms of unrest which the private sector employees would not resort to viz., go slow, tool down, pen-down, work-to-rule etc., instead of direct action as a result we see that the mandays lost are more in the private sector than in the public sector enterprises.

Table IV
Industrial Disputes by Sectors

Sector	*1986*	*1987*	*1988*	*1989*
(a) **Public Sector**				
No. of Disputes	389	422	564	361
Workers involved (000)	678	1,007	802	351
Mandays lost (000)	2,572	5,237	6,633	2,937
Wages lost (Rs. in crores)	6.11	10.26	15.46	14.15
	(281)	(355)	(445)	(296)
Value of production lost	30.06	108.25	71.62	65.04
(Rupees in crores)	(208)	(300)	(394)	(266)
(b) **Private Sector**				
No. of Disputes	1503	1357	1181	659
Workers involved (000)	967	763	389	256
Mandays lost (000)	30176	30121	27314	12244
Wages lost (Rs. in crores)	39.20	43.62	46.49	10.86
	(837)	(672)	(615)	(230)
Value of production lost	783.52	531.43	622.62	218.43
(Rupees in crores)	(758)	(619)	(540)	(201)

Source : Pocket Book of Labour Statistics, 1990. p. 85.

Although a multitude of causes, blended together, result in industrial disputes, it is not always easy in specific instances to ascertain the particular cause or causes involved. Surface manifestations of unrest and dissatisfaction which appear to be responsible for work-stoppage may cover deep-seated and more basic causes which cannot be observed at first sight. In 1931, the Royal Commission on Labour observed "Although workers may have been influenced by persons with nationalist, communist or commercial ends to serve, we believe that there has rarely been a strike of any importance which has not been entirely or largely due to economic reason." Even now the situation is not different.

Neither all strikes can be regarded as justified nor all strikes are unjustified. There are some pre-conditions which must be fulfilled to make a strike justified. Under the following circumstances the strikes can be justified : (i) It should be launched only for economic demands such as basic pay, dearness allowance, increment, leave and other fringe benefits which are primary objects of a trade union.[3] But if a strike is launched for political or other reasons and not for any trade union objects, it would be un-justified;[4] (iii) The demand of the workmen should be reasonable and legitimate so that there is a prima facie justification for the demands. When demands are excessive and unreasonable or when the demands which were settled were tried to be reagitated then any strike to enforce the said demand cannot be said to be justified;[5] (iv) If the facilities like provident fund is withdrawn or closed, strike would be justified; (v) where there is any unfair labour practice on the part of management strike would be justified;[6] (vi) If there is no response from the management inspite of referring a demand and having reminders, the strike is justified.[7]

Role of Government

The Government has been playing a variety of roles in the formation, maintenance and direction of the structure of industrial relations. In India the Government has been playing, particularly after independence, a comprehensive and dominant role in shaping the pattern of industrial relations. In the mixed economy we have in this country, the state has now emerged as a model employer; one significant aspect of its role is to evolve norms through tripartite forums to act as guidelines for shaping industrial relations. The government also accepts the responsibility of ensuring, conformity to these norms through the administrative and judicial machinery. State intervention primarily aims at preserving industrial peace and has, therefore, focussed attention on : (a) the avoidance of industrial disputes, and (b) expeditious settlement of industrial disputes when they do arise. Though in its policy pronouncements, considerable importance is assigned by Government to building up of a stable bipartite relationship between management and labour, the machinery for setting industrial disputes by Government intervention is often pressed into action in performance to the method of bipartite negotiations and collective barganing.[8]

The Table V exhibits the disputes resolved by different methods of settlement. It indicates the growing role of government intervention in disputes settlement which is not a good sign for good industrial relations. Disputes have not been largely resolved by mutual settlement, which is quite essential for healthy labour management relations.

Table V
Disputes Resolved by Different Methods of Settlement (Percentage Distribution)

Year	*Government Intervention*	*Mutual Settlement*	*Voluntary Resumption*
1976	44.4	20.5	34.1
1977	44.3	27.3	28.4
1978	43.3	31.1	25.6
1979	30.7	29.9	39.4
1980	28.6	33.6	37.8
1981	32.6	33.5	33.9
1982	26.5	31.0	42.5
1983	27.6	28.1	44.3
1984	37.1	23.7	45.2
1985	42.1	26.7	31.2
1986	46.7	29.3	24.0
1987	42.0	22.1	35.9

Source : Compiled from various issues of Pocket Book of Labour Statistics, Labour Bureau, Ministry of Labour.

Industrial Relations and Productivity

Industrial relations, like social relationship in any other walk of life, are based on reciprocity; continue to change; and affect the overall functioning of industrial organisations including productivity. Industrial relations affect productivity in a variety of ways. If the relations are cordial and amicable, different parties involved have the required motivation and morale; they try their best to perform their assigned tasks properly and to adjust and accommodate with each other; demonstrate their concern for each other, understand each other's problems and difficulties and lend their maximum cooperation in solving them, they try to forget their grievances and complaints; observe the laid down rules and regulations and show their willingness for coordinated action.

However, if, on the contrary, industrial relations are tense and strained, various associated parties lack the required will to do work sincerely as also in esprit de corps; harbour baseless and unnecessary grouse and grumb and try to find faults in others; attribute their own wrong doings to others by indulging in projections and justify their all kinds of actions even if they are apparently unjustified and wrongful; quite often engage in unnecessary leg pulling backbiting and character assassination; do not show any concern even about the real problems and difficulties of others, do not feel bothered about discharging their assigned duties and responsibilities properly; do not demonstrate any willingness for unified action; and finally become the victims of alienation a subjectively experienced feeling of normalessness; isolation and self-estrangement.

Thus healthy industrial relations create such climate as is conductive for effective functioning of all types of 'human factors' which occupy the central place among determinants of productivity. Industrial relations bring about peace which in turn, create prosperity through enhancement in productivity.

Conclusion and Suggestions

Problem of labour-management relations might have begun with the beginning of the modern industrial activity. According to the Royal Commission of Labour, "Before 1918 strikes were rare." This does not indicate that the workers had no grudge or complaint against their employers or they were quite satisfied with their work environment. But since practically the entire labour class was illiterate, ignorant of their rights, and suffered from class consciousness for there being no organisation among them, the grievances and complaints could not be fully expressed and, hence there were no signs of industrial unrest as such. But at present the concept of labour-management relations has changed tremendously mainly due to the following reasons :

(1) Awareness amongst workers for identifying their strength;

(2) Impact of workers struggle in different parts of world;

(3) Growing importance of 'human factor' for large scale production;

(4) Impact of International Labour Organisation; and

(5) World-wide acceptance of democracy.

Now the role of workers is not only limited to the work but they are also participating in management. They have been playing an important role in works committees and other committees.

"In the building of the new society both labour and management have great responsibility, it is for them to make whatever adjustments are necessary in their mutual relationship and to ensure that the production and prosperity of the nation do not suffer on their account."[9]

From the foregoing discussion the conclusion emerges that the problem of industrial relations is on the increase in India. It is a multidimensional problem and there can be no single solution. If the dispute can be settled by conciliation machinery, the employer-employee relations might remain more cordial, whereas under Adjudication Machinery, the settlement is sometime imposed upon rather than willingly accepted. Amicable settlement are possible through the negotiation and discussion directly between management and employer, when this is not possible, a third party like a government personnel may mediate and try to bring the parties i.e., management and labour, to a mutual agreement.

Work-stoppages as a result of strikes and lock-outs produce adverse effects on workers, management and the society. To workers they mean loss of earnings and to the management, loss of value of production. Loss of production creates scarcity which leads to price rise having an adverse effect on the economy.

Keeping in view, the facts, we would try to settle an industrial disputes expeditiously to minimise the setback both to industrial production and also to industrial relations. Commenting upon the importance of harmonious labour-management relations the National Commission on Labour[10] says, "Economic progress is bound up with industrial peace for the simple reason that industrial harmony leads to more co-operation between workers and management which results in higher productivity and thereby contribute to prosperity."

In the field of labour management, better understanding can be maintained and a good relation can be cultivated if the following steps are implemented :

(i) There is an urgent need to stop all the violent activities whether it is on workers; side or management side because it adversely affects the understanding and faith between labour and management. Most of the unnecessary lock-outs are due to violent activities of workers either directly or indirectly. At the same time management should also refrain from such violent activities.

(ii) Management must take the workers into confidence before an action is taken. Workers may be involved at various stages of management also, winning the hearts and minds of the worker will be a sound step for maintaining cordial relation between labour and management.

(iii) Strikes and lock-outs must be declared after all other efforts have been used to solve the problem. The ultimate sufferers of industrial disputes being the workers.

(iv) The management team in negotiation process must have some understanding amongst themselves. They have some understanding amongst themselves. They must look into the issue from a comprehensive view-point, anticipating possible lines of approach from the union side as well as from their side.

(v) There is a need for promoting workers participation in management in the real sense, workers participation envisages involvement of the working class in programmes to improve productivity and progress of a particular industry. Both management and workers should strive hand in hand to improve the overall relationship between them. "Industrial Democracy is as indispensable for "Industrial Peace" in a country".

(vi) Both management and workers have to realise that their interests are interwoven and that instead of depending on outside help, the state or a political party, they have to develop a mechanism based upon mutual commitment and understanding.

(vii) Trade unions working should be regular, executive meetings and general meetings must be called regularly. The members must understand the real meaning of 'Trade Union'. The returns must be submitted properly. There is a need for inculcating 'work culture' in the industries. Trade unions should also be involved in welfare activities in order to improve the general standard of living of members.

REFERENCES

1. Kapoor, T.M. (Ed.), Personnel Management and Industrial Relations in India, Bombay, 1968, p. 106.
2. Singh, V.B., Climate for Industrial Relations, 1968, p.-9.
3. 'Swadeshi Industries' *Vs.* 'Their Workmen' All India Reporter, Supreme Court, 1258.
4. 'Match Well Electricals (India) Ltd.' *Vs.* 'Their Workmen' 1962, Labour Law Journal, 289, (Punjab High Court).
5. Ambika Jute Mills Ltd., *Vs.* 'Their Workmen' 1954, Labour Law Journal, 835.
6. Associated Cement Co. Ltd., *Vs.* Its Workmen, 1952, Labour Law Journal, 225.
7. Giri, V.V. Labour Problem in Indian Industry, (Bombay, Asia Publishing, House, 1972), pp. 284-85.
8. Punekar, S.D. Labour Welfare, Trade Unionism, and Industrial Relations, Bombay, Himalaya Publishing House, 1978, p. 268-69.
9. Giri, V.V., *op. cit.* p. 214.
10. Report of the National Commission on Labour, 1969, p.-52, Ministry of Labour, Government of India.

9

Human Resource Valuation In India: A Managerial View Point

G.S. Batra*
&
B.S. Bhatia**

Introduction

In any organisation the most important input is the human element. The success or failure of a company very much depends on the persons who man the organisation. It is a matter of common knowing that capital issues of even new undertakings are oversubscribed, if they are floated by competent persons. This is because the investor in the capital market places high value in the human ability rather than any other factors like net worth, yield, price earnings ratio which are not available in the case of a new company. Even among nations, countries like Japan, West Germany and Korea are able to make rapid strides, thanks to the human resources - not in terms of numbers but in terms of quality, devotion to work and loyalty to the nate. In the Asiad at Delhi, we saw how the two Koreas secured a large number of medals quite out of proportion to their size, strength and resources. This was possible because of the emphasis on the development of human resources. Japan, a country which is not endowed with much of natural resources, is not handicapped at all, thanks to it human resources with the help of which that nation can surmount any difficulty. History is replete with examples of several great personalities like Christ, Budha, prophet Mohamed,

* Faculty Member, Deptt. of Business Management, Punjabi University, Patiala, Punjab.

** Professor, Deptt. of Business Management, Punjabi University, Patiala, Punjab.

Sankara and Vivekananda to realise what single individual can achieve without any material resources. In business also the greatest asset is the human resource of the enterprise and not the plant, equipment or the magnificent buildings it owns. It is worth recalling what Alfred Marshal said long ago that 'the most valuable of all capital is that invested in human beings'. However, it is unfortunate that the balance sheets do not exhibit this most vital asset, while capital invested in other assets is shown. This is one of the severe limitations of present day financial statements which hinder the uses of these statements from making full use of them.

Generally, the productivity of investment in industries is known from the rate of return it gives. So far, these rates of productivity are considered in respect of physical assets investment only. To find out the productivity of investment in respect of human beings in any enterprise. Human Resource Accounting (HRA) will be helpful. The Human Resource Accounting is also scaling tool that generates and reports the quantitative control information about the contribution of human resources for promoting industrial productivity. It can help the management in taking many vitial decisions relating to selection, lay-off, transfers, training, promotion, etc.

The American Accounting Association's Committee on Human Resource Accounting has defined human resource accounting as under:

> "Human resource accounting is the process of identifying and measuring data about human resources and communicating this information to the interested parties".

Thus, the basic premises underlying the theory of Human Resource Accounting are :

(1) People are valuable resources of an enterprise,

(2) The usefulness of manpower as an organisational resources is determined by the way in which it is managed, and

(3) Information on investment and value of human resources is useful for decision making in the enterprise.

It helps in developing financial assessments for the people within the organisation and monitoring of these assessments in the light of set accounting policy of the concern from time to time. The purpose of HRA is to improve the quality of human resources decisions made both internally externally concerning an organisation. However the specific objectives of HRA may be outlined as under :

(1) to assist the management in taking suitable decisions regarding investment on human resources.

(2) to provide information to all people concerned regarding the earning potential of human resources of the organisation.

(3) to assess the efficiency of human resources in obtaining productivity and profitability, and

(4) to provide comparative information regarding costs and benefits associated with investment in human assets.

Rationale of Human Resources Accounting

The accountants in the past have not given due consideration to this important asset working in the enterprise. In our traditional accounting practices, the heavy amount incurred on the recruitment, placement, selection, training and development of the personnel is generally treated as revenue expenditure and hence it is debited to profit and loss account of the period during which such amount is incurred. But today, it is argued that these expenditures incurred by an enterprise to get the benefit of the services of its manpower force in future is against the accounting principle to treat them completely of a revenue nature. In fact, such expenditure should be capitalised and is shown in the balance-sheet. The failure of professional accountants to treat human resources as asset just like physical and financial assets attracted the attention of academics and in seventies, the concept of Human Resource Accounting was evolved which emphasis that human resources should be treated like physical assets and should be shown in the balance sheet of the enterprise.

Objectives of Human Resource Accounting

The primary purpose of human resource accounting is to facilitate the management of people as organisational resources. It can also be called as human resource management accounting i.e., the application of accounting to the management of human resources.

Rensis Likert, one of the earliest proponents of the subject, has listed the following objectives of Human Resource Accounting :

(1) To furnish cost value information for making management decision and maintaining human resources in order to attain cost effective organisational objectives.

(2) To allow management personnel to monitor effectively the use of human resources.

(3) To provide a sound and effective basis on asset control i.e., whether assets are conserved, depleted or appropriated.

(4) To aid in the development of management principles by classifying the financial consequences of various practices.

Present Value of Future Earning Model

Under this approach, the value of human resources of an organisation is determined according to their present value to the organisation. A number of valuation models have been developed to determine the present value.

This model has been developed by Brauch Lev and Aba Schwartz in 1971. They are of the opinion that determination of the total of a firm's labour force is a straight forward extension of the measurement procedure of an individual value to the organisation. They have divided the whole labour force into certain homogeneous group such as unskilled, skilled, semi-skilled, technical staff, managerial staff etc. and in accordance with different classes and age groups. Average earnings stream for different classes and age groups are prepared for each group separately and the present value for the human capital is calculated. The aggregate present value of different groups represents the capitalised future earnings of the firm as a whole. They have advocated the use of cost of capital rate for the purpose of capitalising the present value of the future earnings of the employees. According to them, the value of human capital represented by a person of age is the present value of his remaining future earnings from his employment. They have given the following formula for calculating the value of an individual :

$$Vr = \frac{I(t)}{(1+R)^{t-r}}$$

Where Vr = the value of an individual r years old

I (t) = the individuals annual earnings upto retirement

t = retirement age

R = discount rate

Rewards Valuation Model

This model has been suggested by Flamholtz. It identifies the major variables that determine an individual's value to an organisation, i.e., his expected realisable value. The expected realisable value of an individual is the present worth of future services expected to be provided during the period he is expected to remain in the organisation. The model is based on the presumption that a person's value to an organisation depends upon the positions to be occupied by him in the organisation. The movement of people from one organisation role to another is a stochasic process with rewards. As people move and occupy different organisational roles, they render services (i.e., rewards) to the organisation. However, the roles they will occupy in future will have to be determined probabilistically for each individual. The model suggests a five steps approach for assessing the value of an individual to the organisation:

1. Forecasting the period will remain in the organisation, i.e., his expected service life.
2. Indentifying the services states, i.e., the roles that he might occupy including, of course, the time at which he will leave organisation.
3. Estimating the value derived by the organisation when a person occupies a particular position for a specified time period.
4. Estimation of the probability of occupying each possible mutually exclusive state at specified future times.
5. Discounting the value at predetermined rate to get the present value of human resources.

This model is certainly an improvement over the Lev and Schwartz. But this model when examined on operational capacity falls short of a practical value in as much as that probabilities will have to be determined for each individual occupying various service states, and these probabilities will have to be determined for all employees for periods on an individual basis. Further, it will be tremendously expensive way to predict career movements of exit probabilities on an individual basis. Moreover, data developed on the basis will involve large variance which will reduce usefulness of the model.

Net Benefit Model

Morse (1973) suggested this approach. Under it the value of human resources is equivalent to the present value of the net benefits derived by the enterprise from the service of its employees. The following steps are involved under this approach:

1. The gross value of the services to be rendered in future by

the employees in their individual and collective capacity.

2. The value of direct and indirect future payments to the employees is determined.

3. The excess of the value of future human resources (as per (a) above) over the value of future payments (as per (b) above) is ascertained. This represents the net benefit to the enterprise because of human resources.

4. By applying a predetermined discount rate (usually the cost of capital) to the net benefit, the present value is determined. This amount represents the value of human resources to the enterprises.

Certainty Equivalent Net Benefit Model

This approach has been suggested by Pekin Ogan (1976) is, in fact, an extension of net benefit approach of Morese. Under it, the value of human resources is determined by taking into consideration the certainty with which the net benefits in future will accrue to the enterprise. The method involves the following steps:

(a) Net Benefit from each employee. (as determined under the previous approach)

(b) Certainty factor at which the benefits will be available in future.

(c) The certainty equivalent benefits will be calculated by multiplying the certainty factor with the net benefits from all employees. This will be the value of human resources of the enterprises.

Accounting Standards in India

The council of the Institute of Chartered Accountants of India (ICAI) has constituted the Accounting Standards Board (ASB) in April 1977. The main function of the ASB is to formulate Accounting Standards (AS). The ICAI is one of the members of the International Accounting Standards Committee (IASC) and has agreed to support the objectives of IASC. While formulating the accounting standards the ASB gives due recognition to International Accounting Standards (IAS) issued by the IASC and tries to integrate them to the extent possible in the light of the conditions and practices prevailing in India. The accounting standards are issued by the authority of the council of the ICAI. The accounting standards are applicable to public sector companies, private sector listed companies and large borrowers of funds from banks and financial institutions in the corporate sector. The accounting standards are intended to apply only to items that are material. It is the duty of the members of ICAI to ensure that the accounting standards are implemented in the presentation of financial statements covered by their audit reports. In the event of any deviation from the standards it is also their duty to make adequate disclosures in their reports so that the users of such statements may be aware of such deviation. In the initial years the standards are recommendatory in character for a period of three years. The ICAI gives wide publicity among the users and educate members about the utility of accounting standards, and the need for compliance with the disclosure requirements.

The ICAI has so far issued the following eleven accounting standards:

AS-1 : Disclosure of Accounting Policies.

AS-2 : Valuation of Inventories.

AS-3 : Changes in Financial Positions.

AS-4 : Contingencies and events occurring after the balancesheet date.

AS-5 : Prior Period and extra-ordinary Items and changes in Accounting Policies.

AS-6 : Depreciation Accounting.

AS-7 : Accounting for construction Costs.

AS-8 : Accounting for Research and Development.

AS-9 : Revenue Recognition.

AS-10 : Accounting for fixed Assets.

AS-11 : Accounting for the effects of Changes in Foreign Exchange Rates.

The accounting standards issued by the ICAI are more or less on the lines of International Accounting Standards with requisite modifications depending upon the needs of the country. All these accounting standards are quite important from the point of view of measurement and disclosure of accounting information. The ICAI is fully aware that the implementation of accounting standards is as important as their formulation. The ASB constantly makes efforts to achieve an ever-increasing degree of compliance with accounting standards. As one of the steps in this direction, the continuing education programmes of the ICAI attach great importance to discussing the implications of accounting standards so that an awareness about their utility in bringing about uniformity in accounting practices may be created. Efforts are also being made to enforce the standards by making them mandatory. Out of eleven accounting standards so far issued by the ICAI, eight accounting standards viz., AS-1, AS-4, AS-5 AS-7 AS-8, AS-9, AS-10 and AS-11 have been mandatory. As regards duties of auditors in relation to mandatory accounting standards, it has been declared by the ICAI that members should examine whether accounting standards statements relating to accounting matters are complied with in the presentation of financial statements covered by their audit, In the event of any deviation from the accounting standards, it will be the duty of auditors to make audit disclosure in their audit reports and draw attention to the material departure from accounting standards so that the users of financial statements may be aware of such deviations.

Through the ASB of the ICAI has brought out accounting standards on most of the important areas in accounting and has ensured their implementation by making accounting standards mandatory, the most regretting fact is that the ICAI has not been able to bring any definitive accounting standard on measurement and reporting of human resources cost and value. The nondisclosure of human resources accounting information in financial statements distorts net income disclosed by profit and loss accounts, total assets figure in balance sheet and also distorts computation of rate of return on capital employed because its components namely net income and total assets are distorted.

Applications of Human Resource Accounting in India.

If we look at the annual reports of public enterprises and private enterprises in India, we find that chairman's reports invariably contains the statements highlighting the significance of human resources. The chairman of these enterprises make their remarks at the annual general meeting of the shareholders that our employees are most important assets and without their significant contribution, the present growth in the operation would not have been attained, I wish to place it as record of my sincere gratitude for the hard work done by the employees of our company. 'I thankfully acknowledge the contribution made by our employees'. These qualitative pronouncements reflect the importance of human resources in an enterprise but the quantitative information relating to their contribution or their value is nowhere recorded or shown in the financial accounts.

In India, human resource accounting has not been introduced so far as a system. The companies Act, 1956 does not require furnishing of any significant information about human resources in financial statements of companies. The Institute of Chartered Accountants of India has issued eleven accounting standards on different technical subjects of accounting but it has not been able to bring any definitive accounting standard for measurement and reporting of cost and value of human resources of an organisation. The existing accounting standards, however, fully support the adoption of human resource accounting for the purpose of meeting their own requirements in true sense. The result of non-disclosure of human resources cost and value information in financial statements of business enterprises, has been that financial statements do not reveal any quantitative information on human resources side and the statement of affairs is improperly reported to different authorities.

The dichotomy in accounting between human and non-human capital is rather fundamental in that while latter is recognised as an asset and recorded as such in the financial statements, the former is totally ignored. With the accelerated growth in science and technology the value of Human Capital is gradually increasing and hence it is essential for a company to reflect the investment in human resources.

Recently, the idea of human resource accounting attracted the minds of many scholars viz., Hermanson, Hekiman Jones, Likert, Flamholtz, Brument & others. The modern thinking of these scholars is that all the assets of the Company including the human asset must be properly treated, analysed and reported by an accounting system in view of the long-term interest of the organisation. So the Human Resource Accounting is needed in this context.

Human Resource Accounting is necessary: (a) disclose what is happening to the energy of human beings and what is its value for management, (b) to find out the productivity of investment on human beings in organisation. It is the scaling tool that generates and reports quantitative control information about the contribution of human resource for promoting industrial productivity.

The application and usefulness of HRA depends on the future efforts and experiments to be made by practicing managers, accountants and academicians. The application of HRA also needs support from the professional bodies and Government.

In the absence of Human Resource Accounting the management may not realize the negative effects of certain programmes aimed at improving profits in the short run. Such programmes may result in decreased value of human assets due to fall in the productivity levels, high labour turnover, low morale etc.

The success of an organisation very much depends on the build-up of quality workforce at all levels. The success stories of BHEL, ITC, Hindustan Lever, Larsen & Tubro and several other enterprises are largely due to the emphasis on human resource development. If this vital asset is not shown in the balance sheet, to that extent the public and investors are handicapped. Human Resource Accounting helps investors and Public by providing the necessary information.

BIBLIOGRAPHY

1. American Institute of Certified Public Accountants, New York, Accounting Research and Terminology Bulletin, p.-9.
2. American Accounting Association, A Statement of Basic Accounting Theory, 1966.
3. Report of the Committee on Human Resource Accounting, The Accounting Review, 1973, pp. 169-185.
4. The Chartered Accountant, New Delhi, Nov. 1989, p.-408.
5. The Chartered Accountant, New Delhi, Nov. 1990, p.-419.
6. Human Resource Accounting (A Study of India Corporate Sector) Journal of Accounting and Finance, Vol. VIII, No. 1, Spring, 1994.

10

Development Banking in Transition in India (A Case Study)

B.S. Bhatia, G.S. Batra & Pervinder Kaur*

Introduction

The process of industrial growth required, as one of its accompanying structural changes within the economy, the development of capital market that will provide an adequate and properly distributed finance to those entrepreneurs, public or private, who are setting up new plants or expanding existing ones. While finance itself produces no output until capital equipment and new materials are purchased with it, the availability of money and credit permits entrepreneur to gain control over real resources which enable them to engage in an industry by producing and distributing products. Thus, capital market consists of a "series or channels through which the savings of the community are made available for industrial and commercial enterprises for public authorities. It embraces not only the system by which the public takes up long-term securities, directly or through intermediaries but also the elaborate network of institutions responsible for short-term and medium-term lendings."

The impact of the PFC in particularly on the industrialisation of the state and the contribution made in terms of diversification of Industrial Structure, regional dispersal of industries, and industrialisation of the backward areas.

* Professor Faculty Member and Research Scholar respectively, Department of Business Management, Punjabi University, Patiala.

The present study is an attempt to evaluate at micro level the working and performance of PFC through an indepth case study. Efforts have been made to look into the performance of Punjab Financial Corporation in an objective manner and that leads to some findings which will hopefully add to positive knowledge on the one hand, and contribute to information system of decision makers interested in improvement in the working and performance of PFC in particular and SFCs in general.

Research Methodology

Secondary data has been collected from the IDBI's annual reports as well as from internal circulars of PFC. Working of PFC has been examined in terms of organisation policies, objectives, financial resources and contributions made by PFC in the process of development of Punjab State. The state of economy of Punjab and efforts for industrialisation through successive five years plans in the state have been studied by referring to Five Year Plans and review of plans and statistical abstracts and economic survey of Punjab.

Operational performance of PFC has been measured in terms of the amount of assistance sanctioned, and disbursed. Industry-wise and region-wise analysis of the assistance provided by PFC has also been made. Fixed index number and chain base index number has been calculated to analyse the increase or decrease in the amount of sanctions and disbursements. In order to capture the trend more precisely the amount of loan sanctioned to disbursed has been regressed on the basis of time. The trend growth rate has been calculated on the semi-log scale.

Profile of State Financial Corporation

The PFC was set up in 1953 to fill up the gap in meeting the financial requirements of medium and small scale industrial units in the State. Although profit is a criterion of efficiency of management of corporation, a financial corporation, however, should not be judged only in terms of its financial record. Of greater significance to the economy is the corporation's contribution in terms of its impact on the thinking; work ethos and the attitude of its clients and of the business community. Financial corporations are channels through which society achieves modernity and entrepreneurial and institutional growth. Thus, its true profitability can be found in and flows from an enhanced sense of business ethics, innovation in techniques and improvement in management practices and the operational workings.

Operational Performance of Financial Corporation in Punjab. Growth of Sanctions and Disbursements

Fixed index numbers of total amount sanctioned have increased from 100 in 1980-81 to 701.73 in 1991-92. It means an increase of more than 7 times in 10 years. The corresponding index number of assistance disbursed have increased from 100 in 1980-81 to 781.48 in 1991-92. This means an increase of 7.81 times in just 10 years. Thus, though both the amount sanctioned and amount disbursed have increased over the years, the amount disbursed have increased over the years, the amount disbursed have increased more than the amount disbursed.

The chain base index numbers have been computed to show the increase or decrease in the total amount sanctioned and disbursed. These show that in the years 1981-82 and 1982-83, amount sanctioned increased as compared to the previous years but in the next two years (1983-84 and 1984-85) it marginally decreased as compared to previous years.

However, in the year 1984-85 amount sanctioned decreased to a large extent. The chain base index number touched 36.93 as compared to 101.96 in the year 1983-84. After that there was a continuous increase in the amount of sanctions till 1986-87 and then a marginal decrease in 1988-89.

The chain base index numbers of amount disbursed is more than 100 for all the years except in the year 1984-85 and 1990-91. The management of PFC claimed that decline in the amount of loan sanctioned and disbursed was due to general recession in those years and increase in the amount was due to their own efforts.

In order to capture the trend more precisely, the amount of loan sanctioned to disbursed have been regressed on the basis of time.

The best fitted model for total assistance sanctioned is :

$$Y = ab^t$$

$$\log^y = a + bx$$

$$\log^y = 3.522 + 0.146552 \times (.004427)$$

$$\text{Growth rate} = 40.1367 \text{ per cent}$$

The value of regression co-efficient is found to be 0.146552 showing a growth rate of 40.13 per cent. The trend growth rates have been estimated on a semi log scale.

The best fitted model for the disbursement is:

$$Y = ab^t$$
$$\log Y = a + bx$$
$$\log Y = 3.3615 + 0.54072 \times (.00569)$$
$$\text{Growth rate} = 63.99 \text{ per cent}$$

The value of regression co-efficient has been found to be 0.5407 showing a growth rate of disbursement as 63.99 per cent. The trend growth rate has been estimated on a semi log scale.

Table I shows compound rates for plan periods for loans sanctioned, disbursed and outstanding.

Table I
Compound Growth Rates for Loans Sanctioned, Disbursed and Outstanding by PFC

Plans	*Sanctioned*	*Disbursed*	*Outstanding*
Annual Plans	16.51	16.80	——
IV-Plan	28.43	20.85	20.83
V-Plan	20.37	22.79	25.17
VI-Plan	16.72	17.48	17.14
VII-Plan	21.43	21.89	20.77
Upto 1989-90	20.64	20.00	21.03

Source : Punjab Financial Corporation, Annual Reports, Various Issues.

Note : Growth rate is for the period 1968-69 to 1989-90.

Table I indicates that sanctions and disbursements of PFC have grown almost at the same rate over the period 1965-66 to 1989-90. The growth rate of sanctions was 20.6 per cent and that of disbursed was 20 per cent per annum. However, if we look at the growth of amount sanctioned and disbursements from the angles of the plan periods, there emerges a distressing trend. After the initial stop rise in growth rates of sanctions from 16.5 per cent per annum during the annual plans to 28.43 per cent during the fourth plan, there is a declining trend whereas in the subsequent plans (during seventh plan), it again rose to more or less at the normal rate of 20 per cent per annum.

The growth of disbursement shows a consistently increasing trend till the fifth plan. During sixth plan, growth rate declined to 17.48 per cent from 22.79 per cent in the fifth plan. During the seventh plan, it again rose to 21.89 per cent but was still below the level of fifth plan. A similar trend is discerned in the amount outstanding. The whole analysis indicates that the corporation has been working under several constraints, partly due to its resource poor position and partly due to various hurdles in the industrialisation of state.

Assistance to Small Scale Sector

The SFCs were established primarily to cater to the financial needs of small and medium scale units. SFCs have a special responsibility to assist the small scale sector. Year-wise trend in the amount of assistance sanctioned to SSI units shows an increase from 58.89 per cent in 1980-81 to 86.38 per cent in 1989-90. In the matter of disbursement also, the share of SSI units in the amount of loan disbursed have shown an increase from 48.67 per cent in 1980-81 to 89.47 per cent in 1989-90.

The shift in the favour of small scale industries in the loan portfolio of PFC in the last few years have been the result of deliberate policies pursued by the Government (Central and State), the RBI, the IDBI and PFC itself. The small scale industries are potential source of employment for the large number of unemployed persons in our country and prevent concentration of economic power.

Table II shows the amount sanctioned and disbursed to SSI alongwith index numbers with base 1980-81 and chain base index numbers.

Fixed index numbers of amount sanctioned to small scale sector have increased from 100 in 1980-81 to 796.30 in 1989-90, showing an increase of nearly 8 times in 10 years. The corresponding figures for amount disbursed have increased from 100 in 1980-81 to 1060.20 in 1989-90 thereby showing an increase of nearly 10 times.

Chain base index numbers have been calculated to show percentage increase or decrease over the previous year. Maximum increase is in year 1985-86 over 1984-85, i.e., to 290.63 from 46.93. After that amount there has been percentages decrease in amount sanctioned till 1988-89 as compared to the previous years. The chain base index number is less than 100 in 1983-84 and 1984-85. Similarly, for disbursement, chain base index numbers were less than 100 in 1984-85 for both amount sanctioned and amount disbursed, chain base index number was lowest in that year. Highest chain base index number of amount disbursed was in the year 1986-87. Rest of the years show gradual increase/decrease over the previous year. Loan sanctioned is generally less than loan disbursed as loan disbursed also includes disbursements in respect of previous sanctions also.

Table II shows percentage of total sanctions and disbursement during the year. The Tables show that per cent of sanctions during the year to total sanctions increased constantly except in year 1986-87 and 1989-90. Per cent of disbursement during the year to total disbursement shows similar trend.

In order to capture the trend more precisely the amount of loan sanctioned and disbursed to small scale sector have been regressed on time.

The best fitted model for assistance sanctioned to small scale sector is :

$$Y = ab^t$$

$$\log Y = a + bx$$

$$\log Y = 3.36249 + .30607 \times (.010334)$$

$$\text{Growth rate} = 50.72 \text{ per cent}$$

The value of regression co-efficient is found to be 0.30607 showing a growth rate of 50.72 per cent. The trend growth rates have been estimated on a semi log scale.

The best fitted model for assistance disbursed to small sector is :

$$Y = ab^t$$

$$\log Y = a + bx$$

$$\log Y = 3.14437 + .184547 \times (.007216)$$

$$\text{Growth rate} = 52.94 \text{ per cent}$$

The value of regression co-efficient is found to be .18454 showing a growth rate of 52.94 per cent. The trend growth rate have been estimated on a semi log scale.

Thus, from the point of view of assistance to small scale sector, the PFC has done a good job. The average assistance to SSI units have been more than 65 per cent. The emphasis is given to small scale units during the period.

It can also be seen from the tables III and IV showing relative share of small scale and medium scale industries in the sanctions of the PFC.

Table II

PFC : Index Numbers of Amount Sanctioned and Disbursed to Small Scale Sector

(Rs. in lakhs)

Year	*Sanctions*			*Disbursement*		
	Amount Sanctioned	*Fixed base Index No.*	*Chain Index Number*	*Amount Disbursed*	*Fixed Index Number*	*Chain Index Number*
1980-81	770.25	100.00	100.00	411.18	100.00	100.00
1981-82	1034.79	134.34	134.34	607.29	147.69	147.69
1982-83	2136.83	277.42	206.49	1095.34	266.38	180.36
1983-84	1820.11	236.30	85.17	1197.14	291.11	109.29
1984-85	854.25	110.90	46.93	678.37	164.98	56.66
1985-86	2482.75	322.33	290.63	900.51	219.02	132.75
1986-87	3837.09	498.16	154.54	2371.74	562.22	263.35
1987-88	5246.96	681.20	136.74	3310.90	805.22	139.59
1988-89	5202.03	675.36	99.14	4065.09	988.64	122.77
1989-90	6133.56	796.30	117.90	4359.34	1060.20	107.23
Growth rate	50.72 (.010334)*			50.94 (.007216)*		

Source : The *Annual Reports* of PFC (1980-81 to 1989-90).

Figures in parentheses are t the values.

It can be seen that percentage share of sanctions going to small scale sector has been consistently greater than that of medium scale industries. The trend growth rate over the period 1970-71 to 1988-89 shows a marginal increase of 0.73 per cent.

Assistance to Backward Areas

An important objective of economic planning is the balanced development of different regions of the country. It is in this context that SFC's in particular can play a crucial role as their operations are not governed by market conditions. By this preferential treatment to industries set up in the backward areas, these institutions can contribute significantly to the balanced development of different regions.

The PFC does not keep itself confined to small scale sector only. One of the aim of the corporation is also to disperse such industries in the backward areas. The industries organised in backward areas provide raw materials for industries situated in more developed areas.

Table III

Total Amount Sanctioned and Disbursed to Small Scale Units by PFC

Year	*Amount Sanctioned*	*Percentage of total sanctioned during the year*	*Amount Disbursed*	*Percentage of total disbursed during the year*
1980-81	770.25	58.59	411.18	48.67
1981-82	1034.79	68.19	607.29	64.54
1982-83	2136.83	76.30	1095.34	74.65
1983-84	1820.11	63.74	1197.14	76.86
1984-85	854.25	80.99	678.37	63.61
1985-86	2482.75	79.09	900.51	76.88
1986-87	3837.09	83.39	2371.74	79.49
1987-88	5246.96	82.46	3310.90	88.15
1988-89	5202.03	79.10	4065.09	89.23
1989-90	6133.56	86.38	4359.34	89.47

Source : Annual Reports of PFC (1980-81 to 1989-90).

Table IV

Sector-wise Average Size of Sanctions by PFC

(Rs. in Lakhs)

Year	*Small Scale*	*Medium Scale*
1970-71	0.9703	3.377
1974-75	1.310	6.531
1979-80	3.735	20.099
1980-81	3.349	20.934
1981-82	3.164	22.981
1982-83	4.198	22.114
1983-84	3.415	29.557
1984-85	1.668	28.641
1985-86	6.130	26.253
1986-87	5.129	31.887
1987-88	5.437	33.800
1988-89	3.368	41.653
1989-90	4.126	35.395
	Trend Growth Rate	
1970-71* to 1989-90	.0836	.1167
	(0.351)**	(7.979)**

Source : Annual Reports of PFC.
Notes : figures in Parenthesis are 't' values.
* Significant at 0.1% level.
** Trend Growth Rates.

The assistance sanctioned and disbursed by PFC to backward sector and non-backward sector is shown in Table V. The percentage of amount sanctioned has decreased from 51.83 in 1980-81 to 41.33 in 1989-90 to backward areas. In case of disbursement also the percentage of amount disbursed has decreased from 54.19 per cent to 42.19 per cent during the same period.

The Table V shows the assistance sanctioned and disbursed to backward areas by PFC over the period 1980-81 to 1989-90 alongwith index numbers with base 1980-81 and chain base index numbers. Sanctions to backward areas have gone up by 4.43 times and disbursement by 4.17 times during the period.

The chain base index numbers reveal that maximum increase in the sanctions as compared to the pervious years were during 1985-86 and for disbursement it was in the year 1986.87.

In order to capture the trend more precisely the amount of loan sanctioned and disbursed to backward areas have been regressed on time.

The best fitted model for amount sanctioned to backward area is:

Y	=	ab^t
log Y	=	a +bx
log Y	=	3.09761 + 0.269809 × (.009305)
Growth rate	=	86.12 per cent

The values of regression co-efficient is found to be 0.2698709 a growth rate of 86.12 per cent.

The best fitted model for amount disbursed is:

Y	=	ab^t
log Y	=	a + bx
log Y	=	2.933608 + 0.24814 × (.0102279)
Growth rate	=	77.06 per cent.

The value of regression co-efficient is found to be 0.24814 showing a growth rate of 77.06 per cent. The trend growth rate is estimated on a semi log scale.

An analysis of the assistance sanctioned by PFC has been carried out according to backward and non-backward region and also on the basis of district wise sanctions.

The percentage sanctions going to backward and non-backward districts during various years are shown in Table VI. They have been fluctuating over time. But the proportions have increased for backward district, i.e., Amritsar, Sangrur, Bhatinda, Hoshiarpur, Faridkot, Guradaspur and Ferozepur.

During the year 1970-71 the backward districts received only 12.75 per cent of the total cumulative sanctions of the corporation and 87.25 per cent went to the non-backward districts. This clearly shows that the backward districts were industrially backward, which they were bound to and financially neglected. However, in the subsequent years their share staggered to 58.18 per cent in 1978-79. Since then it has again been dwindling and it touched as low as 27.40 per cent in 1982-83. In this respect, the PFC is to be blamed to the extent that it has not been able to encourage and promote entrepreneurship in these districts. But the PFC is of the view that it is basically a financial institution which can

Table V

PFC : Index Numbers of Amount Sanctioned and Disbursed to Backward Areas

(Rs. in lakhs)

Year	Sanctions			Disbursement		
	Amount Sanctioned	*Fixed Index Number* (1980-81 = 100)	*Chain Index Number*	*Amount Disbursed*	*Fixed Index Number* (1980-81 = 100)	*Chain Index Number*
1980-81	681.38	100.00	100.00	457.78	100.00	100.00
1981-82	526.60	77.28	77.28	527.68	115.26	115.26
1982-83	767.20	112.59	145.68	604.68	132.08	114.59
1983-84	1158.71	170.05	151.03	654.89	143.05	108.30
1984-85	437.93	64.27	37.79	512.21	111.88	78.21
1985-86	1327.08	194.76	303.03	503.06	109.89	98.21
1986-87	2380.03	349.29	179.34	1299.19	283.80	258.25
1987-88	2612.52	383.41	96.10	1827.46	399.20	99.09
1988-89	2718.51	398.97	104.05	1949.41	425.83	106.67
1989-90	3021.41	443.42	111.14	1911.93	417.65	98.03
Growth rate	86.12 (.009305)*			77.06 (.010227)*		

Source : The *Annual Reports* of PFC (1980-81) to 1989-90).

*Figures in parentheses are t values.

provide from industrial finance from wherever the viable demand for finance comes. The low demand for finance is ascribed to paucity of entrepreneurship, lack of infrastructural facilities etc. which are beyond the scope of corporation. The percentage of sanctions as given in Table VI suggests that the backward district enjoyed fifty percent share.

However, it is heartening to note that the trend growth rate of the sanctions to backward districts over the period, as shown by Table VII, growth rate was 21.68 per cent and 14.69 per cent respectively for backward and non-backward areas. However, PFC has tried to ensure more development in the backward districts.

Table VI
Percentage of Sanctions to backward and Non-backward Areas

Year	*Backward Districts*	*Non-Backward Districts*
1970-71	12.75	87.25
1974-75	26.41	73.59
1978-79	58.18	41.82
1979-80	49.54	50.46
1980-81	51.83	48.17
1981-82	34.70	65.00
1982-83	27.40	73.60
1983-84	40.58	59.42
1984-85	41.50	58.50
1985-86	42.31	57.71
1986-87	57.80	49.20
1987-88	41.90	51.90
1988-89	41.34	58.66
1989-90	42.56	57:44

Source : *Annual Reports* of PFC.

Table VII
Average Annual Growth Rate of Sanctions by PFC to Backward and Non-Backward Areas

Year	*Backward Areas*	*Non-Backward Areas*
1970-71	29.00	198.45
1974-75	265.85	743.61
1978-79	518.48	372.70
1979-80	490.26	499.27
1980-81	681.38	636.16
1981-82	526.60	990.79
1982-83	767.20	2033.06
1983-84	1158.71	1696.59
1984-85	333.87	720.87
1985-86	1327.08	1812.01
1986-87	2380.03	2222.35
1987-88	2612.58	3749.84
1988-89	2718.51	3858.07
1989-90	3021.41	3858.07
	Trend Growth Rate	
1970-71* to 1989-90	21.68	14.694
	(0.325)*	(5.747)*

Source : *Annual Reports* of PFC.
Note : Figures within Parentheses represent 't' values.
* Significant at 0.1% level.

Sector-wise Assistance

The sector-wise assistance of PFC as given in Table VIII shows that it is mainly the term financer of the private sector. 99 per cent of its assistance has gone to the private sector. In terms of amount of assistance in 1988-89, the effective sanctions to the private sector accounted for 95.80 per cent of the total sanctions of the PFC and the percentage of disbursements and outstanding were 97.30 and 96.50 respectively. The assistance to co-operative sector is nil and to the joint sector and public sector negligible.

The reason for the low share of the public sector lies in the fact that

Table VIII

Size-wise Classifiction of Loans Sanctioned (Gross) by PFC

Since inception upto 31.3.90

(Rs. in lakhs)

	1988-89		*1989-90*		*Since inception upto 31.3.1990*	
Size	*No. of Units*	*Amount*	*No. of Units*	*Amount*	*No. of Units*	*Amount*
Upto Rs. 50,000/-	228	82.74	95	37.11	2676	780.24
Rs. 50,000/- to Rs. 1,00,000/-	74	35.74	98	62.72	1247	902.34
Rs. 1,00,000/- to Rs. 2,00,000/-	130	197.80	87	115.55	1731	2805.52
Rs. 2,00,000/- to Rs. 5,00,000/-	305	856.36	313	776.32	2102	6424.28
Rs. 5,00,000/- to Rs. 10,00,000/-	93	695.56	62	498.21	890	6568.32
Rs. 10,00,000/- to Rs. 30,00,000/-	121	2265.33	125	2328.48	875	17180.38
Rs. 30,00,000/- to Rs. 60,00,000/-	51	2443.05	69	3282.57	227	10731.62
Total	1002	6576.58	849	7100.96	9748	45392.68

Source : PFC Reports of respective years.

it enters the field of directly productive activities in large sector. The financial assistance to large sector mainly comes from the central financial institutions. The needs of joint sector are met from the IDBI, the IFCI, the ICICI, the LIC and the UTI. Thus, for all the practical purposes, the PFC is solely the terms loan financer of the private sector for small and medium industries. The main drawback of PFC has been that it has not designed ways and means through which it can shape the private entrepreneurship according to the needs of the modern industry.

In terms of amount sanctioned and disbursements, maximum sanctions have gone to private sector. Private sector received Rs. 5060.92 lacs in 1987-88 which increased to 5665.78 lacs in 1989-90. It accounted for 99.07 per cent in 1988-89 and 85.85 per cent in 1989-90. In disbursements also a similar trend is seen. In 1987-88, it accounted for 100 per cent of disbursements (Rs. 3755.83 lacs) while in 1989-90 it received 98.5 per cent (Rs. 4806.91 lacs) of total disbursement.

Private sector was followed by joint sector as it received 2.96 per cent (Rs. 151.00 lacs) of total amount sanctioned in 1987-88 while no amount was disbursed in that year. In 1989-90 joint sector disbursements were of Rs. 60.35 lacs (1.23 per cent) only.

Purpose-wise Assistance

The purpose-wise classification of sanctions and disbursements of the PFC for the years 1982-83, 1988-89 and 1989-90 is given in Table IX. The table shows that maximum assistance was given to new projects (80.37 per cent) in 1982-83 followed by assistance sanctioned for expansion and diversification (17.71 per cent) and generating assets (3.05 per cent) and supplementary assistance, no sanctions were made for modernisation, rationalisation and balancing equipment. In 1988-89 the new projects continued getting major share of sanctions of PFC (86.36 per cent) followed by expansion and diversification (10.32 per cent). Sanctions to expansions and diversification decreased from 17.71 per cent in 1982-83 to 10.32 per cent in 1988-89 modernisation/rationalisation also got quite a large amount of sanctions (101 lacs) whereas these projects were totally ignored in 1982-83. In 1989-90, new projects again got maximum share of 87.95 per cent (Rs. 5010.78 lacs) of total sanctions followed by expansion and diversification (7.80 per cent), but it decreased from 10.32 per cent in 1988-89 to 7.80 per cent in 1989-90.

In disbursements also, new projects got major share in 1982-83 (86.10 per cent) as well as in 1988-89 (95.62 per cent) and 1989-90 (93.4

Table IX
Sector-wise Assistance by PFC

(Rs. in lakhs)

	1987-88				1988-89				1989-90			
	Efficive Sanctions		Disbursements		Effective Snactions		Disbursements		Efficitive Sanctions		Disbursements	
	No. of Units	Amount	No. of Units	Amount	No. of Units	Amount	No. of Units	Amount	No. of Units	Amount	No. of Unit	Amount
Public	2 (.25)	80.00 (1.51)	—	—	2 (.26)	74.50 (1.43)	—	10.00 (.219)	1 (0.15)	34.00 (.59)	1	4.99 (.10)
Joint	4 (.50)	151.00 (2.96)	—	—	5 (.66)	143.00 2.75)	2 (.32)	116.92 (2.43)	—	—	2 (.01)	60.35 (1.23)
Co-operative	—	—	—	—	—	—	—	—	—	—	—	—
Private	795 (99.52)	5060.92 (95.52)	664 (100)	3755.83 (100)	750 (99.07)	4976.12 (95.80)	613 (99.67)	4434.64 (97.3)	655 (0.85)	5665.78 (99.4)	570 (.99)	4806.91 (.986)
Total	801 (100)	5297.92 (100)	1664 (100)	3755.83 (100)	757 (100)	5793.62 (100)	615 (100)	4555.56 (100)	656 (100)	5699.78 (100)	572 (100)	1872.25 (100)

Source : Annual Reports of PFC of respective years.
Figures in parentheses shows percentage to total.

per cent). The disbursements to expansion and diversification projects decreased from 9.36 per cent in 1982-83 to 3.96 per cent in 1988-89 but increased to 7.80 per cent in 1989-90 whereas modernisation projects got only (0.31 per cent) of total disbursement in 1988-89 and 1.16 per cent in 1989-90 as compared to 2.34 per cent in 1982-83.

Thus, in terms of proportions of sanctions the corporation has gone out in a big way to assist the new projects and the new enterpreneurs. The emphasis of the corporation is on new projects and it has been gradually withdrawing itself from the old and well established firms which is evidenced by the declining advances for the purpose of expansion/diversification and modernisation etc. The reasons for this trend can be that old/existing firms, may not have been interested in such changes and did not availed such help from the corporation. The sanctions for expansion/diversification decreased 17.71 per cent in 1982-83 to 10.32 per cent in 1988-89 and 7.80 per cent in 1989-90 whereas disbursement decreased from 9.3 per cent (1982-83) to 3.96 per cent in 1988-89 but increased to 5.07 per cent in 1989-90. A negligible supplementary assistance is given in the form of cash over run and purchase of generating assets.

On the whole, above analysis shows that loans have not been sanctioned and disbursed in a balanced way. Modernisation/rationalisation/ balancing equipment have remained seriously neglected inspite of the fact that technological changes are rapid in modern business world.

Industry-Mix Assistance of the PFC

The activities of the corporation cover a wide and varied field of industries. All the industries are grouped in six broad industrial groups. Table X shows the share of these groups in sanctions and disbursements of corporation during various plan periods. The traditional industries like agro, forest and textile based industries continued occupying the first place in all the plan periods followed by engineering goods in sanctions as well as disbursements. These were followed by rubber and chemicals, services, basic metals and metal products respectively whereas assistance for cement and non metalic industry groups has been insignificant.

The share of traditional groups declined from 48 per cent during the annual plans to 39 per cent in the 7th plan. Engineering goods improved from 14.52 per cent to 22.00 per cent during the same period. In basic metal group improvement is marginal i.e., from 12.27 per cent to 13.63 per cent. The services, industries were ignored in annual plans but they

Table X
Organisation wise Assistance Sanctioned and Disbursed

(Rs. in lakhs)

Sectors	*1987-88*			*1988-89*			*1989-90*			*Since inception upto March 1990*		
	Sanctions		*Disbursement*	*Senctions*		*Disbursement*	*Senctions*		*Disbursement*	*Sactions*		*Disbursement*
	No. of Amt		*Amount.*	*No. of Amt*		*Amount.*	*No. of Amt*		*Amount.*	*No. of Amt*		*Amount.*
1. Public Ltd.	15	590.02	327.47	14	501.12	393.44	8	175.84	327.87	160	3197.65	2642.54
										(2.30)	(9.22)	(9.55)
2. Pvt. Ltd. Co.	88	2004.54	1413.28	94	2366.84	2048.46	103	3312.91	2406.25	768	14816.0	10886.68
										(11.01)	(42.79)	(39.39)
3. Co-operative Societies	1	4.20	26.70	—	—	2.81	—	—	6.74	9	118.65	87.90
										(.120)	(.342)	(.81)
4. Partnership Concern	227	1886.74	1350.54	149	1438.93	1316.87	136	1336.63	1442.61	2925	11915.34	10489.66
										(42.19)	(34.31)	(37.96)
5. Sole-Proprietor	471	842.42	636.77	500	886.73	793.98	408	871.90	688.76	3056	4578.43	349.60
										(44.08)	(13.20)	(12.64)
6. Hindu Undivided Family	(—1)	—30.00	1.07	—	—	—	1	250	—	14	36.36	33.29
										(.20)	(.10)	(.12)
Total	801	5297.92	3755.83	757	5193.62	4555.56	656	5699.78	4872.25	6932	34664.49	27632.66

Source : Annual Reports of PFC of respective years.
*Figures in parentheses shows percentage to total.

received quite a good share in 4th (22.59 per cent) and 5th (17.37 per cent) plans. This analysis shows that there has been an up-swing in the favour of non-traditional industries.

The industrial group wise analysis of sanctions and disbursements of PFC indicates that the share of traditional industries increased from 37 per cent to about 40 per cent and that of engineering goods industries recorded a decline from about 35.53 per cent to 19.98 per cent during the first to seventh plan period. But the rank of this industry is same in the 7th plan, as has been in the annual plans. Cement and non-metalic industries were neglected through all the plans.

Conclusions

The Punjab Financial Corporation was set up to finance small and medium sectors of industry in the State of Punjab. The growth rate of sanctions and disbursements of the corporation during the period under study was about 20 per cent. An appraisal of growth rate of sanctions reveals that the fifth and sixth plan was the peak period of activity of the corporation.

A purpose wise analysis of the assistance by the PFC reveals wide gaps. Rationalisation, modernisation and rehabilitation etc. have remained neglected inspite of the fact that these aspects of industrialisation are very important in the changing economic scenario.

The pattern of distribution of loans according to the forms of organisation reveals that major beneficiaries continue to be partnership tune, private limited companies and sole proprietory concerns which reveals that the pace of growth of partnership firms and private limited companies are predominant in the loan portfolio of PFC.

Although the PFC has helped in the growth and diversification of the small sector through its financing, yet its functioning is more like that of a commercial bank that than that of a development bank. It has not done much in the field of promotion of diversification, modernisation and rationalisation. Instead of emphasis on the small sized units, its assistance is biased in favour of medium-sized units. Ths objective of development of backward areas also has not been fulfilled to the extent desired.

The bias in the functioning of the corporation flows from the fact that it combines in itself the function of finance of both the medium and the small sectors. The problems of small scale units are different from those of the medium scale units in several ways.

They have a special set of organisational and technical problems which call for the services of a specialised institution. Some of the peculiar problems of small units like uncertainty about continuity of management, the kind of security it may be able to offer, the absence of a corporate status, etc. have deterred the PFC from financing the small industrial undertakings progressively. Therefore, it is desirable to have separate organisation for financing the medium scale industries and the PFC should work for the small sector only.

The appraisal of the sanctions of the PFC against the assistance applied for reveals that it leaves much to be desired for in its attitude towards the seekers. It should review the cases in such a way that it provides greater opportunity to dynamic elements. Many persons who had no connection with the industry in the past have come forward during recent years and have become industrial entrepreneurs. The emergence of new entrepreneurs from the ranks of traders, civil servants, landlords, technicians and professional prople should be particularly helped by the PFC not only with finances but also by providing guidance and advice as well. Thus PFC should function as an engine of growth in the small scale sector.

Recommendations

To improve the recovery performance, it is suggested that PFC should make an indepth review of default portfolio, reasons for default should be analysed on case basis and appropriate recovery strategies should be adopted in order to recover the due amount keeping in view the difficulties of loanee concerns.

The trend of arrears concerns the Corporation since it impinges upon the optimal utilisation of the available funds. In order to reverse the growing arrears, the Corporation should device suitable plans so that it is in a position to recycle its resources.

The Corporation should be made accountable for better management and efficient operations so that the objectives for which it has been set up are accomplished without any problem.

The internal control system in PFC is very weak right from the sanction of the loan till the inspection and recovery thereof. It is therefore, suggested that PFC should have proper discipline in following the internal control system so that the benefits which it envisages to pass on to the industry are really given to the deserving cases.

Industrially backward districts needs special consideration of the corporation while financing the industrial units so as to promote balanced regicinal development in the state.

To improve, the functioning of the corporation, a system of efficiency could be employed. There is need to develop performance appraisal system, management audit, achievement assessment in relation to the corporation alongwith built in system of reward cum punishment for increasing the managerial efficiency.

The main criteria for judging the performance of the corporation should be financial and working results. The true picture of accountability of the Corporation should be based on the principle of greater the autonomy greater the accountability. Hence the Corporation should have fair autonomy in day-to-day administration.

To monitor and periodically review the qualitative performance of the corporation, consumer councils may be set up so that the Corporation achieves its desired objectives.

To provide a push to genuine promotional and financing activities, a review of Corporation's portfolio is necessary. The researcher having taken a look at the functioning of the Corporation, suggests having of such activities from the Corporation which have lost relevance to the policy regime.

One major factor that has proved to be a drag on the efficient functioning of the Corporation is the multipoint interference in its day-to-day decision making. The idea of memorandum of understanding may be implemented in case of Punjab Financial Corporation, since it represents a genuine desire to give autonomy to the Corporation. At the same time the Corporation could be made accounted for better management and efficient operations of the enterprise.

BIBLIOGRAPHY

1. Bhattacharya, S.N., *Development of Industrially Backward Areas—The Indian Style,* New Delhi, Metropolitan, 1981.
2. Jain, P.K., *Financial Institutions in India,* Trivent Publications, Delhi, 1985.
3. Joshi, S., *Financial Institution: Role in Industrialisation of Backward Regions,* Indian Management, 1987.

4. Hempten, Johm, J., *Financial Decision Making,* (Third Edition) Prentice Hall, New Delhi, 1983.
5. Indian Investment Centre, *Specialised Financial Institutions,* New Delhi, 1980.
6. Khan, M.Y., Development Banking — The Indian Experience, *Lok Udyog,* July 1981.
7. Misra, P.N., *Development Banks and the New Entrepreneurship in India,* National Publishing House, New Delhi, 1987.
8. Nagrath Anita, A Peep into the Performance and Role of State Financial Corporations, *Lok Udyog,* No. 14 (7), October 1980, pp. 53-59.
9. Sharma, C.P., *Industrialisation and Development Banking,* Deep & Deep Publication, New Delhi, 1989.
10. Vahhorne, James C., *Financial Management and Policy,* (Sixth Edition), Prentice Hall, New Delhi, 1983.
11. Appa, Rao, B., and Sujatha, "Recovery Performance of SFC's: An Analysis", *Lok Udyog,* 19 (5), August 1985, pp. 21-27.
12. Singha, Kanhaiya, "Financial Institutions and Industrial Development", Rama Shanker Singh (ed) *Industrialisation in India,* Deep & Deep Publications, Delhi, 1990.
13. Gupta, R.K. and Vashishat, A.K., Haryana Financial Corporation and Inter-district Disparties, *Journal of Accounting and Finance,* Vol. VI, No. 1 spring 1992.
14. Gupta, R.K., "Financial Services of Development Banks in India, Udyog Yug, Vol. 12, No. 3, Jan. 1992.
15. Dangwal, R.C. and Negi, K.S., "Institutional Financing and Industrialisation of Garhwal Region", *Journal of Accounting and Finance,* Vol. 12, No. 2, Fall, 1992.
16. Bhatia, B.S., "Role of Public Sector in Industrialisation", Kulwant Rana (ed), *Indian Industry in the Nineties,* Commonwealth Publishers, New Delhi, 1992.
17. Chander Subhash and Singh Paramplal, "Role of Punjab Financial Corporation in Financing the Industries in Punjab" Indian Journal of Public Enterprises, Vol. 8, No. 14, June, 1993.

11

Strategic Renaissance of Stock Markets : An Appraisal of Recent Stock Market Reforms

G.S Batra*

Introduction

In the preceding two decades, there has been an exponential growth in the Indian Capital market. The observers in the secondary market have noted that all is not well with the functioning of stock exchange. The regulatory system, with the SEBI at the apex, has been having problems in bringing about the desired changes in the functioning of stock exchanges. The present paper aims at a critical examination of the basic features of the secondary markets : particularly evaluating the efficacy of the interventions made by the SEBI as well as the ones which have been introduced by the Government of India. The author makes suggestions for streamlining the working of the secondary markets in India.

The capital market in India has witnessed spectacular growth during little over a decade only. To speak in terms of figure's companies raised funds worth Rs. 4200 crores from the stock-market during 1990-91 as compared to Rs. 100 crore during the seventies. Similarly, the number of listed companies on various stock exchanges has gone upto about 6500 during 1990-91 from about 2500 during 1980-81. The daily turnover on the various stock exchanges has gone upto Rs. 400 crore during 1991-92 from Rs. 15-20 crores during 1980.

---

* Faculty Member, Deptt. of Business Management, Punjabi University, Patiala.

The Indian stock market is said to be deficient mainly in the following respects :

1. Lack of control over the fair disclosure of financial information,
2. Non-development of secondary market,
3. Passive role of public financial institutions in checking the malpractices,
4. Manipulation of security prices,
5. Insider trading,
6. Unofficial trade in the primary market, and
7. Existence of improper control over brokers and subbrokers.

Behaviour of Stock Prices

Despite the difficulties experienced by the stock markets following the crash in stock prices in April 1992, the year 1992-93 was characterised by large volumes of funds raised from the capital markets. Available data for 1992-93 is given in table-I. During April-October 1992 the total volume of new issue activity measured by approvals issued by CCI up to May and clearances of prospectuses by SEBI increased by 67 per cent in the case of non-government companies. In the case of Government companies, there was a sharp decline in the volume of issue of bonds in 1992-93, compared to the previous year. The total capital issues planned by Government and non-Government companies in April-October 1992 were Rs. 9,111 crore, 25 per cent higher than in the previous year.

The behaviour of stock prices in 1992-93 was dominated by the crash which followed the exposure of the scan in April 1992. Stock prices were relatively stable in the third quarter of 1991-92. However, they began to rise again in January. This rise accelerated in the second half of February and especially in March. Reserve Bank of India's all-india Index Number of Ordinary Share prices which stood at 851.4 (Base : 1980-81) in the last week of January increased to 1099.6 in the last week of February and rose sharply to 1485.4 by the last week of March. Thereafter it increased to a new peak of 1659.6 in the first week of April 1992. Between the last week of January 1992 and the peak level in April 1992 the Index had increased by 94.9 per cent, with most of the increase occuring in March.

Establishment of SEBI

The Capital Issue (Control) Act, 1987 was repealed in May 1992, and the office of the Controller of Capital Issue (CCI), was subsequently abolished. With the abolition of CCI, prior government permission was no longer needed by Companies to access the capital markets. Companies were free to approach the capital market without prior government permission subject to getting offer documents cleared by SEBI. Control over price and premium fixation has also been removed and most issuing companies are free to fix the price of their securities for public as well as rights issue.

The need for reforms in the capital market has been evident for some time. As in the case of banks there has been an impressive expansion in quantity but without adequate improvement in quality. The functioning of the stock exchanges shows many shortcomings with long delays, lack of transparency in procedure and vulnerability to price rigging and insider trading. To counter these deficiencies it has been announced in the Budget Speech of 1987-88 that Government would establish a Securities and Exchange Board of India (SEBI) to regulate the capital markets. The SEBI was set up as a non-statutory board in 1988 with the intension of giving it statutory powers but this was not done at that time. The Government gave high priority to achieving this objective; an ordinance establishing SEBI as a Statutory body was promulgated on 30th January 1992. With this, SEBI acquired necessary powers to perform its functions.

Indian companies have been permitted to access international capital markets through Euro-equity issues aimed at mobilising capital for modernisation and import requirements. Several companies have been given such permission. Up to the end of January 1993, two companies have raised around $ 250 million from the Euro-market.

A number of steps havo been taken in the course of 1991-92 and 1992-93 by the Government and SEBI to introduce improved practices and greater transparency in the capital markets in the interest of healthy capital market development.

The act governing SEBI provided the following powers to SEBI.

1. SEBI is authorised to conduct inspections of various mutual funds. These inspections have been conducted and SEBI has submitted a report on each inspection which brings out various deficiencies of individual mutual funds. Corrective

steps are being taken to set right these deficiencies.

2. The process of registration of intermediaries such as stock-brokers and sub-brokers has been provided under the provisions of the Securities and Exchange Board of India Act, 1992. The registration is on the basis of certain eligibility norms such as capital adequacy, infrastructure etc.

3. Companies issuing capital in the primary market are now *required to disclose all material facts* and specific risk factors associated with their projects. Proposals are under consideration to improve the disclosure of information regarding the basis of calculation of premium while leaving companies free to fix the premium.

4. Merchant banking *has been statutorily* brought under the regulatory *framework of SEBI.* The merchant bankers are now to be authorised by SEBI. They will have to adhere to stipulated capital adequacy norms. Merchant bankers have to abide by a code of conduct which specifies a high degree of responsibility towards investors in respect of the pricing and premium fixation of issues, and disclosure in the prospectus or offer letter for issues.

5. The Government has given formal approval for the setting up of the *National Stock Exchange of India (NSEI)* by financial institutions and banks with IDBI as the nodal agency. The NSEI is expected to serve as a model exchange integrating the stock markets all over the country by providing nation-wide stock trading facilities and electronic clearning and settlements.

6. In order to induce companies to exercise greater care and diligence for timely action in matters relating to the public issue of capital, SEBI has advised the stock exchanges to collect from companies making public issues, a deposit of one per cent of the issue amount which could be forfeited in case on non-compliance with the provision of the listing agreement and, non-despatch of refund orders and share certificated by registered post within the prescribed time.

7. Regulations on insider trading under the provisions of the SEBI Act have been notified. Such regulations will help in protecting and preserving the market's integrity, and in the

long run help inspire investor confidence in the market.

8. RBI has liberalised the investment norms evolved for NFIs by allowing companies to accept capital contributions and issue shares of debentures to NRIs or overseas corporate bodies without prior permission.

9. The Government has allowed foreign institutional investors (FIIs) such as pension funds, mutual funds, investment trusts, asset or portfolio management companies etc, to invest in the Indian Capital market provided they register with SEBI.

10. To make the governing body of a stock exchange more broad based SEBI has issued guidelines for its composition. According to these guidelines the governing body of the stock exchanges should have five elected members, not more than four members nominated by the Government or SEBI and three of four members nominated as public representatives, besides its executive director.

11. The trading in stock exchange is now for three hours instead of two-and-a-half hours.

12. SEBI has set up an advisory committee for primary and secondary capital markets to provide wider consultation with the investors etc.

SEBI has ensured better disclosure to investors. Now the companies are regulated to supply the details of the issue, project, promoters, salient feature of the stock invest scheme and risk factors in an abridged prospectus alongwith the application in non-detachable form.

Every company entering the capital market must clearly state in its prospectus, the 'rusk factors' that is, the negative aspects associated with its project for the investors to form an unbiased decision.

The stock invest instrument is designed to minimise investors problems over over-subscription, refund delays. The noval idea being that the money which is used to subscribe to an issue will continue to earn interest even after the share application is made for the investor. The investor will not loose any interest on the money invested in the capital issue. Under the scheme funds remain in bank under lien till the date of allotment, besides earning interest thereon for that period. The liquidity of the investor is not affected.

Underwriting is now mandatory for the issue of capital to the public. If the issuing company does not receive 90 per cent of issued amount from public subscription plus accepted development from underwriters within 120 days from the date of opening of the issue, the company shall refund the amount of subscription.

Credit Rating Agencies

There are now two credit rating agencies in the country, viz., Credit Rating Information Services of India Limited (CRISIL) and Investment Information and Credit Ration Agency of India Limited (ICRA). Their main function is to rate debt instruments of companies. In 1991-92, CRISIL assigned ratings to 155 debt instruments of 103 companies worth Rs. 5866.5 crore while ICRA rate 47 debt instruments of 34 companies worth and Rs. 1161.8 crore. Guidelines issued by SEBI make credit ratings mandatory for companies issuing debentures to public.

From its inception till 12 November, 1992 CRISIL rated a total of 491 debt investments issued by 315 companies (including 5 in public sector) involving a total sum of Rs. 20,980 crore. During the 15 months ended 30 November, 1992 ICRA rated 119 debt instruments of 81 companies involving a total sum of Rs. 3537.87 crores. It has also completed two credit assessments and two general assessments during this period.

CRISIL also completed the credit assessment of 70 small companies upto November 1992. Credit assessment, a special product developed initially for the State Bank of India, is now used by other pubic sector banks as well as an important input in their decision making process on terms of lending. Beside, CRISIL has started providing technical assistance and training to foreign rating agencies.

Secondary Market

The governing boards of the stock exchange will be reconstituted soon with 50 per cent non-brokers. It has been experienced that a broker-dominated governing body has seldom been able to take disciplinary action against erring brokers.

The Insider trading on confidential information and cornering of shares is another malpractice rampant in stock exchange. Detailed guidelines have been issued to curb rampant insider trading which goes unchecked.

Over the Counter Market (OTC)

OTC Exchange of India, a company incorporated on October 1990 under section 25 of the Companies Act, 1956, will blaze a new trial in the capital market by giving small and medium sized companies an access to the capital markets, and investors a convenient mode of investment. OTCEI has also been supported by the SEBI for listing of smaller companies.

SEBI requires registration of all the mutual funds, existing as well as new. Private funds will be allowed. Code of advertisement had already been issued to the mutual funds regarding their honesty and fairness to disclose the risk factors involved in their funds. They are now advised not to give rosy pictures of high returns to investors and to make unreasonable comparisons of their funds with other funds.

Investor Protection Fund (New Provision)

In the interest of investors, clause 329 of the Companies Bill, 1993 proposes to establish an Investor Protection Fund to which will be credited the amount of dividends remaining unpaid or unclaimed after a period of 4 years from the date of transfer thereof to the general revenue account of the Central Government in pursuance of the provisions of the proposed clause 328 (section 205-A0, and any income on the investment made out of the amount credited to the fund. The fund shall be operated by the Government. The money credited to the fund shall be utilised 'for protection of investors' in accordance with the rules to be made by the Government, which investors will be covered by the fund and what will be purposes for which the amounts in the fund will be utilised will be decided by the Government. There is no indication in the clause of these aspects. It appears that any person entitled to a dividend transferred to the general revenue account and subsequently to the Investor Protection Fund, my claim the amount of dividend from the authority operating the fund any time even after it is transferred to the fund but the clause is silent of this matter.

According to a study conducted by the Society for Development of Capital Market, the average investor is still very conservative, abhors risk and prefers to bank his savings with the UTI. The middle class in particular, go in for the mutual funds in a big way. Market players like issuers, merchant bankers and underwriters were trying to get a safety net for themselves without honouring mutual contractual obligations, while the investor alone was left to suffer the consequences of failure of issues.

Elaborate guidelines have been issued by SEBI for the purpose of protecting investor's interest. These guidelines relate to issue of shares, debentures, new financial instruments and bonus shares.

Evaluation of the Working of SEBI

Notwithstanding the fact the SEBI's functioning has come under sever criticism, it is able to make a dent into the jungle of stock market. In spite of the hesitant attitude of the Govt. in tackling the situation, SEBI started its activity on a firm note. The constituents, which enjoyed the degree of freedom more than permitted levels, would normally be unwilling to curtail their activities. Even the stock exchange have come into conflict with SEBI regarding the exercise of powers relating to calling for periodical returns, prescribing maintenance of certain documents, approving by-laws, and licensing of dealers in securities in certain areas. As a matter of fact, Central Government has the authority to exercise these powers under the Securities Contracts Regulation Act, 1956. These are now sought to be transferred to SEBI through the new legislation.

It is true that SEBI has tussle with almost every participating institution in the capital market in respect of own or the other issues. Instead of taking up the entire work with such a great speed, it should have implemented its policies in a sequential manner allowing the participant institutions to learn the art of compliance. More so, SEBI should have taken at least public financial institutions and governing boards of stock exchanges in to confidence, while formulating the guiding for different issues.

Some Challenges

With the likelihood of more mutual funds arriving on the scene in the coming months, there may be competing demand for resources of individual savers. The mutual funds will certainly by helping small investors who cannot maintain a portfolio of their own involving large amounts as they will have the benefit of profitability of the portfolios built up with a balanced package. If proper codes of conduct are observed and the mobilised resources are properly deployed, it can surely be expected that the pool of resources will get augmented significantly and the resources so gathered can be deployed for hastening industrial development and improving returns on investment.

Investor protection left a great deal to be desired, with many companies flouting the rule relating to interest payment. Despite the fact that a three-tier brake system is now coming to the fore, investors need adequate legal protection under the circumstances.

Besides investors education which can go a long way in giving the much needed protection to the small investors, a separate legislation to protect the investors is necessary.

Conclusion

The process of reforms in the capital market has only just begun. It needs to be deepened to bring about speedier conclusion of transactions, greater transparency in operations, improved service to investors, and greater investor protection while at the same time encouraging the corporate sector to raise resources directly from the market on an increasing scale. Major modernisation of the stock exchanges to bring them in line with world standards in terms of transparency and reliability is also necessary if foreign capital is to be attracted on any significant scale.

The capital market requires reforms in many areas an many of these are inter-connected. As a result SEBI has to proceed simultaneously, on several fronts like companies, Brokers, merchant bankers, mutual funds, various market players etc.

SEBI powers need to be enhanced to ensure strict compliance with the rules and regulations. Stringent action should be taken against those who violate the rules, heavy penalties should be levied.

It is recommended that the functioning of stock exchanges needs modernisation in trading practices, computerization, integration of various stock exchanges across the country, substantial increase in the number of trading hours, scripless trading, steps for the availability of increased floating stocks, slowing down the process of permission to private sector mutual funds and FII's, speedier and comprehensive development of requisite regulatory framework, promotion of 'Self-Regulatory Organizations', construction of 'ideal' equity prices indices, activation of secondary markets for debentures and other 'much less traded instruments', speedier incorporation of useful recommendations in the existing regulatory framework and also developing the same for trading in 'futures and 'options' business, introducing and strengthening of financial base of Customer's protection Funds on various stock Exchanges.

BIBLIOGRAPHY

1. Navin Chandra Joshi, Over-The-Counter-Exchange : Will it Click? *The Economic Times,* April 29, 1992.
2. Rangamani, P.T., "Companies bill to promote immodernisation, equity Cult", THE HINDU, May 27, 1993. p.-18.
3. Kurup, N.P., SEBI Shows Teeth, PNB Monthly Review June 1993.
4. Securities and Exchange Board of India, "Its Role, Power function and Activities", by V.H. Panda, Chartered Secretary, New Delhi, September, 1992.
5. Dalal Street Journal, Bombay, September 7-20, October 5-11, 1992.
6. SEBI draft : Towards more transparency—I by J.R. Verma, V. Raghunathan and M.C. Bhat—The Economic Times, Bombay, June 1992.
7. SEBI guidelines for investor protection : Some suggestions—K. Sethuraman—The Economic Times, Bombay, June 1992.
8. Business India, Bombay, September, 28 to October 11, 1992.
9. Reserve Bank of India, Bulletine July, 1992.
10. Batra G.S., Emerging trends in Financial Market, Seminar on Recent trends in Financial markets in India Kurukshetra University 1994.

12

Managing Transition in Indian Economy : An Evaluation of Recent Public Sector Reforms

Dr. G.S Batra*
Dr. B.S. Bhatia**

Introduction

Liberalisation of business is gaining growing attention as a strategy for survival, competition and growth. The limitations of national markets, the diversity and unevenness of resource endowment of different nations, complexity of technological developments, differences in the levels of developments and demand patterns differences in production costs and efficiencies, technological revolution in communication and other fields etc. mandate globalisation. The political transformation in the USSR, Eastern Europe and economic reforms all over the world have given an added impetus to globalisation.

The deregulation and the delicensing initiatives have been undertaken with a view to increase production, improve quality and market and products and services abroad in competition with other multinational companies. This resolve has found consistency in the last three budgets of the Government of India.

There is growing realisation on the part of the Government that instead of doing some business, it should concentrate on creating an

* Faculty Member, Deptt. of Business Management, Punjabi University, Patiala, Punjab.

** Professor, Deptt. of Business Management, Punjabi University, Patiala, Punjab.

environment in which business prospers and entrepreneurial instincts are aroused so that the investors may get maximum output and reward from the efforts. Radical liberalisation has been ushered to make the Indian economy progressively market oriented and integrate it with the emerging global economic structure in a more meaningful way.

In an otherwise promising outlook for the Indian economy, a major factor for concern is the country's external payment situation. The external payment situation has continued to remain difficult on account of several mediumterm factors such as :

(a) Deceleration in the rate of growth of domestic oil production.
(b) The repayment obligations to I.M.F.
(c) The liberalisation of imports which has been highlighted considerably in the wake of the massive trade imbalance.
(d) The economic survey has also stressed the role of high fiscal deficits leading to a continuous dose of money creation and consequent inflation to be contributing towards the current account deficit.

Rationale of Liberalisation Strategies

By introducing new industrial policy in July 1991 the government has turned the system of economic regulations inside out. It removed industrial licensing except in respect of 18 specified cases. It also removed the there should limit of assets in respect of MRTP Companies and provided for foreign investment upto 51 per cent and in some cases upto 100 per cent equity in FERA Companies. It was also decided that a part of government's shareholding in Public Sector (first it was 20 per cent, then it is extended upto 49 per cent of equity) will be offered to mutual funds, financial institutions, the general public and workers. Accordingly the government has already generated Rs. 3,038 crores from the sale of Public Sector Undertaking (PSU)—shares during 1991-92 and about Rs. 3,000 crores in 1992-93. Thus, Indian economy is passing through some structural changes. Whether these fundamental changes can be managed successfully against the long-established specific way of life and mind-sets of the Indian people, remains to be seen.

In this paper an attempt has been made to evaluate the recent public sector reforms introduced recently. The path of Privatisation being adopted by the government is also examined in the Indian context.

Performance Evaluation of Public Enterprises

Despite the dominating role, the Public Sector has played in the

Table I
Profitability Profile of Central PSEs

1	*1981-82*	*1990-91*	*1991-92*	*1992-93*
	2	*3*	*4*	*5*
1. Operation Enterprises	188	236	237	237
(i) Profitable Enterprises	104	123	133	131
(ii) Loss-making Enterprises	83	111	102	104
Rs. Crore				
2. Capital Employed	21935	102083	117991	139933
3. Gross Margin	4012	18312	22223	25217
4. Gross Profit	2654	11102	13675	15978
5. Net Profit	445	2272	2355	3396
6. Profit of Profit-making Enterprises	1293	5394	6079	7346
7. Losses of Loss-making Enterprises	848	3122	3723	3951
Per cent				
8. Ratio of Gross margin to capital employed	18.29	17.94	18.83	18.02
9. Percentage of gross profit to capital employed	12.10	10.88	11.59	11.41
10. Ration of Net profit to capital employed	2.03	2.23	2.00	2.43

Source : Government of India, Economic Survey, 1993-94.

economic development of the country, yet it suffers from various problems.

One of the important problems of public enterprises is their economic inefficiency as indicated by low profitability. Though the profits of public enterprises has increased from Rs. 455 crore in 1981-82 to Rs. 3396 crore in 1992-92 as per Table-I. This return is too small keeping in view the huge investments made in public enterprises. Thus, there has been something fundamentally wrong with public sector units which were never in a position to perform competitively, as far as economic efficiency is concerned.

As on March 31, 1993, there were 245 Central Public Sector Undertakings (PSUs), excluding nine companies with Central Government investment but without direct responsibility for management, six insurance companies and three financial institutions. Of these, eight were in the construction sector, 72 in services and 165 in manufacture.

Out of 237 operating PSUs, as many as 131 were profitable during 1992-93 as compared to 133 during the previous year. Profits of these profit-making enterprises went up from Rs. 6079 crore in 1991-92 to Rs. 7346 crore in 1992-93, and increase of 20.8 per cent. But the losses of the remaining loss-making companies increased from Rs. 3723 crore to Rs. 3951 crore, an increase of over 6.1 per cent, during the same period. The overall rate of return over capital employed in the PSUs increased from two per cent during 1991-92 to 2.43 per cent during 1992-93. But the gross margin (i.e. before depreciation, interest and taxes) of PSUs as per cent of capital employed declined from 11.59 in 1991-92 to 11.41 in 1992-93. The heavy capital investment in the past combined with a massive interest burden is reported to have reduced the gross margins of PSUs.

Public enterprises have been suffering from high costs of production and low capacity utilasation and over capitalisation. Though one may argue that the public enterprises units will have higher cost due to their social obligations, one finds little justification in areas of competitive industries where both public and private sector units function side by side. How can one justify the high cost of public enterprises when they operate under similar business environmental conditions of private enterprises? Being not competitive they lose their market base both in the domestic market as well as international markets. This leads to low capacity utilasation due to reduced demand. Low capacity utilisation is a drag on the public enterprises, thus increasing its cost of production further.

Poor managerial efficiency has been another weakness of public enterprises which has an adverse impact on their performance. The managerial weaknesses of the public enterprises mainly stem from structural procedural rigidities, lack of initiative in decision-making, red tapism, instability in leadership, weak motivational base etc. All these factors led to absence fo professional management, which is so essential for effective functioning of the public enterprises. In addition, too much political interference hindered enthusiastic managers, who were willing to take innovative decisions but were kept on leash by political interference.

Public enterprises have been suffering from too much accountability on one hand and lack of autonomy on the other. There is close on public enterprises by the parliamentary committee and nominated board of directors, thus leading to inflexibility in the functioning of public enterprises. To respond to a change in the environment, they have to go through a lengthy procedure and by the time the concurrence for a decision comes the opportunities have been lost. Such things are common in case of public enterprises leading to functional rigidities. Due to functional rigidities the public enterprises become obsolete with the passage of time.

At the same time, there is inadequate accountability in that, no clear cut guidelines are available for judging the performance of public enterprises in attaining social-economic objectives. This lack of accountability for social objectives have been the excuse under the guise of which they try to conceal their inefficiencies an defend their dismal performance.

Public enterprises suffer from over dependence in government for finances. Though it is stated that they contribute to the state revenues in the form of dividends, the outflow from the exchangure is more that the inflow, as the loss incurring units are more as compared to the profit earning units.

Hence, public enterprises suffer from several weaknesses which ultimately contribute to the budgetary deficit of the country. It is stated that governments in many developing countries over-tax themselves by getting involved directly in the industry. The consequent burden on budgets and demand for credit have been important causes of economic difficulties of developing countries. Under the conditions of serve resource constraints, the participation of private sector in the development process is not an option but an essential one. Thus, privatisation is a necessity arising out of changes in environmental conditions.

The Rationale and Strategies of Privatisation

The ideas that propel privatisation are :

(i) Those who want cheap and efficient goods should turn to private sector (supposedly efficient and cheaper).

(ii) Those who want wide choice must allow competition between private and public sector.

(iii) Those who want entrepreneurial development they must unlock opportunities and provide alternatives in private sector.

That means private sector would provide a wide variety of cheaper, more efficient goods and services and encourage new entrepreneurs.

Different strategies can be adopted by India privatisation of PSUs.

1. *Cold Privatisation :* Public enterprises are required to relate their activities and strategies to the market conditions. Public enterprises are distanced from the government, though the ownership continues to be with the government.

2. *Managerial privatisation :* While the ownership of PSUs continues with the government, the Board of Directors comprise experts from the private sector.

3. *Joint ventures :* A private enterprise owns a part of equity in PSUs and the government owns the balance. The joint venture model is considered to be a transitional arrangement, leading to eventual total disinvestment.

4. *Franchising :* PSUs may develop new technology in new products/services, which are then franchised to private sector companies for more production, so that PSUs need for invest in additional manufacturing facilities.

5. *Leasing :* The assets, particularly, the idle and the underutilised ones, are leased out to the private sector. Ownership continues to be with PSUs.

6. *Contracting-out :* Certain stages of production of PSUs may be contracted out to the private sector though the final product is still manufactured by the PSUs. With competitive bidding, the production cost of final output can then be brought down.

7. *Disinvestment :* The government sells whole or part of its equity in PSUs to private enterprises and/or the investing public.

Recent Public Sector Reforms

The Government of India announced a New Industrial Policy in July

1991 which contains the following four major decision in respect of the Public Sector :

(1) Reduction in the list of industries for the public sector from 17 to 18 and introducing selective competition in the reserved area;

(2) Disinvestment of shares in PSES to raise resources and encourage wider participation of general public and workers in the ownership of the PSEs;

(3) Policy for sick public enterprises to be same as that for the private sector ; and

(4) Improving performance through the performance contract or Memorandum of Understanding (MOU) system by which managements are to be granted greater autonomy and held accountable for results.

Governments in the past have undertaken organisational improvements in PSEs based on the recommendations of expert committees, such as, establishment of Holding Companies and the system of MOU, and reference of sick units to the BIFR. Though these have resulted in some improvement, a comprehensive reform of public enterprises was considered necessary to bring PSE operations in consonance with the overall structural changes and the macro-economic stablisation programme initiated the present Government. The desirability of Public Sector reforms has been emphasised by the need to raise the productivity of capital resources employed and to reduce PSE losses so as to reduce the size of the fiscal deficity in successive budgets. As is evident from table-II, the budgetary support as percentage of the total plan outlay of the public enterprises has significantly come down. While their plan investment has gone up by about 25 per cent in 1992-93 over 1991-92, the share of budgetary support in their plan investment has come down from 23.52 per cent to 18.62 per cent. This trend may get strengthened in the coming years following the restructuring of public enterprises leading to higher internal resource generation and mobilisation of larger volumes of extra budgetary resources.

The key elements of the strategy for the reform of public sector include : strengthening managerial autonomy; promotion of private sector competition in areas where social considerations are paramount; reduction in budgetary support to public enterprises in view of severe budgetary constraints; and increasing dividend payments to ensure adequate return on

Government's equity; partial divestment of equity in selected enterprises to mobilise non-inflationary resources and to widen public and private sector participation in pubic sector in order to introduce a greater sense of accountability; restructuring or closure of unviable enterprises and creation of a safety net to protect the interests of workers.

Table II

Public Enterprises : Plan Investment and Budget Support

Year	*Plan Investment*	*Equity*	*Loan*	*Budget Support Total*	*Share of Plan Investment*
1	*2*	*3*	*4*	*5*	*6*
		Rs. Crore			**Per cent**
1991-92	30783.10	4539.84	2289.19	6829.19	22.18
1991-92	29421.22	4185.02	2735.24	6920.26	23.52
1992-93	36750.15	4367.33	2476.74	6844.07	18.62

Source : Government of India, Economic Survey, 1992-93.

Recommendations of the Rangarajan Committee on Disinvestment of Shares

The committee on Disinvestment of Shares in Pubic Sector Enterprises was reconstituted by the Government in November 1992 with Dr. C. Rangarajan as the Chairman. The Committee has since submitted its report to the Government. The major recommendations of the Committee are given in Table III.

Disinvestment of Shares

Disinvestment of Shares of PSUs in India has been made during the last two years by inviting bids, earlier for a packet of shares (a pocket comprising good performance with poor ones), and later for individual shares. Minimum bid size has also been lowered from Rs. 2.5 crore per bid earlier to Rs. 1 lac in the last bid to broad base the tenders. However, the average price realised per share has reduced over the year, the actual realisation for the 1992-93 falls short of the target and a view is expressed that the Government has received much lower price than the worth of the shares. There has been poor response to the sale of shares of 15 PSUs in the third phases there was no bid for a number of PSUs; 95 per cent of the bids received were below the minimum reserve price; and 83 per cent of the total bids were to a single institution, namely, UTI.

Non-acceptance of the any bid received in the third phase in March 1993, would adversely offset the budgetary calculations for the year, it is viewed as signal that the Government was not desperate to disinvest at any price.

It is expected that such disinvestment would bring in forces of market and competition in the working of such enterprises, would introduce autonomy, and improve their overall operation performance. This, however raises questions such as : How such disinvestment would ensure autonomy to management? How far such privatisation would bring in additional savings in the country? Would it lead to additional savings by private sector, or would it be mere channeling private savings by earthwhile public sector?

Table III

Recommendations of the Rangarajan Committee on Disinvestment of Shares in Public Sector Enterprises

1. The target levels of disinvestment for the medium term should be consistent with the Industrial Policy. In general, the percentage of equity to be disinvested should be 49 per cent in industries reserved for public sector and 74 per cent in other cases.
2. Instead of year-wise targets of disinvestment , a clear action plan should be evolved.
3. A number of steps need to be undertaken which may include corporatisation of the PSEs, restructuring of finances with a proper debt-equity gearing, and an independent Regulatory Commission for the concerned sector, if necessary.
4. The choice of method of valuation of shares of a PSE needs to take into account the special circumstances affecting PSE's operations, such as, the past focus on social responsibilities rather than pure commercial considerations.
5. A scheme of preferential offer of shares to workers and employees in PSEs may be devised.
6. Ten per cent of the proceeds of disinvestment may be set apart by the Government for lending to the PSEs on concessional terms to meet their expansion and rationalisation needs.
7. A Standing Committee on Public Enterprises Disinvestment may be constituted to oversee the action plan for reform, restructuring and disinvestment as well as monitoring and evaluation of progress made.

Source : Government of India, Economic Survey, 1993-94.

Table IV
Disinvestment of Public Enterprises Equity

	No. of Shares sold (Crore)	*Total Realisation (Rs. Crore)*	*Average Realisation (Rs. Crore)*
1991-92			
Ist Phase Dec. 1991	51.62	1427	27.65
2nd Phase Feb.1992	35.59	1611	45.25
	87.21	3038	
1992-93			
Ist Phase October 1992	12.87	682	53.00
2nd Phase Dec. 1992	31.06	1184	38.10
3rd Phase March 1993	No Sale		
	43.93	1866	

Source : Government of India, Economic Survey, 1992-93.

How the funds raised from disinvestment are planned to be utilised? By utilising these funds for meeting operating expenses or revenue deficit, will it not amount to meeting of operating expenses out of the sale proceeds of jewellery? Further, Privatisation of chrononically loss-making units either by way of sale of individual assets or by outright sale, no doubt would reduce financial burden on the government, would require political will. In the words of Samuel Paul "private parties are reluctant to buy loss-making units and the political risks of closing public enterprises are high".

WAYS FOR IMPROVING PERFORMANCE

Restructuring Strategies

Various attempts have been made to improve performance : the establishment of Holding Companies, the system of Memorandum of Understanding, and reference of sick units to BIFR. They have not been effective in significantly improving the level of profit and the return on investment of government.

Holding Company

The Holding Company concept was tried out in the case of steel enterprises by the creation of the Steel Authority of India Limited (SAIL), and the takenover textile mills which were put under the

National Textile Corporation (NTC). The experience did on the whole help to improve coordination between buying, marketing, product-mix etc. and hence improve performance. But the improvement was limited and to some extent helped by safety price increase, and one-time earnings.

M.O.U.

The M.O.U. System assumes the grant of full operational autonomy and a measure of strategic autonomy to the public enterprises; without this the M.O.U System will serve no useful purpose. "It is an instrument which defines clearly the relationship of the PSU with the Government and clarifies the respective roles of the PSU as well as the government in order to achieve better performance. The MOU is also an attempt to bring a proper balance between accountability and autonomy. Since public enterprises were started with a plethora of objectives (such as to maintain a reasonable price level, act as model employer, promote regional development, undertake R & D and so on" the MOU helps to differentiate between the performance of these "Enterprise objectives", and the objectives for managerial performance. The MOU also makes a distinction between "explicit" and "implicit" losses. "The former are those losses that show up as such in the financial statements" of the enterprise. The "implicit" losses, on the other hand, represent the difference between the maximum possible profits and the existing level of "profits".

No doubt the MOU system is well-conceived to evaluate performance when there are multiple objectives. With profit parameters getting 50% weight in the MOU, public enterprises are now in greater consonance with the structural changes in the economy. The performance of some enterprises have improved over the last three years. The MOU gradings of enterprises for 1991-92 have a highly significant correlation to growth in net profits. However, the level of profits is not adequate and must improve. There is a good case for giving profit performance a much greater weight in the MOU. The objectives of full operational autonomy and some strategic autonomy have not yet been achieved. The MOU has not been able to distance the Government from the enterprise and managements continue to be subservient to the government representatives.

Reference to BIFR

In December 1991, the sick industrial companies act, 1985 was amended to enable chronically sick public enterprises to be referred to the Board of Industrial and Financial Reconstruction for rationalisation. Under the Act, for reference to BIFR, the enterprises must have been incorporated for 7 years, eroded net worth completely, and had two years of continuous cash losses. The Economic Survey states that as on 31st December 1992, there were 91 public sector companies referred to BIFR, of which 9 were rejected, 11 were under scrutiny, and 71 (38 Central and 33 States). Awaiting examination. The BIFR process is slow. Meanwhile the Budget has to bear the losses of the sick enterprises-both those waiting BIFR scrutiny and others.

Conclusion

None of the attempts has succeeded in sufficiently improving the return on Government's investment. A comprehensive reform of public enterprises was considered necessary to bring PSE operations in consonance with the overall structural changes and the macro-economic stablisation programme. The key elements of the strategy for the reform of the public sector that Government has put forward are :

—strengthening managerial autonomy;

—promotion of private sector competition;

—reduction of budgetary support;

—creation of safety net to protect the interests of workers;

—partial divestment of equity; and

—restructuring or closure of unviable enterprises.

The strategy proposed for the reform of the public sector has been partially implemented. Private sector competition is now entering the oil refining, tele-communication, and other areas like power generation. Budgetary support as a proportion of total public enterprise outlays has dropped from 27 per cent in 1990-91 to 14 per cent in the 1993-94 budget. Dividends are expected to rise from Rs. 654 crores in 1991-92 to Rs. 737 crores and Rs. 883 crores in 1992-93 and 1993-94. Partial divestment of equity shares has been taking place in bulk lots. Market interest in the shares seems to have decline, and there are doubts whether the PSE's will in addition raise the funds from the market, required for plan outlays. The National Renewal Fund has been formed to enable reduction of excess staffing and appears to have been effective at the NTC. However, the funds available may be inadequate if it is to apply to all public enterprises. BIFR has yet to decide regarding restructuring or closure of enterprises referred to them. However, the key element for improving performance is to let public enterprise managements function autonomously.

BIBLIOGRAPHY

1. Birla, S.K., Industrial Growth : Challenges of the Nineties? Survey of Indian Industry, ed. The Hindu, Feb. 1991.
2. Bureau of Public Enterprises (Government of India), Public Enterprises Survey, Annual report.
3. Mani Pande, "Disinvestment and Winding up to Public Sector", Alive, May 1992.
4. Natraj, R., Public Sector Performance in the Eighties, Economics and Political weekly, December 14, 1991.
5. Prahlad, Basu, Government Failure Overshadows Managerial Failure, Economic and Political Weekly, May 26, 1990.
6. Hemming, Richard and Mansoor Ali M., Privatisation and Public Enterprises, Occasional Paper No. 56. Jan. 1988. IMF, Washington, D.C.
7. Minhas, B.S., Public versus Pravate Sector : Neglect of Lessons of Economics in Indian Policy Formulations, Artha Viynana, March 1991, Vol. XXXIII, No.1.
8. Srinivasan, T.S., Privatisation and Deregulation, Economic and Political Weekly, Vol. XXVIII, Nos. 15,16, April 11-18, 1992.
9. Vyasulu Vinod et. al. Towards a Political Economy of the Economic Policy Changes, Economic and Political Weekly, Sept. 21, 1991.
10. B.M., Liberalisation of Economic Policies : World Bank's New Push, Economic and Political Weekly, No. 32, Vol. XXII' August 8, 1988.
11. B.M. Government's Privatisation Plans come into Open, Economic and Political Weekly, Vol. XXIII, No. 17, April 23, 1988.
12. Lata Arun, Scope of Privatisation in India through Divestiture and Denationalisation, Asian Journal of Economics Vol. 6, No. 3, 1987.
13. Mukhopadhyay, J.K., The Privatisation Phenomenon and its Relevance to Developing countries tries, Forum of Free Enterprise, July 1988, Bombay.
14. Paul Samuel, Privatisation : A Review of International Experience, Economic and Political Weekly. Vol. XXIII, No. 6, Feb. 6, 1988.

15. Pendse, D.R., Privatisation and Economic Growth, Forum of Free Enterprise, June 1985, Bombay.

16. Reddy, V.Y., Privatisation: Where are the gain? Financial Express, July 19, 1988.

17. Sandesara, J.C., Privatisation : The Wheel is turning, The Economic Times, April 13th and 15th, 1988.

18. Ravi Ramamurti and Roynold Vernon (Ed.) Privatisation and Control of State Owned Enterprises, EDI Development Studies, The World Bank, 1991.

19. Ahluwalia, Montek Singh, Policies for the Nineties, Business India, 15th Anniversary Issue, Bombay, 1993.

20. Mishra, Girish, Global Economic Liberalisation : Some Implications, World Focus, No. 146, New Delhi, Feb. 1992.

21. Ummat, R.C., Liberalising Indian Economy, World Focus, No. 146, New Delhi, Feb. 1992.

22. Government of India, Economic Survey, 1992-93, 1993-94.

23. International Monetary Fund. Annual Report, 1991.

24. Washington, D.C., Year Book 1991, 1992.

25. Batra, G.S., Leading Issues in Public Enterprises, Anmol Publication, New Delhi, 1993.

26. Singh, Sukhpal, "Dunkel Proposals-Implications for the rural sector" ed. Dunkel and its implications for Indian economy, 1994.

13

Management of Tourism in India (A Case Study)

G.S. Batra*

Introduction

Tourism has a unique multiple-effect on national economy. In the eighth five year plan of India, it has been recognised as an important commercial activity. It is the fastest growing industry of the world and has tremendous potentialities for earning foreign exchange, yielding tax revenues, providing employment, promoting the growth of the ancillary industries and development of industrially backward regions.

Objectives and Methodology of Study

This study aims at studying the problem of management of tourism in India with special reference to Punjab. The State Governments have been giving top priority to develop tourism in the States for their economic development and to solve to some extent the problems of unemployment.

The objectives of the present study are:

1. to analyse the recent trends in tourism industry in India;
2. to examine the performance and development of State tourism corporation in Punjab;
3. to highlight the problems of tourism management;

* Faculty Member, Department of Business Management, Punjabi University, Patiala, Punjab (India).

4. to give suggestions regarding the functioning of STDC's; and

5. to identify the prospects and potential of tourism at state level.

Sources of secondary data are memorandum and Articles of Association of Punjab Tourism Development Corporation Ltd., Economic Survey, Statistical outline of Punjab, Various reports of State Tourism Public Sector Undertakings, Plan Documents of Government and other published material.

Rationale of Tourism as Industry

There can, perhaps, be no second opinion about the fact that tourism is an industry, like any other 'industry' it has to be planned and developed on scientific lines. It needs organisational and managerial skills. It requires the best brains engaged in the related industries for the production and marketing of the product that is tourism. The impact of tourism on national economy is becoming increasingly important todays because of the growing size of the tourist market. From the economic angle tourism is especially important in a developing country like India. In the process of political and economic changes that India is undergoing, international trade especially of non-traditional items has assumed an importance which it never had before. The quality and the content of international trade is an indication of the economic growth of a country. There is a marked difference between the technologies of the developed and the developing societies. One of the easier methods suggested for closing the chronic gap in 'our balance of payments' arising out of developmental expenditure is the establishment of the tourist industry. The reason for this is that unlike other industries it does not demand much technological sophistication. Yet the fact remains that developing countries in general and India in particular, have not been able to make a significant dent in this area. Incidentaly, we have the ninth largest budget in the world but, however, our share of market constitutes no more than 0.20 per cent to 1 per cent of the world tourist market. However, tourism industry has taken rapid strides in the recent years as an instrument of all round economic growth. The wide ranging achievements in this field have led to a marked improvement in general standard of living. The most notable advances seem to be the income and employment generating effects and the foreign exchange earning potentials.

Till recently India did not realise the importance of fully tapping the tourism potential. "The contribution of tourism is term of foreign exchange accruals is shown under the item 'invisibles' in the balance of payment data. Apart from tourism (travel), transportation, insurance, investment income and transfer comprise the invisible group. Tourism and private transfers have emerged as the major benefactors to the nation by way of their contribution in terms of net foreign exchange inflow".

International tourism to India has had a phenomenal growth since independence and better than any other industry, the number of foreign tourists visiting Indian increased from 16,829 in 1951 to 4.65 lakhs in 1975 and further it reached the peak of 8.60 lakhs in 1982. The total number of tourist arrivals in 1986 was 14.5 lakhs and 17.07 lakhs in 1990-91 as per table-I.

As per table I, during August 1992, foreign tourist arrivals including nationals of Pakistan and Bangladesh were recorded at 151341 as compared to 141830 in the corresponding month during 1991, thus registering an increase of 6.7 per cent.

As per table II, tourism forms a major source of foreign exchange for India. India earned Rs. 35 crores foreign exchange in 1972 which increased to Rs. 104 crores in 1975. After the year 1975 earnings have been increasing continuously and reached to Rs. 180 crores in 1986 which comes to 1.4 per cent share of world tourism.

India has reached a stage where she can be recognised the world over as a leading tourist destination. Tourism industry in India is worth Rs. 4,000 crores and largest earner of foreign exchange, besides providing employment to 5.3 million people.

Table I
Tourist Traffic in India

Year	*Tourists (in lakhs)*
1975	4.65
1982	8.60
1986	14.50
1990	17.07

Source : Govt. of India, Department of Tourism, Various Annual Reports.

Table II
Foreign Exchange Earnings from Tourism in India

Year	*Foreign Exchange Earned Rs. in crores*
1972	35
1975	104
1986	180
1990	245
1991	290

Source : Govt. of India, Deptt. of Tourism, Various Annual Reports.

Recent Trends

With passage of time tourism has grown into a fulfledged industry. Tourism, primarily is a service industry because it does not produce goods but renders services to various classes of people. In view of their special nature and complexity of their contribution to the tourist product, they may be described as tourist industry.

Tourism has emerged as the fastest growing industry in the world. In 1990 along, the number of world travellers was 429 million who spent a staggering USS 249 billion. These numbers increased to 450 million and USS 278 billion respectively for the year 1991, a 4.895 per cent change over the previous year.

The world travel and tourism council estimated that in 1990 the industry was worth more than USS 2.5 trillion, 5.5 per cent of the world's gross national product. Atleast 7.5 million people in the European community alone depend on tourism for their livelihood.

The council projects that tourism will be the world's biggest industry by the year 2000. In India, tourism pipe dreamers see a Rs. 10,000 crore a year by the end of the century and increase in India's of the total global traffics from the present level of 0.4 per cent to one per cent in the next five years.

Tourism Development in India

The Government of India set up three separate corporations viz. India Tourism Hotel Corporation, India Tourism Corporation Ltd. and Tourism Transport Undertaking Ltd. in 1965 in the department of tourism on the recommendation of the Jha Committee (1963). The main

Motels, Tourist Bungalows, Tourist Huts, Holiday Capms, Rest Houses, Circuit Houses, tented colonies etc.

(b) To provide catering facilities to tourists by way of hotels, restaurants, cafeterias, canteens, coffee Houses which are managed by STDCs.

(c) To provide cheap accommodation to middle class or low income tourists at various places by carrying on business of Youth Hostels, Retiring room facilities at Railway Stations and Airports, camping sites, pavallions and Dormitories, Yatrikas etc.

(d) To provide better transport facilities to tourist by establishing transport units, travel and transport counters in the state. STDCs have their own tourist buses, coaches, taxies besides State Road Transport Corporation buses, private buses, cars and taxies, railways and airlines.

(e) To provide entertainment to tourist by organising fairs & festivals, dance, music, night clubs, sports, swimming pools and son-et-lumiere (Sound and Light show) at various tourist attraction places in the states.

(f) To provide shopping facility by establishing and managing shops (duty free shops, bazars, emporia etc.) at various places of tourist attraction to tourist in the states.

Performance of Punjab Tourism Development Corporation

Before the formation of the Corporation the Tourist complexes were run by the State Tourism Department. In order to bring elasticity in the running of Tourist Complexes on the commercial lines, it was deemed necessary to form the Corporation. The corporation came into existence on 26.3.1979.

The corporation is wholly owned by the Punjab Govt., and it has shareholders i.e., the Governor, Secretary Tourism, Finance Secretary and other Senior Officers of Punjab Govt. The number of Directors on the Board is eight, which are nominated by the Govt. from time to time.

The Management of the Corporation is vested with the Board and Managing Director. Govt. however, has the power to issue from time to time "Some directives as it may consider necessary making broad policies and the Company is bound to give immediate effect to the directives so issued".

functions of these corporations were to construct the manage hot the public sector, to produce materials for tourist publicity a provide facilities of road transport to tourists. Due to mismanag of these units, "the government set up in October 1968 a public undertaking, namely the Indian Tourism Development Corp Ltd., (ITDC) in Delhi under the auspices of the department of by amalgamating these three separate corporations".

ITDC is not only a profit-making organisation in the cou is doing so in the face of stiff competition from private sect and transporters enjoying a lead of several decades in the trac its inception the Corporation has been making profit and valuable foreign exchange for the country.

Tourism at State Level

Tourism has been declared a concurrent subject to be har by the Union and the State Governments under the const India.

The States have realised the importance of tourism and an effective role by investing in tourism from their own r a big way. Each state has followed the Central governmer up a tourism machinery. India's tourism is managed betw sector and public sector and has assumed the role of mixe Both the sectors await each other's initiative, thereby slowi rate of developing infrastructure. While planning and m in the hands of government, real service in this trade lies entrepreneurs.

In India every state has a separate state tourism corporation to promote tourist trade in the state. These co working under the Ministry of tourism on the pattern Tourism Development Corporation (ITDC).

Functions of State Tourism Development Corporati

STDCs have started commercial activities whi publicity and development of new tourist places in t in the hands of the State Directorates of Tourism. The r activities or functions of STDCs are as follows:

(a) To provide comfortable accommodation f both from within the country and abroad attraction places by carrying on the busin

The Corporation has floated a Holiday Home Club Scheme with the objective to provide assured and comfortable accommodation to the members. The corporation has also set up a Tour and Travel Wing which has conducted many Tours in India and abroad.

PTDC had a authorised capital of Rs. 800 lakhs and paid up capital of Rs. 521.5 lakhs in 1991-92 as shown in Table III. The corporation has been incurring losses since 1980-81. Table IV indicates that the losses of the corporation, which were Rs. 23.50 lakhs in 1981-82 increased to Rs. 36.66 lakhs in 1991-92.

Achievements of PTDC

Under Centrally Sponsored Scheme, the corporation has provided accommodation facility at Floating Restaurant Sirhind, Tourist Complex, Kartarpur and Madhopur and Phagwara. The construction work at Tourist Complex, Ropar is likely to be completed shortly. The corporation is also constructing a Yatri Niwas at Jalandhar.

The corporation has also envisaged the plan under Centrally Sponsored Schemes for setting up a Tourist Complex at Nadampur, Dasuya, Moga, Goindwal Sahib, Hoshiarpur, Patiala, Yatri Niwas at Mohali and Madhopur and Tourist Complex Katori/Dunera also. Under the wayside amenities, the corporation has also planning for setting up the complexes at Sanghol, Barnala and Talwara. In addition to above a 5-Star Hotel-Cum-Convention Hall is being set up at Chandigarh with the Collaboration of ITDC.

Due to disturbed law and order situation in the State the Tourist traffic decreased in the State of Punjab. The initial period of 3 years was gestation period and losses were due to teething-troubles. The second major reason is that, at the time of formation of the corporation, it was burdened with capital cost of complexes transferred to it by the Department of Tourism. The corporation had to bear not only the depreciation of the building transferred to it, but, also expenditure on maintenance of buildings, equipments, wayside facilities such as approach road, street lighting and horticulture. In other states a substantial expenditure incurred on infrastructure and maintenance is provided by the State Govt. Further, another continuing factor is lack of adequate publicity of culture heritage and places of tourist interest in the Punjab. Due to huge cahs losses, corporation could not make adequate investment on development of new complexes. However, in compliance of Government instructions to adopt economy measures every possible efforts were being made to reduce cut the expenditure.

Table III
Capital Structure of Punjab Tourism Development Corporation

Capital Structure	*Figure in Lakhs*		
	1986-87	1987-88	1991-92
(a) Nominal Capital/ Authorised Capital	800.00	800.00	800.00
(b) Paid-up-capital	434.64	444.64	521.15
Contributed by			
(i) State Government	434.64	444.64	521.15
(ii) Central Government	—	—	—
(iii) Others	—	—	—

Source : Various Annual Reports on the working of State Public Sector Undertakings and Annual Reports of PTDC, Bureau of Public Enterprises, Govt. of Punjab.

PROBLEM AREAS OF TOURISM DEVELOPMENT CORPORATIONS

Absence of Clear-cut Objectives

Every business enterprise strives to fulfil its objectives and its success depends upon the extent to which it is able to attain these objectives. In case of the PTDC its objectives are quite ambiguous, vague and it becomes more complicated due to the multiplicity of objectives which are quite conflicting in nature. Moreover, fulfillment of social objectives or safeguarding the public interest are vague terms and it becomes difficult to achieve them. As mentioned earlier, the state Government has not yet come forward with a clear-cut statement regarding the objectives of PTDC.

Table IV
Financial Results of Punjab Tourism Development Corporation

Years	*Profit/Loss (Rs. in lakhs)*	
1981-82	—	23.50
1982-83	—	36.67
1983-84	—	30.87
1984-85	—	35.43
1985-86	—	27.90
1986-87	—	20.20
1987-88	—	16.58
1988-89	—	48.54
1989-90	—	27.28
1991-92	—	36.66

Source : Annual Reports of PTDC and Bureau of Public Enterprises, 1981-82 to 1991-92.

Financial Problems

PTDC suffers from various financial problems and constraint. Some of these are as follows:

a) PTDC suffers from the over capitalisation and the overhead expenses in PTDC are quite large relatively;

b) there is rigid financial control over PTDC; and

c) we find unsound capital structure of PTDC because of which it is required to meet fixed interest charges considerably. The losses in PTDC flow essentially due to its wrong financial structure.

Management Problems

Success of any enterprise depends considerably upon the competence and quality of management. Earlier, there has been shortage of competent managers to man PTDC, which with the result that the civil servants had to shoulder the burden of management of PTDC. They bring their bureaucratic culture and style of management which is undoubtedly, not suitable to run business enterprises on commercial lines. The result has been redtapism, adherence to precedence and playing safe and avoiding taking risks, regionalism and nepotism etc.

Excessive Control

Excessive control, formal or informal over PTDC also towards the initiative of the management and it affects their efficiency adversely. There is a large number of agencies wielding control over them. We have the Minister concerned, the secretariat officials, the legislature, the Audit Board, the Consumer councils and the various committees appointed to look into the affairs of PTDC. Besides this, there are local politicians who also interfere in the day-to-day working of PTDC. Such controls stifle the initiative and curb the autonomy of the management of State Enterprises like PTDC and affect their efficiency adversely.

The CPU in Punjab has so far submitted 39 reports on the working of state enterprises in Punjab. These reports have resulted in improvement in the working and performance of state enterprises. However, according to the recommendations of the CPU, the state enterprises should be delegated with proper amount of authority and the adequate balance between autonomy and accountability should be made. Though there is no dispute regarding the role of the state enterprises in the economic development of Punjab, these enterprises are being criticised for the poor profitability and poor service to the customers. CPU has not examined the working of PTDC even once since its inception in 1971.

The corporation has also taken maximum steps to face the situation by creating more infrastructure at Floating Restaurant, Sirhind, Tourist Complex, Madhopur, Kartarpur and Phagwara. The corporation has also set up a Tour and Travel Wing which has conducted tours in India and abroad. Besides, this corporation has also opened liquor vends. With the results, the corporation has improved its working and increased profitability by increasing turnover and hailing losses. In addition to this, the management has fixed the norms of food cost etc. The Inspection of the complexes is being conducted by the officers of the corporation regularly.

Conclusion

Tourism in India, today, has come of age. Tourism has become a common part of the local scenario. Like in many other developing countries, tourism in India has helped in generating not only valuable foreign exchange; providing employment but also as a medium of national integration, cultural assimilation and a means for promoting international understanding. India has reached a stage; where she can be recognised the world over as a leading tourist destination. The traditional image of India as a cultural destination only to be replaced with more vibrant holiday and leisure tourist destination.

Tourism industry in different states enjoys a very bright prospects as the country possesses rich cultural heritage and tourist spots which offers a diversity of attractions and places of historical and archaeological importance. In other words, we have an excellent product to sell. But the potential of tourism industry as a source of foreign exchange earner and employment remains largely untapped. Tourism has as a good potential for growth as any other export industry; thus the need is to extend 'industry status' to tourism at par with export industry. Besides, minimum financial involvement by the government, this industry does not substantially consume the scarce resources of the country.

Hence, much efforts shall be made to tap the great tourist potential it has. A thrust of the current government's policy should be to promote domestic tourism to enable people of this subcontinent to get to know their own country.

Upgrading the standard and the capacity of fleets by PTDC's is expected to match the facilities of transportation upto the international standard which will in turn help the government in earning maximum foreign exchange.

This will also make tourism more broad based and will also help in increasing the economic activity in the proposed areas which are totally untouched. The diversification of the tourist-traffic will dispurse the population pressure and also enable the Government to solve the economic problems existing in the different states.

BIBLIOGRAPHY

1. Ashworth, Gregory and Goodall Brian, Marketing Tourism Places, Routledge, New York-London, 1990.
2. Bhatia, A.K., International Tourism Fundamentals and Practices, Sterling, New Delhi, 1991.
3. Cox, Kathleen, The Himalayan Countries, Fodor's London, 1990.
4. Gupta, V.K., Tourism in India, Gian Publishing House, New Delhi, 1987.
5. Journal of Tourism and Hotel Management, Department of Management Studies, University of Jodhpur, Jodhpur, Vol. IV, 1989-90.
6. Kaul, R.N., Dynamics of Tourism, Vol. I, II, III, Sterling, New Delhi, 1992.
7. Kumar, Maneet, Tourism today - An Indian Perspective, Kanishka Publishing House, New Delhi, 1992.
8. Lea John, Tourism and Development in the Third World, Routledge, New York-London, 1985.
9. Marphy, Peter E. Tourism A Community Approach, routledge, New York-London, 1985.
10. Pearce, Douglas, Tourism Today — A Geographical Analysis, Longman, New York, 1990.
11. Seth, Pran Nath, Successful Tourism Management, Sterling, New Delhi, 1990.
12. Sharma, K.K., Tourism in India, Classic, Jaipur, 1991.
13. Shelley, Leela, Tourism Development in India, Arihant Publishers, Jaipur, 1991.
14. Singh, S.N. Geography of Tourism and Re-creation, Inter-India, New Delhi, 1986.
15. Seth, P.N., Successful Tourism Management, Allied Publishers Pvt. Ltd., New Delhi, 1985.
16. Joshi, N.C., "Tourists Industry Needs Boosting", Yogna, Vol. 34, No. 19, Publication Division, Patiala House, New Delhi, October 16-31, 1990.
17. Srivastava, K.K., "Tourism in India", Yojana, Vol. 27, No. 10, Publication Division, Patiala House, New Delhi, June 1-15, 1993.
18. Acharya Ram., Tourism in India, National Publishing House, New Delhi, 1977.

14

Accountability of State Enterprises : Recent Trends

Dr. G.S Batra*
Dr. B.S. Bhatia*
Harvinder Singh**

The public sector enterprises involve complete separation between ownership and management which results in the absence of any control or vigilance by the proprietors and shareholders. The management is placed in the hands of those who have hardly any stake in the enterprises they manage. This gives rise to the need for putting such enterprises under some suitable control and for making the management responsible and answerable to some authority. There could be no better than the Parliament which represents the shareholders and consumers and which is responsible for safeguarding the interests of the nation. The public enterprises have such an important influence on the total national income, capital formation and consumers of their services that the parliament cannot afford to be indifferent to their working. There is the risk that, if left free, the public enterprises may develop into powerful centralised monopolistic bureaucracy exploiting the community at large. This would dead to state capitalism which is worse than private capitalism. The public accountability therefore is unquestionable. The problem has become particularly crucial in racet years because of two major developments. Firstly, the public enterprises have fast grown in number as well as in

* Faculty Member and Professor, Deptt. of Business Management, Punjabi University, Patiala.

** Research Scholar, Deptt. of Business Management, Punjabi University, Patiala.

size. Secondly, the organisation of public enterprises has undergone important changes. The departments managing these enterprises were fully responsible and accountable to the minister concerned who in turn was responsible to the legislature. Whereas the emergence of statutory corporation has given rise to the problem of safeguarding the national interest by exercising the necessary control and at the same time maintaining the freedom of the Board of the corporation.

Various reasons go to justify the need for and importance of public accountability. The accountability of public enterprises is justified on the economic, political and administrative grounds. It is seen that these enterprises follow the general national policies in accordance with the national priorities. Public enterprises are established with public money and it may draw from public resources for further investment by way of diversification and expansion. As the administrative ministry is accountable to parliament, the ministry concerned must make the management accountable to it and be watchful so that the management may not involve themselves in wastages or scandals etc. The public enterprises are controlled and managed by officials, who have no personal or financial stake in the enterprises. Many may come on deputation from Govt. services and may be like flying birds from one place to another. Professional managements develop because there is no other resource, but it will run the enterprises with personal care and attention, there is no guarantee of it. Under these circumstances managements accountability is the only way to ensure that autonomy and professionalism do not lead to misuse of their freedom and position. Being business enterprises, there may be justifications for considerable autonomy in their internal affairs. When such autonomy is provided the need for ensuring accountability commensurate with autonomy becomes a delegate task. More and more power is being delegated to the management with a view to bring about greater operational efficiency and this in turn, attracts their accountability.

Objectives and Scope of the Study

The primary objective of the study here is to examine the nature, content, adequacy and impact of the legislative control over public enterprises in the state of Punjab. An attempt has been made to evaluate in broad terms whether the level of such control is 'optimum', considering the requirements of their functional freedom and operational efficiency.

Since this paper is on the issue of legislative control, no attempt has been made to present a review of the economic aspects of the functioning of the various government undertakings of the state. Primarily, this has been done to delimit the areas of study and to provide it with a more in-depth treatment of the various significant aspects of the foci. contents and possible impact of the Committee on Public Undertakings in Punjab. The period selected for analysis corresponds to the terms of the 6th to 9th Punjab Vidhan Sabha, spanning in the years 1972 to 1987.

Legislative Control

Legislative control is the most suitable, effective and important method of enforcing accountability in Indian Public enterprises. The Parliament as the trustee of the nation has a right to assure itself that in broad terms the financial and managerial policies followed by public enterprises are sound and promote the ends of public policy underlying their establishment. This is particularly necessary because the member of the Board or the Chief Executive having no financial stake in the concern and being in no way, linked to the fortunes of the enterprises. Since public money is invested in public enterprises, public in General is interested in their efficient functioning. It has been rightly accepted that "The public must have the final word in the control of industries it owns".

In the words of Lord Harcomb "very real problem of accountability to Parliament ultimately arising from the vast amount of capital and of income and expenditure involved in concerns which are under public ownership, the charges upon consumers and users of necessities of Civilised life which they provide and the treasury guarantee of the interest paid on the stock issued in respect of various nationalised industries."

"Members of Parliament are the trustees of the public wealth whose duty is to safeguard the interests of the public and to protect the public enterprises from the high handed action of the executive."

Parliament exercises continues control over public enterprises Apart from the Parliament interest as representative of the tax-payers there is an overall social interest, the quantum, however should depend not so much on the ideology of minimum control over autonomous corporations but on what is necessary for the efficient and economical working of the public undertaking.

Although, in deciding the ultimate extent of Parliamentary control political ideology and social sentiments play an important role, it is generally accepted that "......." the legislature should not attempt too close a control, in particular that it should not normally interfere in day-to-day running of the industries, but confine itself to questions of major policy and exceptional circumstances. Detailed interference will lead to delays, over caution and lack of confidence on the part of those running the enterprises."

The nature and extent of legislative control over a public enterprises to a large extent depends upon its form of organisation. So far as departmentally administered undertakings are concerned, there is hardly any difference between industrial or commercial enterprises and government departments in regard to the nature and scope of legislative control and the ministerial responsibility to the legislature. In case of such enterprises, the control is absolute because the capital and the operating budgets of the units are presented before the house in the form of demand for grants. This tends to impair initiative and boldness of the persons at the helm of the affairs. There is no autonomy in running these enterprises.

Public corporation on the other hand are set up under a special Act of the legislature. The Act governing a public corporation specifically defines and determines the relationship between the legislature and the corporation. The Act also specified the rights and powers of the legislature, corporation and of the minister in regard to the working of the corporation and duties and obligations of the minister. The public corporations are independent of government and cannot be looked upon as merely one of the many departments of govt. These are autonomous bodies with the necessary public control commensurate with national interest.

Government companies registered under the companies Act, necessary enjoy greater autonomy and are subject to limited parliamentarily control. The rights and powers of the government are governed by the provisions of the Articles of Association of the company. While govt. control and therefor, legislative control over departmentally managed undertakings can be as complete and as desired by the government and Parliament, the corresponding position in respect of the corporate and other autonomous undertakings requires careful considerations.

Parliament has a right to call these enterprises and the govt. to account, to be fully informed about them and to scrutinize and criticize their performance although all or some of these rights have on occasions been disputed sometime by spokesman of the govt. and sometimes by the Chief executive of these undertakings on the ground that it is unwarranted interference or erosion of their autonomy.

Legislative control in exercised primarily through

1. Questions in the legislature,
2. Debates in the legislature,
3. Legislature Committee.

The Committee on Public Undertakings

CPU is the most important, powerful and effective legislative tool of enforcing legislative accountability and control over public enterprises in India. It came into existence on the 1st May 1964 in central shpere. Before establishment of the CPU only two committees viz. public accounts committee and estimates committee were studying the financial and administrative accountability of public enterprises. The public accounts committee examines the reports of comptroller and auditor general in order to acertain that the money granted by parliament has been spend by the government within the scope of the demand, whereas estimates committee works as a continuous economic committee and suggests alternative policy in order to bring efficiency and economy in administration.

Functioning of the CPU

It is not just the committee's performance but also the response of the government and the media which influences the level of effectiveness on public undertaking, whether at the national or the state level. All the state enterprises in Punjab which were earlier within the purview of PAC considering the volume of work and need to appraise the effectiveness of the public enterprises have come under the ambit of CPU which was constituted in Punjab in 1971. The CPU during 4 assemblies (6 to 9) from the period 1972 to 1987 submitted 39 reports on the general working and reports of C.A.G. of state enterprises in Punjab. The committee examined the general working of Punjab small industries and export corporation, Punjab financial corp., Punjab State Handloom and textile development corporation, Punjab Hosiery and knitwear development corporation. Punjab State electricity Board and Audit paras of C. & A.G. of India etc. The CPU has tried to study all the undertaking within its purview.

Since the inception of CPU, small number of the undertaking have been examined by CPU. There are some enterprises which have been examined only once. This type of tendency detracts from the effectiveness of control and supervision of CPU over the enterprises. This type of general examination of the undertaking cannot prove more fruitful either for the legislature or for the management of these enterprises. All the state enterprises should be categorised according to their nature of operation such as manufacturing, trading, financing etc. and then important areas should be taken for examination such as management, finance, production, personnel etc.

Output of the Committee

The CPU of Punjab submitted in all 39 reports during the period spanning 6th, 7th, 8th & 9th Vidhan Sabha. The information about the number of reports brought out by the CPU per sessions during the 4 assemblies. Of the 39 reports, 17 reports were submitted in the 6th assembly, 3 reports in the 7th assembly, 12 reports in the 8th assembly and 7 reports in the 9th assembly. In the 6th assembly produced large number of reports per session, which went down during the 7th assembly period. Highest number of reports were submitted in the 6th assembly that is 17. In the 8th assembly as many as 12 reports were submitted by the committee during 3 years period before the president rule was imposed in the state.

Number of Recommendations

Another index of measuring the efficiency of CPU could be the number of recommendations, conclusions and proposals contained in its reports. The valid point should be that instead of producing a very large number of reports and recommendations, CPU should try to reduce their number by focussing upon broader issues of policy and horizontal studies.

Frequency of Examination of State Enterprises

One of the criticism that can be levelled against the CPU is it paid excessive attention to comparatively larger or sensitive enterprises at the cost of the smaller ones. Such an approach adversely affects the balance that is generally aimed to be struck between the needs of operational autonomy and those of control. In the absence of adequate legislative control, ministerial over control is likely to fill the void, thus making the task of small enterprises extremely difficult. In the different assembly periods as is evident, for example in the 9th assembly working of major enterprises like PSIDC, PFC, etc. could not be proved.

More so frequent revisioning of the same enterprises would result in the wastage of time, resources and energy in the connection and submission of requisite papers and regards. Besides vigorous and repeated examination of chief executive of undertaking would affect their initiative to take decisions whereas frequent summoning of departmental representatives might also strain the relationship between the CPU and the government. The British select Committee circumspect approach in this connection has been quoted by coombs in the following words.

"The committee is probably too modest in thinking, it takes too long to get through the nationalised industries, at its rates so far it could certainly examined the whole lot at least once in a life time of any parliament, which will be surely enough if the country wants to get or retain men of calibre and self respect in the top management of these large industries.

Type of Reports

Except for action taken reports, their hardly exists any guideline or accepted conventions about the CPU reports. To some extent this is desirable to give reasonable latitude to the committee to follow its own pattern of reporting, depending upon the nature of inquiry that seems to be useful and the points that require to be emphasized as per its own perception. As for as the type of reports or nature of inquiries is concerned, CPU has not followed any consistent pattern while in the 7th Assembly more than half reports pertained to the audit objections raised by the C. & A.G. in the 8th Assembly the main reports were much higher. It is important that each type of report has its own merits and hence no particular type of report need to be over emphasized at the cost of others. The main reports through a complete and general review of an undertaking, enable the members of the CPU to appreciate the circumstances in which an enterprise is operating.

Regarding examination of the paragraphs of the audit reports submitted by the C.&A.G. is the CPU could have been able to do a better job if were supported by requisite expertise in financial administrative matters. On the other hand action taken reports are useful so long as they allow the CPU to obtain feed back on its earlier recommendations from the govt. as well as from the subject undertaking. This turn gives an opportunity to the committee for self appraisal and also for strengthening its relations with the government and the subject enterprise besides such a feed back helps the committee to become realistic and practical in its approach.

Horizontal Studies

Studies involving simultaneous examination of similar issues facing different undertakings have been supported on the ground that these enable the committee not only expand and deepen its inquiries but also help facilitate evolving a common approach to the development of the public sector in the state.

During four Assemblies the CPU of Punjab produced only one horizontal study on public enterprises in comparison to six reports published by the CPU during the 5th Lok Sabha along.

The CPU laid increasing emphasis on horizontal studies with 5 of them put up in the 6th Lok Sabha where as CPU in Punjab has not given much attention to conduct horizontal studies of public enterprises.

New Trends in the Reports of CPU

A comparison of all types of reports of the CPU in the four assembly period from 1972 to 1987, point out certain changes in the method of reporting by the committee. It is to be noted here that the last four reports of the British select committee adopted on approach which has quite different from the one followed in the four reports. In these reports of the select committee, there was a singular emphasis on the point that any review of a nationalized industry must be related to the ends which a nationalized industry undertakes. Large number of reports of the CPU on different state enterprises bear a subtitle "Objectives of establishment and achievement" giving the impression that in these reports an attempt has been made to assess the overall performance of the enterprises vis-a-vis their broad objectives. Actually CPU in Punjab has concentrated on individual lapses instead of stressing upon the broader objectives.

Legislature being over worked and it does not gets adequate time, hence the quality of debates suffer. To remove this defect, it would be better if the parliament/legislature can set apart two or three days during every session for reviewing the working of public enterprises as is done in case of foreign affairs and other important matters.

Conclusion

The committee on public undertakings set up in the Punjab Vidhan Sabha in 1971 is certainly the most important development in the history of legislative control over public undertaking in the state. Not only has this committee brought consistency and direction in the accountability of state enterprises and it has also lent to the legitimacy to the public sector in the state. The committee has been evaluating performance of public enterprises from all aspects and the limitations imposed on its function have not in any way hindered its work. The committee has thrown much right on the problem and the workings of the state enterprises through its reports in this respects.

The recommendations of the committee on public undertakings are no doubt in the nature of advice "But as the representative body of entire parliament, the committee enjoys much prestige and its recommendations are by convention, regarded as view of parliament and the ministry as a rule, implements them."

Since 1971 CPU has submitted 39 reports covering the different aspects of the state enterprises like technical and economic, feasibility/ viability study, project reports, operational working, personnel and organisational problems. The CPU undertakings studies into the various problems of state enterprises and by serving as an instrument for the expression of view points of the representatives of executive departments and state enterprises, it has succeeded in bringing the state govt. the boards and the legislatures closer.

BIBLIOGRAPHY

1. Ananda Rao, C.R., Public Enterprises and Parliamentary Committees in India, Chugh, Allahabad 1982.
2. Batra, Satish K., Legislative Control Over Public Enterprises, Printwell Jaipur, 1988.
3. Gadkok, D.N., Parliamentary Control Over Government Expenditure, Sterling, New Delhi, 1976.
4. Ghai, Y., The Legislature and the Public Enterprises, United Kingdom, ed(s) Commonwealth Secretariat relationship between parliament and Public Enterprises, 1981.
5. Ananda Rao, C.R. Autonomy and Accountability of Public Enterprises in India vis-a-vis the Committee on Public Undertakings, Lok Udyog July, 1989.

6. Bhatia, B.S. and Gurdeep Singh, Accountability of Public Sector Enterprises. Indian Journal of Public Enterprises, Allahabad, Vol. 6, No. 10, June 1991.

7. Changing Role of Public Sector in India, Indian Journal of Commerce, September 1991.

8. Memorandum of understanding in Public Enterprises, The Management Account, Vol. 26, No. 11, November 1991.

9. Disapp, H.C., Parliamentary Control and Accountability of Public Undertakings, Indian Journal of Public Administration New Delhi, April-June 1961.

10. Sadique, A.S.K. Autonomy and Accountability, Lok Udyog, Vol. 14, No. 4, July 1980.

15

Strategic Management of Industrial Sickness in India—Challenges for 90's

B.S. Bhatia and G.S. Batra*

Introduction

In the past few decades, the accent in management literature and in research has been upon the achievement and success of companies doing business. The subject of company failure has received virtually little attention from writers, academicians and management specialists.

The failure of a business is an event which brings a lot of mental pain to entrepreneurs, managers and to their families. The society is also affected by business failure, as unemployment goes up, availability of goods and service decreases and the cost goes up, The shareholder loose their savings, creditors loose their cash and future business. Thus a coherent framework setting out the causes and symptoms of industrial sickness and developing a model predicting the potential industrial sickness is the need of the hour. Such a coherent and systematic body of knowledge about corporate sickness would serve to minimise, if not eliminate, such losses by providing ample warning in advance to those concerned.

The area of industrial sickness is so wide and varied that it has become a universal problem. Even in the most highly developed countries of the world, the problem of industrial sickness exists, though, the incidence may be lower in comparison to the less developed countries where industrialisation, as a result of low level of technological and

* Professor, and Faculty Member, respectively, Department of Business Management, Punjabi University, Patiala.

managerial know-how, has not been an exhilarating experience. This problem concerns the highly industrialised countries like U.K., U.S.A., Japan etc., as well as the developing countries like India. It has been rightly observed that during the time of crisis in the automobile, steel and ship-building industries all over the world, British leyland received more than Rs. 900 crores (half a billion pounds) in the form of government support. The European Steel Industry, including the British, suffered from considerable over capacity. There was a great deal of sickness in ship-building industry in many countries. General Motors had to retrench a part of its workers, and half to freeze wages in order to avoid further retrenchment.[1] "The tragic fall of Rolls Royce (U.K.); or the Penam Railways (U.S.A.) and number of large enterprises in Japan and other countries were wound up in recent years".[2]

Industrial sickness is the key event of modern industrial age; and incidence of sickness has been growing in such large proportions that in the wake of industrial development, a large number of new units covering all types of units in large, small and medium sectors are added in this category. The rapid growth and magnitude of industrial sickness is puzzling issue not only for present time but also for all times to come; especially for India during the next century. It has become a matter of grave concern for all; concerned directly or indirectly with the industrial units, not only for the crores of rupees locked up in lacks of sick units but also for the fotunes of numerous classes to be affected. "The failure of a unit is an event which brings a lot of mental torture to entrepreneurs, managers and to their families". The society is also affected by the phenomenon of sickness as un-employment spreads widely, availability of goods and services decreases and the prices soar up. The share holders lose their hard earned savings, creditors lose their cash and future prospects of business.

Industrial sickness has, perhaps not come up over-night but it is spreading like silent cancer in all sectors of industrial economy in India. Obviously, an industrial backward state like Rajasthan cannot be an exception. The socio-economic implications of industrial sickness are so grave that it may disturb the whole industrial climate and become an obstacle in the way of making healthy industrial climate. "The Central and State Government have a loose grip of the problem of growing sickness in industries. They have been causing great concern as they erode public money in a big way which affects the budget of these governments".[4]

The sixth plan document has also rightly recorded, "the phenomenon of industrial sickness not only tends to aggravate the problem of unemployment but also renders infructuous capital investment generally creates adverse climate for the industrial growth".[5] The Seventh Plan has also shown its anguish over this problem and its intensity. It calls for concrete steps to arrest its magnitude. Banking industry, itself loses more than Rs. 700 crores in a year by a way of loss of interest due to granting of various concessions, writing-off bad debts, loss of interest due to non-cycling of the funds locked up in the sick industries and due to additional administrative expenses on management of credit to sick units.[6]

It means that the industrial sickness directly and indirectly affects the profitability of the banking industry. If the finance provided by the term lending financial institutions, Central and State Governments in the form of loans, subsidies and other tax reliefs to sick industrial units is considered, the amount blocked in sick industries will be beyond imagination. The locked up capital due to industrial sickness today exceeds Rs. 10,000 crores, if reschedulement of payment is considered as an inability to meet the obligations in time.[7] It is bound to increase with the increase in quantum of assistance to such a huge number of sick units. Thus, in case, this problem is allowed to grow without taking preventive and curative measures, it will seriously impede the utilization of installed capacity, reduce output, block scarce capital, create further unemployment check further investment and tax revenue of the government.

Symptoms of Sickness

Some important symptoms of sickness are as under:

(a) Persistent shortage of cash or liquid assets.

(b) Constantly worsening trend of current ratio (normally less than 1 : 1), with current assets progressively falling short of current liabilities.

(c) Unsatisfactory debt equity ratio i.e., a progressive increase in debt in relation to equity or owner's funds or continual erosion of networth due to constantly occurring cash losses for three years. This tendency reduces the capability of a unit to face rough weather as the equity which has capacity to absorb shock, is too eroded to struggle with adverse circumstances.

(d) Defaulter case in payment to suppliers, employees, bank and financial institutions.

(e) Frequent request, in case of heavy defaulter, for rescheduling the payment of the installment and demand to waive off interest during the closed period or (in some cases, interest over due become more than principal sum).

Dimensions of Industrial Sickness

Of late, the phenomenon of sickness in the industrial sector has widely spread. It is like a disease which increases with the treatment. The situation has deteriorated to a much extent in the last couple of years. During the year 1986 the growth in number of sick units was 23.5 per cent which increased to 39.5 per cent during the year 1987. Similarly, the amount locked up in these units jacked up by 28.3 per cent in 1987 against 14.1 per cent in 1986. As per latest estimation (March, 1990), the total amount locked up in sick units has been estimated around to Rs. 10,000 crore thereby meaning that nearly 10 per cent of the total bank credit. The industrial sickness not only affects production and employment opportunities in the economy but also it has other socio-economic repercussions. Moreover, the industrial sickness has posed serious problems to the banks in maintaining their profitability. Due to grave consequences of industrial sickness on the economy, the issues has become a serious concern to the government, Reserve Bank of India, commercial banks, financial Institutions and Entrepreneurs too.

The magnitude of industrial sickness came in to lime light of large in the early seventies and since then a number of policy measures were adopted to arrest sickness in industries. Among the various measures a mention may be made of the few, viz., providing financial assistance on concessional and liberalised terms, providing raw materials and other inputs from Government quota on reasonable rates, fiscal and financial relaxation by the government, identification of specialised bank branches for extending and monitoring industrial finance, introduction of Health Code System for effective monitoring and follow up at micro-level, formation of Board for Industrial Finance and Reconstruction (BIFR) for expediting the process of rehabilitation, setting up of monitoring forms exclusively for sick industries in the Administrative Units of banks, etc. But the situation has not improved rather it has further widened. The alarming situation has put certain basic questions, viz.,

(a) whether the various measures undertaken were ineffective or there has been weaknesses in the implementation process;

(b) the entrepreneurs of so-called sick units were more attractive of various incentives and concessions offered to them rather than making honest efforts dealing with the crux of the problem;

(c) whether the Government Policy towards industries revival and their growth was not favourable; or

(d) whether required infra-structure and needed support was lacking.

These are some of the conflicting issues which need a great deal of debate. An attempt has been made in this paper to highlight briefly, the dimensions of industrial sickness, causes of sickness and various problems being faced in nursing programme. Finally, suggestions have been given to tackle this task in an effective manner.

Cure of Sickness

The prevention of sickness is not, by itself, a panacea for the disease of industrial sickness. What is needed, is a positive approach to find out proper remedies for it. In this connection, it should never be forgotten that even closed units can be revived and rehabilitated through proper treatment and remedial measures. There is no specific formula for the cure of sick unit, and each unit will have to be diagnosed keeping in view the root causes of sickness and proper remedies will have to be prescribed.

Is the Unit Rehabilitable?

A sick unit, like a human patient, looks forward for proper treatment and its rehabilitation. But it is very unlikely that every sick unit can be rehabilitated even with the best of attention and sympathy. Besides, it is hardly desirable either for commercial banks, or term lending institutions to pump additional funds without knowing about the capacity of potential viability in a reasonable period. It is useless to provide assistance and postpone failure of enterprises which are bound to close. Thus, any kind of assistance should not be extended unless a sick unit tends itself to viable working.

Although, there cannot be any uniform prescription for the rehabilitation of sick units but an entrepreneur or the agency/agencies, while considering rehabilitation of a sick unit, may have to distinguish a unit which is rehabilitable from the one which is not. Normally, a sick unit may require three types of treatment: (1) rehabilitation; (2) rehabilitation with change of management-merger/amalgmation; and (3) allowing the unit to languish, or to do mercy killing by forcing its closure by sale or otherwise. Some broad parameters such as competency of management, location, condition of plant and machinery, labour relations, networth erosion and possible generation of surplus funds in reasonable time so as to attain viability, may be taken into account while deciding whether the unit is rehabilitable.

Rehabilitation of Sick Unit

Rehabilitation of a sick unit is indeed a very difficult task which, admittedly, cannot be the sole responsibility of banks, or financial institutions, or any one agency. It calls for concerted and co-ordinated efforts on the part of all concerned. Rehabilitation of sick units assumes vital importance for putting to productive use the investment already sunk into them. From the point of view, of national interest also, in India, rehabilitation of sick units is vital, as their revival will result into a higher G.N.P. and tax revenue, restoration of employment in sick units.

Formulation of Suitable Rehabilitation Plan

The decision of rehabilitation of a sick unit is dependent upon the conclusions of the viability study which brings to light, in detail, the strengths and weaknesses in the various functional areas.

A suitable, rehabilitation plan of sick unit covers the history of the unit, its present state and plans for the future stating therein the specific causes that led to the decline of the units performance and the remedial action now proposed to be taken.

History of the unit would describe type of its organisation, qualification, past experience, year of establishment, the line of production, a review of its operational activities in the form of equity profits and employment.

The present state of the enterprise should be analytical. It should describe about the location; production function indicating about the plant and machinery, its lay out, utilization, materials management; marketing including working results in terms of sales turnover, finance function including assets and liabilities, past net profit or loss, position of working capital finance, debt equity and current ratios, statutory liabilities in the form of Income-tax, P.F., Electricity and Water charges etc.

Plan for the future should be based on the present state of the unit and the remedial action, proposed to be taken for eradication of causes that led the enterprise to sickness. It should contain the need for improvements of management skills and the manner in which it will be accomplished. The plan may also state how the management proposes to tackle raw materials, power cuts, depressions, changes in Government policies etc. It may also work out B.E.P. on the basis of plan for future and its requirement of financial assistance and the method by which the assistance, if granted, shall be repaid.

Conclusion

The magnitude of industrial sickness has touched alarming point and its unprecedented growth in the small sector is a matter of great concern to one and all involved in the task of industrial development. This calls for concerted efforts and pragmatic approach measures to arrest and reverse the trend rather than following turn a round strategies. The important criteria should be the proper diagnosis and right identification of weaknesses of the unit in the incepient stage by the entrepreneurs and financial institutions with going deeply into definitional aspects. The whole exercise calls for attitudinal changes at all levels. Though sick units deserve all encouragements all precautions are necessary and a clear distinction needs be made between a 'genuine' and 'induced' sickness. The banks have significant role in improving the position if adequate care is adhered right from the project appraisal to monitoring and follow up. The modes operandies of financial institutions and promoters of industrial units needs better alignment and co-ordination in the overall interest.

Merger of viable sick units with the healthy units should be allowed and encouraged as an effective measure for cure of industrial sickness, and the unviable sick industrial co-operatives alongwith induction of professional management should also be encouraged.

The RBI, financial institutions and banks should play a more dynamic role and shoulder group accountability alongwith the promoters. The various measures for rehabilitation should, however, be initiated at the incipient stage of sickness without having waited for a long period of 7 years.

REFERENCES

1. Pillain, K.N., Perumal, "Turning round a Sick Unit - A Practical Approach" *The Economic Times,* June 6, 1984.
2. Viswanathan, R., "Industrial Finance" p. 268.
3. Srivastav, S.S., & Yadav, R.A., "Management and Monitoring of Industrial Sickness" p. 1., Concept Publishing Company, New Delhi.
4. Mahajan, Y.S., "Sick Industries — A Drain on Economy" *The Economic Times,* December 27, 1986.
5. Sixth Plan Document (1980-85) Planning Commission, Government of India.
6. Agrawal, R.C., "Industrial Sickness and its Effects on Bank Profitability" *The Economic Times,* March 19, 1986.
7. Srivastav, S.S., & Yadav, R.A., "Management and Monitoring of Industrial Sickness" Preface IX.
8. Batra G.S., Industrial Sickness in India, The Chartered Accountant, 1992.

16

Role of Public Sector in Industrialisation (A Case Study of Garhwal Mandal Vikas Nigam)

R.C. Dangwal*

Abstract

Two public enterprises were created in the mid' 70s in the northern part of Uttar Pradesh for the economic upliftment of the two hill regions, viz. Kumaun Mandal Vikas Nigam and Garhwal Mandal Vikas Nigam. In the present study the performance of one of the public enterprises has been closely followed and its role in economic upliftment of the area analysed.

Garhwal

Garhwal is situated between $29^0 45'$ N to $31^0 27'$ N latitudes and $77^0 45'$ E to $80^0 7'$ E longitudes. The region comprises the five districts of Chamoli, Dehradun, Pauri Garhwal, Tehri Garhwal and Uttarkashi and has an area of about 11.325 square miles. This region lies in the northern part of Uttar Pradesh and rises from a height of 300 m to more than 6000 m above sea level. Garhwal is conspicuously different from other parts of the state due to its topography, soils, climate and vegetation. The area gets a relatively higher rainfall in U.P. and many of its peaks are permanently covered with snow.

According to the census 1991, the population of the region is 29.34 lakhs with the population density at 65 per square km.

---

* Lecturer in Commerce, H.N.B. Garhwal University Campus, Srinagar (Garhwal).

Garhwal happens to be one of the (economically) poorest region of the states. It has a (money order cum) agriculture based economy but the land holdings are very very small and uneconomical.

The need for a recognised body aimed towards economic upliftment of the faltering economy was being felt for quite sometime. The resultant, 'Hill Development Corporation', however, was soon converted to Kumaun Mandal Vikas Nigam for development of Kumaun (another neighbouring developing hill region). This lacuna was filled in with the birth of a corporation, Garhwal Mandal Vikas Nigam (GMVN) on 31st March 1976.

GMVN

The Nigam has a sole membership of the Government of Uttar Pradesh and is a Government Company within the meaning of the Indian Companies Act, 1956. The authorised and subscribed capital has witnessed a five fold increase from Rs. 1 crore and Rs. 65 lakhs on 31st March 1977 to Rs. 5 crores and 3.21 crores respectively on March 31st, 1985. It is headed by a Managing Director who is generally an I.A.S. Officer, with the board of Directors and a Chairman.

Presently, the Nigam is involved in several businesses which can be grouped as:

1. Promotion of tourism which includes conducting package tours, managing tourist rest house and canteens, organising mountain climbing and trekking, winter sports (skiing) and ropeway installation.
2. Industry: Give active units (all within Garhwal) namely, resin and turpentine oil unit, woodwool factory, integrated wood industry, cement concrete block unit and a flush door factory.
3. Marketing of local and other products such as LPG gas, petrol and diesel, truck transport, fruit and vegetables (local) etc.
4. Construction unit which builds rest houses for the Nigam and other structures.
5. Joint ventures with Venus Cement Ltd. is in operation.

Laid Objectives of G.M.V.N.

The Nigam has been formed to help accelerate the pace of economic growth in Garhwal through direct participation or extending assistance to local industries in various ways. The Memorandum of Association of the Company states that it can aid, assist, promote or establish, develop, execute industrial projects, or enterprises or programmes for manufacture, production, or distribution of plants, machinery etc., and other materials, substances, goods or things of any description which in the opinion of the Company is likely to promote or advance the economic industrial and agricultural development in Garhwal. Industries under any organisational structure (company, firm, sole etc.,) can be financed by the Nigam i.e., providing capital, credit, means, resources, and technical managerial assistance. Further, the company is also empowered to take up small River Valley Projects in the area, develop tourist traffic or trade by development of hotels, restaurants etc., own or run transport facilities, exploit mineral resources, undertake projects for plantation of orchards, poultry farming, commercial crops etc., establishment of warehouses and cold storages, exploit forest resources, marketing of local produce, produce medicines from herbs etc. Besides, the subsidiary objects include, rights to enter into a joint venture with any body or person, to conduct a survey in the area for ascertaining availability of raw material etc.

Annual Progress of the Nigam (1976-77)

Until 31st October 1976, the Nigam was managed by the Kumaun Mandal Vikas Nigam Limited and on November 1, 1976, the control over the affairs was handed over to the Managing Director of the Garhwal Mandal Vikas Nigam Limited. Consequently, the remaining five months of the financial year passed away in 'taking over' the different business and grasping the state of affairs.

1. Tourism

As established by the previous body, exploitation of tourism potential in Garhwal was given top priority by the management. However, since summers (the main tourist season) was already off, implementation of new schemes was not possible. Nevertheless, programmes were drawn up to increase accommodation facilities in various tourist places (in accordance with desire of the government). The Bus fleet for package tour was increased to fifteen.

2. Industry

(a) Integrated wood industrial unit manufactured furniture, drawing board, tenis racket and door parts. It was decided to

Table I
Annual Performance of GMVN (Sales-Unit Wise)

(Rs. in lakh)

Item of Sales	1977-78	1978-79	1979-80	1980-81	1981-82	1982-83	1983-84	1984-85	1985-86
1	2	3	4	5	6	7	8	9	10
Industry									
Resin & T. Oil	*	37.16	62.58	44.99	61.85	68.68	86.58	106.79	52.33
Resin Tapp.	18.44	23.18	*	*	*	*	*	*	*
Wood Industry	.44	.63	1.23	3.64	7.96	17.78	6.74	12.81	17.78
Wood Wool	.52	1.53	2.52	2.94	7.11	7.63	15.11	20.86	32.26
Cement Concrete	*	*	*	.16	2.74	2.97	3.45	3.81	4.41
Flush Door	*	*	*	*	*	*	34.50	39.52	29.08
Tourism									
Package Tours	7.87	7.51	15.76	15.62	27.14	—	3.30	38.00	35.00
Rest House	2.62	3.37	3.83	8.32	8.43	46.46	—	20.28	23.00
Canteen	—	.15	1.01	1.14	3.10	—	—	7.24	7.67
Mont. and Trekg.	*	*	*	.26	1.12	—	3.14	3.60	3.00
Skiing	*	*	*	*	*	*	*	*	*
Ropeways	*	*	*	*	*	*	64.71	94.47	99.00
Marketing									
Gas	—	1.94	3.10	—	22.50	64.13	12.77	17.16	10.00
Truck	.12	4.16	8.27	—	16.20	15.00	28.05	35.59	10.00
Petrol etc.	8.50	10.04	18.60	25.56	26.62	27.66	2.38	23.62	—
Fruit	1.08	.71	1.28	—	1.18	2.00	—	55.27	17.00
Construction	—	1.09	—	—	—	—	—	—	—

Notes :— indicates non-availability of data.
* indicates non-operations of unit.

Source : Data have been completed from the various annual reports of the Garhwal Mandal Vikas Nigam Limited.

reorganise and to instal a seasoning plant. The industry is totally dependent on the forest department for the supply of wood.

(b) *Wood Wool Factory:* Apart from problems of demand, the factory is facing difficulties in obtaining a suitable quality of raw material (wood). It is a new industry and the production began in the current year.

(c) *Resin and Turpentine Factory*: This factory was expected to commence production by the end of the year. Further, the Nigam was in correspondence with the Forest Department for increase of area of lease for tapping the required raw material (resin).

3. Marketing

On experimental basis, only four trucks of oranges were transported from district Chamoli to Delhi. This would enable the Nigam to formulate plants for future, in this respect. The Nigam was also endeavouring to market apples for the local producers and thinking in the lines of purchasing trucks to facilitate marketing of the various local produce (vegetable and fruits).

Besides, the above said projects, several other proposals were drawn up as follows:

1. Match splint factory;
2. Paper plant;
3. Watch Factory;
4. Handicraft;
5. Cooking gas;
6. Pine needles hard board manufacturing;
7. Woolen Factory;
8. Seasoning plant;
9. Cold storage for fruits and vegetables.

1978-79

1. Industry

(a) *Resin and turpentine oil unit:* By the end of its third year of its establishment, the unit had already commenced production, earned a good amount of profit and, had become the largest industrial establishment of the Nigam.

(b) *Resin Extraction (tapping) unit:* This unit was to be shut down in view of the government's directions to the forest deptt. for exclusive extraction of resin. In the current year, the unit had incurred a loss.

(c) *Wood Wool Factory:* this increased the volume of its operation in the year but still ended in a loss.

(d) *Integrated wood industry:* The unit although, improved a little, still required reorganisation.

2. Marketing

A fleet of seven trucks, a petrol pump and a gas agency had begun operations and plans were being made to expand the fleet and increase the number of gas agencies.

3. Tourism

The Nigam conducts tours for various tourist spots of the region, besides, arrangements were made to provide more accommodation for the incoming tourists.

4. Construction

Under this activity, several rest houses were being constructed by the Nigam in different parts of the region.

'Garhwal Anusuchit Janjati Vikas Nigam' (GAJVN) is a subsidiary of GMVN and an investment of Rs. 12 lakhs has already been made in the company by the GMVN.

1979-80

1. Industry

(a) *Resin and turpentine oil:* The unit earned profit once again but there is a big gap between the installed capacity and the capacity utilised.

(b) *Wood based factories:* Although the volume of sales increased during this year the losses in both the wood based units persist.

(c) *A new cement* concrete unit (block) was coming up in the current year, the production was expected to begin soon.

2. Tourism

The Nigam having a fleet of 20 buses and 25 rest houses conducted regular tours for thousands of tourists in the year. However, tourism still happens to be running in a loss.

3. Marketing

Local produce such as apples, potatoes, beans, etc., as well as other items such as cooking gas are being marketed by the Nigam to the tune of several lakhs.

4. Construction

Work has also increased more than two folds in the current year as compared to 1978-79. Plants were being made to establish additional units for manufacture of telescope, paper, cement, magnesite etc. The subsidiary of the Nigam, GAJVN continued to incur losses.

1981-82

1. Industry

(a) *Resin and turpentine oil:* This unit increased its sales volume still further. The profits were also higher this year.

(b) *Wood wool factory:* The factory plans to manufacture Thermo-boards after the reorganisation process is completed. In comparison with the previous year, the sales have more than doubled in the current year.

(c) *Wood industry:* The process of reorganisation being completed, doors, windows etc., are being produced with the help of most modernised machines. Although the sales have increased more than twice, the unit is yet to earn profits.

(d) The cement unit has begun production but resulted in a loss.

2. Tourism

Activities have been progressing. The income for the year increased more than 50% in comparison with the previous year. The year ended with a profit.

3. In the field of marketing

Three more gas distribution agencies are coming up rapidly and the existing outlets are marking sound profits. As regards local produce, about twice the quantity of apples of previous year were marketed in the current year, also better rates were fetched to the producers. Besides, oranges, other citreous fruits were also marketed in the current year, another matter praiseworthy is that marketing of local produce fetched profit this year.

4. Construction unit

This unit completed more work this year, about 50% more when compared to 1979-80.

The subsidiary continued incurring losses.

In the front of upcoming units, preliminary work regarding mini-cement plant, resin derivatives, flush door factory, paper plant and a ginger plant has been commenced by the Nigam.

Efforts are being made by the Nigam to obtain permission for new gas distribution outlets at several towns of Garhwal. Furthermore, Government permission with respect to installation of a Ropeway at Auli (Joshimath) has been obtained and construction work in this regard is scheduled to commence soon.

1982-83

1. Industry

(a) *Resin and turpentine oil unit:* Although the profits this year have increased four folds, as compared to last year, the full capacity is not being utilised mainly, due to a low supply of raw material.

(b) *Wood wool unit:* The sales volume of this unit has been more or less constant but, the profit have come down to one third, in comparison with the previous year.

(c) *Wood industry:* Sales this year were thrice that in 1981-82 resulting in the first ever profits to the unit.

(d) *Cement Concrete unit:* Which provides concrete blocks to the Tehri Dam Project recorded a marginal increase in it's sales.

2. Tourism Activities

Brought an increased revenue to the Nigam but, ended with a loss.

3. Marketing

An increased sale of local produce also resulted in a loss to the

Nigam. The gas agency and the petrol pump outlet however, earned profits.

4. The Construction Unit completed thrice the amount of jobs of the previous year.

The Flush Door Unit at Kotdwara commenced production this year. The Ropeway Scheme is yet in the construction stage. Apart from this the Nigam is making efforts to obtain permission for additional gas agencies in Garhwal. The subsidiary of the GMVN, GAJVN continues to incur losses.

April, 1984 - December, 1985

By the end of the year 1985, the Nigam had a total turnover of Rs. 379.96 lakhs and a profit of Rs. 14.10 lakhs.

1. Tourism

Income from all tourism activities totalled Rs. 64,76 lakhs which is almost equal to that of twelve months in 1984-85 (March), Rs. 69.57 lakhs. Profits came to Rs. 8.97 lakhs for the period. The number of rest houses under control of the Nigam, reached 46, and that of the package tours totalled 223. During the year winter Sport (Skiing) had been commenced at Auli, Joshimath in the region while, the Ropeway scheme is still in progress.

2. Industry

The five active plants produced items to the tune of Rs. 135-36 lakhs with sales reaching Rs. 122.82 lakhs and securing a profit of Rs. 3.76 lakhs in the period.

The subsidiary GAJVN continued to incur losses.

3. Marketing

Local produce, gas, motor spirits etc. accounted for an income of Rs. 175.38 lakhs and a profit of Rs. 1.32 lakhs whereas 1984-85 fetched a profit of Rs. 3.84 lakhs with an earning of Rs. 173.99 lakhs.

4. Construction

In the year 1984-85 construction work totalled Rs. 55.27 lakhs and profits came to Rs. 1.96 lakhs. However, the current year was low for this department with profits of Rs. 0.25 lakh from a total work of Rs. 17 lakhs.

An investment to the tune of Rs. 10 lakhs had been made in a joint venture scheme with Venus Cement Ltd. Production in this unit had commenced in the current year. Besides, a Cement Concrete Block Unit was expected to be ready by March 1986 and Wood Treatment Plant was being established at *Muni-Ki-Reti.* Also, proposals are on the way to Government for approval such as an Electronic Typewriter Unit, Trout Fish Hatchery Farm, T.V. and Radio Unit (Production-cum-training).

Financial Analysis

A Financial analysis of the Nigam's affairs may tend to project a biased picture because of it's unusual nature; promoting economic development in a (economically) backward region rather than profit earning. Nevertheless, such an analysis may not entirely be a futile exercise, all the more, because much of the Nigam's resources have been directed towards establishing than, merely aiding/assisting in the industrial development.

Within it's years of existence GMVN has had a tenfold increase in it's sales. The initial three years witnessed losses but, since the past 3/4 years profits have been coming up from several units. In this duration several more units have been established, the existing modernised and plans, for fresh schemes have been drawn up. However, it is clear that the Nigam is touching profits (Table II) only due to one unit namely, Resin Turpentine Oil Factory (Tilwara). In the light of recent imports of resin and a tightening of the control over tapping of resin by the forest department it is feared, that the 'Loan Bread Earner' may have to face a tough fight thus, shaking the very grounds on which the Nigam stands, today. The Resin Unit regulates the profit trend of the Nigam, e.g., in 1978-79, 1980-81 and 1981-82 when the Unit earned low profits, the Nigam incurred losses, similarly, the year 1984-85 saw the Nigam's profits touching a new high when, the Resin Unit recorded it's most favourable year.

The Integrated Wood Industry at Gavana and the Cement Concrete Unit at Tehri have shown profit in only one year (each) of their existence. The Flush Door Factory is yet to show a profit. Similarly, the Tourism and the Marketing Divisions have been incurring losses almost every year since inception, excepting the recent two years.

The Gross Profit Margin (Table III) as well as the net profit margin have more than often been Negative. The Overall Inventory Turnover

Table II

Profit of Garhwal Mandal Vikas Nigam Limited : Unit-wise

(Rupees in lakh)

Net Profit	*1977-78*	*1978-79*	*1979-80*	*1980-81*	*1981-82*	*1982-83*	*1983-84*	*1984-85*	*1985-86*
1	*2*	*3*	*4*	*5*	*6*	*7*	*8*	*9*	*10*
Industry									
Resin	*	7.57	30.02	2.48	3.65	14.85	22.19	48.13	18.71
Resin & Tapp.	—	(-) 1.50	*	*	*	*	*	*	*
Wood	—	(-) .55	(-) .75	(-) 3.40	(-) 1.88	.42	(-) 1.52	(-) .41	(-) 3.00
Wood Wool	—	(-) .87	(-) .54	(-) 1.54	1.38	.54	.92	3.50	5.57
Cement Construct	*	*	*	(-) .87	(-) .87	(-) .05	(-) 1.03	(-) .93	.64
Flush Door	*	*	*	*	*	*	(-) 28.42	(-) 16.62	(-) 18.15
Tourism									
Package Tours	—	(-) 6.74	(-) 3.17	(-) .56	(-) 1.51	(-) 3.32	(-) 2.96	.35	5.00
Rest House							(-) 1.11	2.34	3.17
Canteen							(-) .22	(-) .75	.80
Mont. and Trekg.	*	*	*	*	*	*	.73	.97	.50
Skiing	*	*	*	*	*	*	*	(-) .03	—
Ropeways	*	*	*	*	*	*	*	*	*
Marketing									
Gas	—			—	2.43	.86	(-) .14	3.50	.79
Truck	—			—	(-) .96	(-) 2.58	(-) 4.42	(-) .47	.18
Petrol etc.	—	(-) 1.55	(-) 1.16	—	.41	.08	.51	.82	.25
Fruit	—			—	(-) .62	(-) .72	.07	.14	—
Construction	—	—	—	—	—	3.48	3.97	1.96	.25

Notes :— indicates non-availability of data.
* indicates non-operations of unit.

Source : Data have been compiled from the Annual Reports of the Garhwal Mandal Vikas Nigam Limited.

Rate has been fluctuating greatly but this could be explained as due to the Construction Unit which may include huge sums of Work-in-progress. The return on investments as well as on Capital is very discouraging being often Negative.

Table III

Profitability Ratio Analysis of GMVN (In % and Ratio)

Ratio	**G.P.M.%*	***N.P.M.%*	****OITR%*	*****ROC*	******ROI*
1977-78	(-) 23.79	(-) 23.97	65.9	(-) 4.62	(-) 7.13
1978-79	(-) 7.66	(-) 8.73	27.4	(-) 3.12	(-) 5.13
1979-80	17.82	16.25	15.6	7.12	11.7
1980-81	(-) 1.1	(-) 10.6	2.26	(-) 3.5	(-) 6.96
1981-82	4.27	(-) .77	4.16	(-) .37	(-) .68
1982-83	5.17	3.5	5.38	1.99	3.82
1983-84	2.79	.79	11.25	.55	1.08
1984-85	7.89	4.05	13.29	3.33	6.39

* GPM stands for Gross Profit Margin.

** NPM stands for Net Profit Margin.

*** OITR stands for Overall Inventory Turnover Rate

**** ROC stands for Return on Capital.

***** ROI stands for Return on Investment

Note : The above calculations are based on data noted from the relevant Annual Reports of the Garhwal Mandal Vikas Nigam.

Objective Fulfilment

The main-objects for which GMVN has been created can be explained in a nutshel as expediting the (economic) development process of Garhwal through direct and indirect means is by participation (establishing industries etc.) and assistance (extending help to other existing and new units). Of course, in deciding whether a project is likely to promote or advance the economic industrial and agricultural development in the Garhwal Mandal it is the discretion of the Nigam. Nevertheless, the question whether the laid objectives are being closely followed cannot escape scrutiny.

A deeper study of the various projects in operation, schemes recently floated and plans now being drawn reveals that, the Nigam is a force to be reckoned with amongst the (few) local industrialists.

Besides, being a Public Enterprises, business like a Cooking Gas Agency and Petrol Pumps are being simply handed over to it. Generally, however, it is an individual entrepreneur who takes up such (small) distribution outlets.

Garhwal which has several tourist attractions such as, Badrinath, Kedarnath, Gangotri, Shrines, Hem Kund Sahib, Valley of Flowers, Mussoorie etc., holds a great potential for Hoteliering, (passenger) Transport, Package tours etc. But unfortunately, no individual dare compete with the Nigam (which has no shortage of funds and seems unaffected by losses) in such areas of business.

For the past few years, the Nigam has been marketing local produce-potatoes, oranges, apples etc., in accordance with it's main objects. But although, the Nigam is not expected to earn profit out of it's dealings with the local producers, yet it seems unreasonable to simply waste away revenue through losses in such transactions.

Further, the Nigam is presently engaged in a ropeway installation scheme in Garhwal. This is a sound step in keeping with the objectives of the Nigam since, such establishments will help to attract tourists.

One of the main objects of the Nigam is to "take up small River Valley Projects.......for checking soil erosion.........extension of irrigation facilities." It is also well-known that there is no dearth of water in Garhwal (what with two rivers Alaknanda and Bhagirathi flowing through it), but, since the water is at a low level as compared to the town areas, and there being a scarcity of pumps for lifting it, the water is barely used for irrigation purposes. Also, rains are quite generous with Garhwal but no efforts (for water-catchment) have been made by the Nigam in this direction.

Lastly, the first object of the Nigam reads as "to assist promote or establish........." but hardly any evidence of an assistance being extended to entrepreneurs whether, financially or technically is available.

Visible Trend in Future Schemes

In it's monthly progress statement of December 1985, the Nigam's proposed projects are stated as, manufacture of Electronic Typewriter and alive fish Hatchery Farm, Television and Radio etc. Perhaps, it will enhance the cause of economic development more if, the Nigam encourages entrepreneurs and provides consultancy and, if possible, extends financial assistance to deserving and needy units in the region (as sought in it's memorandum) instead of increasing it's area of active participation. It must actively participants, River Valley Projects, Cultivation of fruit-belts, construction of Cold Storage, Schemes for growing grass and fodder for cattle, Commercial projects Feasibility Surveys etc., could be undertaken by the Nigam.

Suggestions

While summarising the evaluation, it will be appropriate to point out the areas which need prompt attention of the Body. Thus, the Nigam must effect an efficiency increase in Truck Transport marketing of local produce, management of Rest Houses and Canteens, Cement Concrete Unit, Integrated Wood Industry and the flush Door Unit. Furthermore, the Nigam, while evolving future schemes, must concentrate on those projects which provide a platform for more industries is laying the infrastructure. Also, yearly allocation may be made for needy and deserving units and arrangements made for providing technical assistance (free consultancy). Projects that will contribute towards agriculture development need to be taken up urgently.

Conclusion

GMVN must not forget the purpose for which it has been created, it must remember that it's object is economic development of Garhwal whether, through participation or assistance; constructing a commercial base to support and invite further development and lending assistance is a noble cause befitting the Nigam. Also, should it feel that it must run industries then, the golden rule of business must be foremost in mind is unless running in profits a unit has no right to exist (excepting the initial years).

REFERENCES

1. Memorandum and Articles of Association of GMVN.
2. Annual Report of 1976-77.
3. Annual Report of 1978-79.
4. Annual Report of 1979-80.
5. Annual Report of 1981-82.
6. Annual Report of 1982-83.
7. Balance Sheet of 1984-85.
8. Monthly Progress Statement of Dec. 1985.

17

Management Control Over Public Enterprises : Emerging Dimensions

Dr. G.S Batra*

Ministerial control over Public Enterprises is highly significant and effective. It is generally believed that the Minister should have control over the Public Enterprises. From the initial stage of development of Public Enterprises in the U.K. and other countries, the Minister has been entrusted with the task of controlling these enterprises.

Hanson has very aptly remarked that "There is no need to argue that Ministers of the government should possess certain powers of control over public enterprises. It is only through ministerial directives that enterprises can be brought into line with the requirements of current public policy. The alternatives are either no effective control at all or control by bodies without political responsibility." There is a general practice in this regard as pointed out in the U.N. Rangoon Report : "The Principles of ministerial control over Public Enterprises is accepted in almost all the countries in the ECAFE region and the present stage in the development of these countries make it essential such enterprises should be coordinated into national economic programmes at the ministerial level."

Ministerial or governmental control is the most important method of enforcing accountability over different forms of pubic enterprises in India. Of all the agencies of accountability, ministerial accountability is more effective and real than is publicly admitted. Public Accountability of public enterprises is canalised through ministers to parliament. It is the main way in which full control is retained over the State

* Faculty Member, Deptt. of Business Management, Punjabi University, Patiala.

enterprises. In relation to public enterprises parliament has three main functions—viz.,

—to pass or amend legislation,

—to provide finance, and

—to supervise administration.

But parliament is too big and too busy to successfully govern individual enterprises under its jurisdiction. It is the ministers who have been vested with specific powers of control over the public enterprises. The degree to which the accountability of the enterprises to the people successfully rests on the degree to which the ministers are accountable to parliament.

In order to ensure accountability the government usually reserve certain powers which are exercised through the minister which are:

1. power of appointment and removal of top officials and members of the Board;
2. power to require the Corporation to submit a budget for approval of government when so provided in Statute;
3. power to dictate the policy of the enterprises;
4. power of prescriptive or to issue directives in public interest;
5. power to carry out a supplementary or test audit or in case of some statutory corporations, the power to audit vesting in the C.& A.G. of India, who is constitutional authority;
6. power to call for information, report and returns;
7. prior approval of capital expenditure and other cases where it exceeds a ceiling fixed depending on the size, complexity and type of management;
8. prior approval in all matters of borrowing, investment and distribution of profits; and
9. prior approval of rules and regulations of corporations established by Statute.

Devices of Ministerial Accountability

Ministerial accountability over public enterprises in India may be established through one or other or a combination of the following devices :

1. issue of general policy directions;
2. issue of specific directions;
3. approval or veto of specified categories of actions and policies;
4. informal control;
5. appointment of governing board and managers of an enterprises; and
6. participation in management as a member of the governing board.

The ministers should control public corporations, but their control should as confined to matters of general policy only. They should not interfere with day-to-day administration in which the enterprises should enjoy freedom.

Emerging Issues

There are a few issue involved in the question of ministerial control.

The problem of distribution of enterprises among ministers. The general rule is that if an enterprises is a manufacturing one, it should be placed under the Ministry of Industries; and similarly agricultural enterprises under the Ministry of Agriculture, banks and financial institutions under the Ministry of Finance, and defence enterprises under the Ministry of Defence. The general principle may be that an enterprise should be attached to a Ministry within whose general sphere of responsibility it falls. But the question as to which Ministry should control a particular enterprise is not easy answer.

Prof. Hanson places the following four factors which should decide the placement of an enterprise under a particular Ministry:

(i) the stage of economic development reached in the country;

(ii) the demands made on ministers' time and energy by a particular sector of public enterprises;

(iii) the quality of the machinery that the government has established for inter-ministerial consultation, and the preparedness of the concerned Ministers to use it effectively; and

(iv) the role that the government has assigned to public enterprises and the kind of agencies it has chosen for the development of public sector.

With the increase in the number of enterprises, the Minister's responsibility becomes wide. Under the circumstances the decisions are delayed, which mar the efficiency of enterprises particularly those which are commercial and where speed and span of control are of vital importance.

A situation may arise when some ministries are overburdened. For example, manufacturing industries go to the Ministry of Industries where there may be excessive concentration.

There may be enterprises in respect of which it is difficult to categorise a particular Ministry. There are always some borderline cases where different ministeries compete for supervisory function. In this regard, competition and conflict between Finance Ministry and Industry Ministry, or between Agriculture and Industry Ministries may always exist.

There is an important problem relating to the enterprises in private sector vis-a-vis enterprises in public sector in a mixed economy like India. In a mixed system private and public sectors are to cordinate and cooperate with one another to achieve the desired goals of the country defined in the national plans and it shall be in the interest of the country to keep enterprises of a kind, whether in public sector or in private sector, under the same Ministry.

There may arise a problem of coordination among various ministries under any one of whom the enterprise has been placed. Inter-ministerial coordination is essential for smooth working of the enterprise.

There is again the issue involved in reconciling the interests of Ministry of Finance and other Ministries. Ministry of Finance is by far the most important one, because it is concerned in one way or the other with all kinds of public enterprises in respect of financing and capital budgeting. Besides, certain decisions would always need approval of the Ministry of Finance even though it is a manufacturing or marketing enterprise. Under the circumstances, there is bound to be some conflict between ministeries in lieu of shortage of resources.

The degree of control to be exercised by the Minister over the Public Enterprises is really a vexed issue and has yet evaded any solution. The extent of ministerial control over Public Enterprises differs from country to country. In some countries, even the extreme situations persist. At one extreme, for instance, Middle-Eastern and

Southern Asian countries, we find Ministers exercising substantial, stricter and even ruthless control over the Public Enterprises and all effective decisions are taken by the Ministers themselves. The freedom given to the administration of the Public Enterprises is severely limited. This is prevent specially in such countries where the legislature is quite strong and is able to wield enough pressure over the Ministers. This is also possible in a country where the able and competent administrators are not available and Ministers feel that the important decisions cannot left in their hands. At the other extreme, for instance, is Latin America. Here we find that ministerial control is quite remote, nominal and ineffective. The minister is the controlling authority for the name sake. He feels that he can wield little effective control as he is not an expert in the field. In Columbia, for instance, the Minister has been made responsible but he does "little more than speak for the enterprise in the legislature". Between these two extremes, however, greater variations are found with regard to the ministerial control, depending upon the various forces prevailing in the particular country.

A large number of public enterprises today are becoming commercial in nature and are run on business principles. That is why a universally accepted principle is that their management should have enough flexibility and autonomy. If it does not possess substantial autonomy, it will not be able to attain the desired level of efficiency. On the one hand there is need for control, on the other hand there should be autonomy, and a proper balance between the two is an important element. To balance autonomy and control is not an easy task. The difficult question boils down to the determination of a right kind of checks and balances.

The degree of control exercised by the Minister differs from country to country. There are countries where Ministers exercise substantial control giving little freedom to public enterprises. On the other hand, there can be a case where ministerial control is remote and nominal. Ministerial interference is not necessary as management is manned by extremely able and competent people who do not, therefore, unnecessarily depend upon the Minister's directives or advice. But both the extremes mentioned above are rare. In between the two are found variations with regard to degree of control exercised by Ministers which may differ from country to country, and from situation to situation within the same country.

Usually, the Minister is empowered to give directions to the company's Board in relation to matters which are of 'national interest'. In the name of 'national interest' the minister can exercise any degree of control. But too much control in the day-to-day management would not be in the interest of the efficient functioning of the enterprise. It would lead to encroachment upon the freedom of the Board. It would encroach upon the autonomy of enterprise. It is due to this reason that Mr. A.D. Gorwala said "If the autonomy of authority is to be preserved. 'matters affecting the national interest' must really be interpreted strictly and not made to cover a wide variety of unimportant details as sometimes happens. In practice it could perhaps be as well to play down that the authority ought to be consulted, before a directive is issued."

In India the ministerial control has not been limited. Control is formal as well as informal; general and specific; and often the Minister's interference goes to an unreasonable limit. He has been found interfering not only in broad matters of policy, but also in matters relating to personnel, labour relations, stores purchase policy, finance etc. He has been found saying that he is particularly careful because the Parliament sometimes insistes on "detailed ministerial responsibility." However, the generally accepted nation is that the role of the Minister should not go beyond the formulation of policies, and he should not interfere in the day-to-day administration, though deviations from it have been frequently noticed in all kinds of enterprises under varying situations. A question has often been discussed whether the Minister should issue general directives only or should issue specific directives also. In various democratic countries like U.K. U.S.A. and France, the Minister issues general directives only. In India too the Minister is supposed to issue general directive but at times interference on some specific issues has not gone unnoticed. Though the general consensus is that Minister should have limited control, the tendency has been towards ministerial intervention even in day-to-day affairs of public enterprises, however indirect it may be. As a rule, enterprises are likely to function better if ministerial control is confined to matters of general policy.

Factors Affecting Management Control

There are various factors which affect the complex problem of minister-board relationship and degree of accountability to be enforced by the minister over Board of public enterprises. These factors exert their influence in varying degree in different countries and are highly complex as they themselves are affected by the political, social, psychological and administrative considerations. Moreover, even if some of these forces are very strong, the countervailing forces may also exist side by side which may really complicate the situation.

The role of government in planning economic development affects considerably Minister's responsibility and control over public enterprises and public expenditure and investment. He has to see that enterprises work in conformity with the overall plans of the country and in the larger interest of the country. His role increases and his influence over the enterprises under his control thus increases.

The nature of the government or the political system also influences the extent of control. In a parliamentary democracy Minister's responsibility is continuous and he draws the support and confidence of the Parliament. If the Parliament supports the Minister, he is successful and it is this support on which he always banks which he tries to earn and enhance. Since he faces the Parliament and people while contesting the elections, he remains alert in supervising the working of enterprises under his control.

The extent of control also depends upon the extent to which the Minister assumes his responsibilities, and the manner in which he interprets them. If he assumes wide responsibilities he would be accountable to the Parliament on a large scale and if he assumes limited responsibilities, his accountability would also be less.

The quality of managerial personnel; beginning from the Chairman and managing director influences the operations of the Minister and his control over public undertaking. If the top men appointed by the Minister are competent people, who have been given free hand in administration, the relationship or control is healthy, useful, and smooth as it is based on mutual trusts, goodwill and understanding of each other. There is no need for interference in such a case. On the other hand, if the quality of managers is questionable, relationship between Management and Minister may not be smooth and under the circumstances control may increase. But this is not all that simple. It has been observed that howsoever competent people have been appointed, the relationship between chairman/MD and Minister and his secretary sometimes is such that the latter dominate and the managers obviously fall into the bureaucratic rut, who do not always get an opportunity of presenting their best. Ministers may prefer to work with men of lesser talents and they may thus leave only the minor decision into the hands of the Management Board. Boards are often asked to report all the major decisions to them for their final approval. This causes considerable delay in case of even small matters. The ministers may even get involved in small matters, which leads to poor relationship, between the Minister and the Board. It may even involve the organisation into some politics, and thus retard the smooth working of the enterprise. The only solution to the problem seems to be that the Minister should resist the demand for persistent interference on his part, and he should limit the number of items needing ministerial approval to the minimum.

In a parliamentary form of government if there exists a strong and powerful pressure group, it could have a considerable influence over the Minister. It might even create a situation which keeps the Minister his toes. Such a group might make the relationship between minister and management weak and tarday, and even lead to interfering in normal working of the enterprise. A U.N. Report : in this connection rightly mentions : "A majority of the Board of some of the most of the important enterprises are named by private groups which can be held accountable to neither the government nor the people."

Mode of financing the enterprise also determines the extent of control. Some enterprises receive their capital in the farm of grains. In their case control should be direct and strict. In case of enterprises which are financed out of loans, and which are to run on commercial lines, the control is of a different kind Ministerial control, other things remaining the same may in such cases be minimum.

Some of the important factors which exert considerable influence in this regard are :

(a) nature of political system;

(b) mode of financing public enterprises;

(c) role assigned to public enterprises;

(d) availability of competent managerial personnel;

(e) government's attutude towards economic planning;

(f) assumption and interpretation of responsibilities by minister; and

(g) existence of strong and significant pressure groups.

All the factors, mentioned above with varying force and degree, are prevalent in our country and with the result the ministers are able to wield considerable influence and exert substantial control over the public enterprises.

Extent of Managerial Responsibility

Along with control goes responsibility of the Minister towards public enterprises. As the Minister is accountable to the Parliament, he should possess some responsibility, because without that he can not be held accountable. In a Parliamentary form of government, a Minister's function are: the formulation of policy, he consults his colleagues and with the help of his Secretary he performs that function. In respect of implementation, he delegates his powers to the Secretary and Head of Departments and keeps an eye on the overall position. It follows that the constitutional responsibility of the Minister to the Parliament, and through Parliament to the people covers action of his subordinates, through whom he gets things done. So far as his responsibility is concerned , as the head of a department, he is accountable for all that goes in the department and therefore, in the enterprise and in the Ministry.

This matter was discussed as early as 1947-48 in U.K. and Herbert Morrison, the then Lord President of the Council and Leader of the House of Commons explained the principles underlying the extent of ministerial responsibility to the Parliament. He was of the view that Ministers were not responsible for the day-today administration of the nationalized industries. His views merit our attention. "A Minister is responsible to Parliament for action which he may take in relation to a board, or action coming within his statutory powers which he has not taken. Thus the Minister would be answerable for any directions he have in the national interest, and for the action which he took on proposals which a board is required by statute to lay before him. It would be contrary to this principle, and to the clearly expressed intention of Parliament in the governing legislation, if Ministers were to give, in replies in Parliament or in letters, information about day-to-day maters. Un due intervention by the Minister would tend to impair the board's commercial freedom of action."

This question was examined by Chagla Commission in the affairs of Life Insurance Corporation of India in 1958 in relation to Mundhra deal, when the Commission held that the "Finance Minister's responsibility was inescapable, call it constitutional, moral, administrative or personnel. "The Finance Minister resigned from the Ministry as a result of it. The LIC had invested a huge sum of Rs. 1.5 crores in six concerns of Mr. Mundhra. Perhaps to help him out of a precarious financial situation. The transaction book place by the Principal Finance Secretary but the Commission rejected the plea that Minister was not in the know of things and had never endorsed the actions of the Principle Finance Secretary. The Commission was of the view that the Minister "can not be permitted to say that his subordinates did not respect the policy or acted contrary to his wishes or directions. "The views of the Minister may also be of significance. He said that it would be impossible for any minister to accept the dictum that "he must take full responsibility for the acts of his subordinates without being permitted to say that his subordinates did not respect his policy or acted contrary to the wishes and the directions expressed by him."

Conclusion

To establish a sound relationship between Government and public enterprises in India, it is very essential that the nature and scope of ministerial accountability is clearly defined.

State enterprises have no uniform statutory provisions regarding the size of the board, composition, tenure or the qualifications of members. It differs from undertaking to undertaking. In some enterprises, directors are nominated by the state Government while in a number of cases some civil servants are ex-officio members of the Board. The purpose is to give due representation to the different departments which might be helpful in the smooth functioning of the enterprise. The tenure of the appointment of full time chairman/managing director and functional directors should normally be for a period of five years subject to their performance being satisfactory.

Management of these enterprises was of the view that CPU had been doing yeoman's service in examining and controlling the state enterprises. MDs of the state enterprises opined that executive control is adequate and all the decisions are influenced by the ministry concerned. They also contended that autonomy in these enterprises is sham and it has affected the operational efficiency of the state enterprises. They were also of the view that the financial control is not wholesome in these enterprises and the finance ministry plays a restrictive role in the efficient conduct of these enterprises. Hence a minister should be held responsible for the successful working of a public enterprise and he must in turn exercise sufficient but not excessive control over them.

The success or failure of a public enterprise considerably depends upon the quality of its Board which is responsible for its direction and goverance. The type of Board that would be more suitable differs from enterprise to enterprise depending primarily in the nature of its functions and its size. For major public undertakings, a functional Board with full time members would be preferable while in case of small size enterprises, the management may be carried on by a Managing Director and a policy Board may be set up to advise him on various issues of policy. In most cases, a combined Board would be more effective than either an exclusively policy Board or functional Board.

With a view to attract the best available persons on the Board of State Undertakings, the salaries and allowances should be such that they provide incentives for work, loyalty to organisation, devotion to public services, uprightness and efficiency in operations and social prestige commensurate with the importance to the undertaking.

BIBLIOGRAPHY

1. Albu, A., Ministerial and Parliament Control in M. Shanks. ed(s). Lessons of Public Enterprises, London, Jonathan Cape, 1963.
2. Dholakia, Bakul, H. The Changing Efficiency of Public Enterprises in India, Somiya, New Delhi, 1980.
3. Jakhar, Balram. The People, the Parliament and the Administration, Metropolitan, New Delhi, 1982.
4. Khera, S.S., Management and Control in Public Enterprises, Asia, Bombay, 1963.
5. Brown, C.C., Restructuring the Board : A Director's Perspective, Management Review, American Management Association, New York, Sept. 1976.
6. Davies, Earnest, Ministerial Control and Parliamentary responsibility of Nationalised Industries, Political Science Quarterly, London, Vol. 21, 1950.
7. Gillis, Malcolm, The Rule of State Enterprises in Economic Development, Social research, New York, Vol. 47, No. 2, Summer, 1980.
8. Kaur, Narinder and Gurdeep Singh, Balancing and Accountability in Public Enterprises, Indian Management Studies Journal, Punjabi University, Patiala, Vol. I and III, 1990.
9. Narain Laxmi, Public Enterprises Management, 1989.
10. Prakash, Jagdish, Administration of Public Enterprises in India, Himalaya, 1992.

and its size. For major public undertakings, a functional Board with full time members would be preferable while in case of small size enterprises, the management may be carried on by a Managing Director and a policy Board may be set up to advise him on various issues of policy. In most cases, a combined Board would be more effective than either an exclusively policy Board or functional Board.

With a view to attract the best available persons on the Board in State Undertakings, the salaries and allowances should be such that they provide incentives for work, loyalty to organisation, devotion to public services, uprightness and efficiency in operations and social prestige commensurate with the importance to the undertaking.

BIBLIOGRAPHY

1. Albu, A., Ministerial and Parliamentary Control in M. Shanks (eds.) Lessons of Public Enterprises, London, Jonathan Cape, 1963.
2. Dholakia, Bakul, H. The Changing Efficiency of Public Enterprises in India, Somiya, New Delhi, 1980.
3. Jakhar, Balram, The People, the Parliament and the Administration, Metropolitan, New Delhi, 1982.
4. Khera, S.S., Management and Control in Public Enterprises, Asia, Bombay, 1963.
5. Brown, C.C., Restructuring the Board : A Director's Perspective Management Review, American Management Association, New York, Sept. 1976.
6. Davies, Earnest, Ministerial Control and Parliamentary responsibility of Nationalised Industries, Political Science Quarterly, London, Vol. 21, 1950.
7. Gillis, Malcolm, The Role of State Enterprises in Economic Development, Social Research, New York, Vol. 47, No. 2, Summer, 1980.
8. Kaur, Narinder and Gurdeep Singh, Balancing and Accountability in Public Enterprises, Indian Management Studies Journal, Punjabi University, Patiala, Vol. I and II, 1996.
9. Narain Laxmi, Public Enterprises Management, 1980.
10. Prakash, Jagdish, Administration of Public Enterprises in India, Himalaya, 1992.